What's for Dinner?

What's for Dinner?

MICHAEL ROBERTS

WILLIAM MORROW AND COMPANY, INC. • NEW YORK

Library of Congress Cataloging-in-Publication Data

Roberts, Michael
    What's for dinner? / Michael Roberts.
       p. cm.
    Includes index.
    ISBN 0-688-08544-X
    1. Cookery.   2. Dinners and dining.   I. Title.
  TX714.R59 1992
    641.5′4—dc20   92-1492
                                                                      CIP

Printed in the United States of America

First Edition

1 2 3 4 5 6 7 8 9 10

BOOK DESIGN BY HELENE BERINSKY

To the memory of my grandmothers, Helen and Pearl

*H*elen used to chase everyone around the house with food, imploring them to eat. Boy, was it annoying, trying to throw a ball or watch TV or just stay up late listening to the adults. And we'd all just finished a meal not thirty minutes past. Well, I was a child of this family and, as well, loved eating a lot, certainly long before I learned that I loved cooking. But when I began to prepare meals for myself, I understood. It had nothing to do with food at all; it had to do with love. And also nudging.

*P*earl used to come on the weekends, wearing a seal coat and a scarf of foxes all clamped together ass to mouth, tails flying. And she'd drop off shirt boxes from Bergdorf's or Bloomingdale's filled with coffee cake or sour cream cookies. Or jars of borscht or gefilte fish. Once, I decided to make a fancy fish mousse and went up to her apartment to grind the fish. The wrong fish as it turned out, but she didn't let on. After I became a chef, she remarked that my potato pancakes weren't really potato pancakes because they weren't cooked in chicken fat. Tradition has its special place in cooking.

Acknowledgments

This cookbook is the result of many things, but mostly I have to thank those responsible for creating my food memories.

Earliest ones are of my mother's cooking and that of both my grandmothers, Helen Picker and Pearl Roberts. They cooked food that's about loving and nurturing, two pretty important ingredients in any recipe. Even the soft-cooked eggs my dad used to make on Saturday mornings count.

Lenore Greenfield was the first person I knew who cooked French food. Zounds! Will Greenfield was our scoutmaster and showed us how to cook over a campfire, my first real cooking.

Throughout college, when I began cooking meals for myself, I'd ring my aunt Suretta Lieblich and shmooze recipes. She's an intuitive cook. Uncle Herman is the herring-and-pickle maven and also introduced me to Bermuda onions.

Richard Ortner bought me a copy of *Larousse Gastronomique* while we were in college and Ron Meyers, our other flatmate, and I were a cooking team. We labeled our style "orangutan." It was baroque and over the top.

Roger Lallemand was my cooking professor at Centre Ferrandi in Paris. He was very old-school, all rules and recipes. Oh, where would my cooking be without rules to bend and recipes to reinterpret?

Good cooking is not possible without the diligence of the specialty farmers and animal husbanders who provide me with the proper ingredients that demand to be prepared with respect.

Cooking is a fabulous thing to do, and anything so fabulous needs to be written about. But writing about it means thinking about it, too. Beginning in 1990, the American Institute of Wine and Food, at the urging of Julia Child, embarked on a project called Resetting the American Table: Creating a New Alliance of Taste and Health. I've been honored to be a participant in this "think tank," and to discover, among other things, the work of Drs. Sidney Mintz, Paul Rozin, Margaret Mackenzie, and the nutritionist Mary Abbott Hess. I've been influenced also by writers of culinary history and cultural anthropology—Reay Tannahill, Margaret Visser, and Lionel Tiger. Harold McGee explains why and debunks much culinary lore. The person who introduced the works of these thinkers to me is my friend and erstwhile editor at the Los Angeles Times Syndicate, Russ Parsons.

It would be impossible for me both to run a restaurant and write books without the support of my crew at Trumps—Jeff Nichols, Mary George, and the whole kitchen, dining room, and administrative staff.

The recipes were all tested by the delightful Patty Krause. And thank you, also, Max Robles.

At William Morrow there's the incomparable Ann Bramson and staff—among them Laurie Orseck, Sarah Guralnik, and copy editors Deborah Weiss Geline and Judith Sutton.

Maureen and Eric Lasher are my agent/protectors. I couldn't be in better hands.

Thanks, D.P.A., for putting up with me, and a bow-wow to Otto and Marcel for keeping the kitchen floor clean.

Contents

Recipes by Category

PASTA DINNERS

POULTRY DINNERS

PORK

VEAL

LAMB

BEEF

SPECIALTY MEATS

Introduction

"What's for Dinner?" It seems like such a simple question; we ask it every day. What we have for dinner—how, when, where, and with whom we take it—tells us who we were, who we are, and may even predict who we shall become.

Dinner is the main meal of the day, and for most of us it's the most social one, too. Families sit down together and recount the day's events, traumas, successes, and peculiarities. Friends get together and debate politics or discuss movies. Hostesses and hosts throw dinner parties. Dinner involves complex social conventions. People come together over food.

Insomuch as dinner is one of my favorite social rituals—no matter whether I'm having people in or whether it's a simple family meal—dinner is my favorite meal to prepare. It grounds the day for me. Part of my attachment to dinner things has to do with the food; partly it's the anticipation of spending some time in the kitchen.

Planning dinner, whether it's a midweek family meal or a Saturday-night dinner party is as important as the actual meal itself. I cherish the impulse to invent in the kitchen—that's why I'm a chef. Yet, home cooks should not overlook the creative aspect either. Cooking dinner may seem like just another daily chore, but for many of us, preparing dinner just may be the most creative activity we do each day. It requires us to be our most resourceful and inventive. But remember always that good dinners begin with good ingredients.

Let the marketplace guide you. Rather than deciding in advance what to prepare, explore the market for seasonal items and specials. If the asparagus is beautiful, use it in a main course such as Seared Scallop Seviche (page 14), or feature it in a vegetable risotto (page 154). Or serve it separately as a first course.

Think of all the food on your plate as ingredients in a recipe, and it's easy to see how your meal will go together. You don't want too many personalities fighting on your dinner plate, so avoid adding strong flavors to every dish you prepare. Harmony is more important to a good meal than culinary showmanship. If you're preparing a peppery entrée, such as Steak Paillards aux Deux Poivres (page 196), prepare simple vegetable accompaniments, baked or mashed potatoes, and steamed spinach, for instance. And, you probably don't want more than one sauce on your plate either. It confuses the palate and doesn't sit well in the stomach.

Don't serve the same ingredient in every course. If your main course is fresh, lovely salmon, don't start with a smoked salmon appetizer, but choose mushroom soup. Then again, if you begin dinner with a mushroom soup or salad, you'll want to save Open-Faced Mushroom, Arugula, and Brie Sandwiches (page 135) for another meal. Don't begin dinner with a cream soup if you're preparing a creamy fricassee of chicken as the main course. Flattened Chicken and Mushrooms (page 298) is a better choice.

There are all kinds of dinners in this book. This is the food I like to eat at home, the cooking that I do for myself, my family, and my friends. This is a book of main courses.

If it's a warm-weather dinner that you want and you'd like to get dinner out of the way before the heat of the day, Cool Dinners is where to look. If it's chilly and you're in the mood for a stew or hearty soup meal, you'll find something you'll love in Kettle Dinners.

We all remember the food we grew up on—sometimes fondly, sometimes not—and for me, food memories are a well of inspiration. When I think of mealtimes past I can often smell and taste them and they connect me to all sorts of past feelings and emotions. But, hey, I don't really want to relive the past. I simply want to recapture the enjoyment as I remember it. So, you'll find lots of good stuff in Fifties Favorites and Other Funky Dinners and Dinners My Grandmother Wouldn't Recognize.

Dinners Without Meat and Politically Correct Dinners are the kinds of meals I try to eat most of the time now. I find this type of cooking energizing and delicious, and it doesn't slow me down. There are recipes that use some familiar ingredients—rice, cornmeal, beans, and barley, for instance—in sometimes unfamiliar ways because they have been elevated to main-course status. You'll find still other recipes using ingredients, such as chick-pea flour and buckwheat flour, largely unfamiliar to many cooks, that you'll want to incorporate into your repertoire of staples.

More and more markets have wonderful supplies of ethnic products unknown to most people outside large metropolitan areas just a couple of years ago. There are chilies, both fresh and dried, and cilantro, used in

Latino cuisines, and miso paste, tofu, and fresh bean sprouts for Asian-style cooking. I love the flavors and aromas of these cuisines and enjoy cooking my versions of them, as you will see in the chapters called Mexican Nights and Asian Flavors. And of course there's still French and Italian cooking—the two cuisines that trapped my interest in cooking in the first place. My favorites from these cuisines are found in Dinner in the French Manner and Dinner in the Italian Fashion.

Busy people don't have time to spend lots of time preparing meals, especially on school and work nights. So *à la minute* is the way to cook dinner. Preparing my Last-Minute Dinners requires very little *mise en place,* or preparation of ingredients. There are recipes for quick-cooking ingredients—boneless breasts of chicken, turkey paillards, shrimp, swordfish steaks—and in most cases the sauces are simple yet wonderfully flavored pan reductions.

Finally we come to feasts. Guess Who's Coming to Dinner is a chapter of recipes for dishes that will fit the "occasion" meal. There are recipes for ham, turkey, and goose that you'll want to prepare for large holiday gatherings, and there are elegant entertaining dishes perfect for dinner parties. With these more *soigné* recipes, you'll want to serve a fitting first course, salad, and dessert to round out the menu.

So here's your chance to look forward to dinner with excitement and prepare the right meal to fit your mood. You may not be able to monitor what the kids eat at school, or know what your partner had on the run at noon, but dinner is the meal that you control. And you can use the preparation time to regain some of the sanity that perhaps got away from you during the course of a hectic day.

Cool Dinners

$\mathcal{F}$or someone like me, who is not particularly fastidious, who dislikes fussy food, and who'd rather have something taste fabulous than merely look impressive, preparing a dinner that is to be served chilled or at room temperature is a joy. It affords the cook time to assemble each element of the dish without the feeling of working against the clock and to adjust flavors as necessary or add a special garnish.

Habit has it that hot food should be served very hot and cold food very chilled, even though neither choice allows us to best taste the subtleties in a dish. It's like sampling a white wine: If you like, drink it well chilled, of course, but to really judge it, sample it lightly chilled so every characteristic stands out. Food also has more taste at room temperature, and there is a large repertoire of dishes that should be served this way.

There are a few points to remember when cooking room-temperature dishes. Aromas are less noticeable in a tepid dish than in a steaming hot one; since our sense of smell excites taste, you must compensate by spicing the dish more generously. Where wine cooked into a sauce may subtly attract us in a hot dish, citrus juice or vinegar in the sauce or marinade of a cool or chilled one will give it that little oomph for recognition.

When sautéing an ingredient for a chilled or room-temperature dish, use an oil, which will remain liquid, rather than butter. Flavored oils such as olive and walnut contribute their own special character to a dish, but they can be quite pungent, so you may want to cut them with some flavorless peanut or safflower oil. With room-temperature dishes—served on a bed of greens or as a composed plate—the role of the dressing is to unify all the ingredients.

Different room-temperature dishes often are happy all together on one plate. Instead of serving the usual starter, main course, and sides of vegetables, prepare a few complementary dishes and serve them together.

Cool or room-temperature dinners are the best ones to serve if you're preparing a buffet, football-Sunday dinner, or New Year's Eve supper. If you're coming back from the theater or symphony, dinner can be waiting for you like a faithful dog. This food has the comfort of an old cashmere throw and shows an elegant offhand style.

These "cool dinners" run the gamut from warm to chilled, and the dishes are mostly cooked ahead. Some, such as the individual Eggplant Parmesan, can be prepared up to a couple of days in advance, refrigerated, and then set out to return to room temperature for serving. Others, such as Tomato and Pastina Aspic with Spiced Crab and the two tartares, are served right from the refrigerator. And the salads in this chapter are basically done in advance, except for the last-minute sautéing of the main ingredient in a few cases to make a warm vinaigrette.

The Salad Goes Where?

Years ago what you did with your dinner salad told a lot about you. Asking for it *after* the main course meant that you had traveled in Europe. When you were invited to a dinner party and the hosts held their forks in their left hands, spearing their food rather than shoveling it, you could be sure that a salad was going to follow the main course. This European custom was greeted with a certain amount of disdain by Americans, who took it as a sign that we were somehow socially inferior to Europeans, and that our palates were less evolved or that we had less refined tastes.

SCALLOP, ENDIVE, AND ARUGULA SALAD

SERVES 4

I make the dressing for this salad by gently warming the scallops in lemon juice and Pernod and then letting their juices bleed. It's light and full of flavor. And the quickly cooked scallops are really creamy.

> *1 pound large sea scallops, halved crosswise*
> *¼ cup fresh lemon juice, plus more for the endive, if necessary*
> *2 tablespoons Pernod*
> *Salt to taste*
> *¼ teaspoon ground white pepper*
> *2 teaspoons chopped fresh tarragon or 1 teaspoon dried*
> *⅓ cup virgin olive oil*
> *2 heads Belgian endive*
> *1 bunch arugula, stems trimmed (about 1 cup loosely packed leaves)*

1. Combine the scallops, lemon juice, Pernod, salt, and pepper in a nonreactive skillet or pot large enough to hold the scallops in one layer. If using dried tarragon, add it now. Cover, and cook over medium heat for 2 minutes. Remove from the heat and let sit, covered, until cooled to room temperature.

2. Using a slotted spoon, remove the scallops and set aside. If you're not serving the salad immediately, place them on a plate and refrigerate.

3. Transfer the scallop cooking liquid to a bowl and beat in the olive oil. If using fresh tarragon, add it now. Refrigerate if not using immediately.

4. Halve the endives lengthwise. Trim out the cores and cut each half into 1-inch lengths. If not serving immediately, toss with a little lemon juice and refrigerate.

5. When it's time to get dinner on the table, combine the endive, arugula, and dressing in a bowl. Toss together and mound on four salad plates. Arrange the scallops over the top and serve.

CLASSIC SALMON TARTARE

SERVES 4

*U*nless you have a reliable source of impeccably fresh fish, you may want to freeze the salmon for a couple of hours to kill any parasites before preparing the tartare. Always buy the freshest salmon available and freeze it yourself; do not buy frozen and defrosted salmon at the supermarket. I like farmed Norwegian salmon for my tartare because it's fattier and has a smoother texture than Alaskan or King salmon, so it's less likely to turn to mush in the freezer. Serve French-fried potatoes with mayonnaise and vinegar along with the tartare, and begin dinner with a room-temperature salad of braised, steamed, or sautéed vegetables.

1¾ pounds skinless salmon fillets
16 anchovy fillets
⅓ cup drained capers
1 tablespoon grated horseradish, preferably fresh
2 tablespoons grainy mustard
1 tablespoon Dijon mustard
2 tablespoons finely chopped fresh parsley
2 tablespoons finely minced shallots
½ teaspoon Tabasco sauce, or to taste
1 egg yolk
¼ cup fresh lemon juice
2 tablespoons virgin olive oil
Toast or sliced dark bread, for serving

1. Wrap salmon airtight and freeze for 2 hours; defrost in refrigerator.

2. Place four plates in the refrigerator to chill.

3. Remove and discard any dark flesh on the skin side of the salmon. Using a sharp knife, chop the salmon fine.

4. Chop 12 of the anchovies together with the capers and place in a bowl. Add the horseradish, mustards, parsley, shallots, and Tabasco sauce, then add the egg yolk and lemon juice and mix well. Slowly beat in the oil until absorbed. (The salmon and the anchovy mixture can be prepared up to 2 hours in advance to this point and refrigerated.)

5. When ready to serve the tartare, add the salmon to the anchovy mixture and mix. Then, using two forks, mash the salmon with the tartare mix to blend. Mound on the chilled plates and garnish with the remaining anchovies. Serve immediately with warm toast or fresh dark bread.

POACHED SALMON SALAD
WITH GRAPEFRUIT VINAIGRETTE

SERVES 4

*T*he woodsy, almost gamey flavor of salmon is perfectly dressed with smoky walnut oil and a sweetly acidic reduction of grapefruit juice. When poaching fish, meat, or poultry for a chilled or room-temperature dish, simmer it briefly and gently (not over intense heat, please). Meat and fish especially should be a bit on the undercooked side. Poultry that poaches at a low temperature remains finely textured.

4 7-ounce skinless salmon fillets
2 cups grapefruit juice
⅓ cup raspberry or cider vinegar
½ cup walnut oil
Salt and freshly ground black pepper to taste
1 small head curly endive (chicory)
24 grapefruit sections

1. Place the salmon in a pan just large enough to hold it and add the grapefruit juice and vinegar. Cover, bring to a simmer over medium heat, and simmer about 6 to 7 minutes. The salmon should remain slightly pink in the center. Transfer the salmon fillets to a plate and place in the refrigerator to chill.

2. Boil the liquid in the pan until it has reduced by one third and thickened slightly, about 5 minutes. Pour the liquid into a bowl and cool to room temperature.

3. When the cooking liquid is cool, vigorously beat in the oil. Add salt and pepper to taste.

4. Remove and discard the dark outer chicory leaves. Tear the remaining leaves into pieces, wash well, and dry in a salad spinner.

5. When it's time for dinner, combine the chicory and grapefruit and toss with half the dressing. Mound on individual plates, place a salmon fillet atop each lettuce mound, and dress the salmon with the remaining dressing.

SEARED SWORDFISH SALADE NIÇOISE

SERVES 4

*T*his classic Mediterranean salad became a classic American one using canned tuna. It's far more delicious with fresh tuna or, better yet, with swordfish. Buy one large piece for slicing into thin paillards. In a hot skillet, they will sear beautifully.

Keep dinner in a Mediterranean vein by starting with a chilled tomato soup. Finish with a plate of cheese and fresh fruit.

½ pound green beans, preferably haricots verts
8 small new potatoes
4 eggs
1 head Boston lettuce
2 cups arugula
2 ripe tomatoes
1 tablespoon minced garlic
Salt to taste
24-ounce slab of swordfish fillet (or 4 6-ounce steaks)
Ground white pepper
⅓ cup olive oil
¼ cup fresh lemon juice
2 tablespoons tomato paste
24 Niçoise olives
4 teaspoons drained capers
16 basil leaves
8 anchovy fillets

1. Bring a large pot of salted water to the boil. Fill a large bowl with ice water. Add the green beans to the boiling water and blanch for 2 minutes. Remove from the boiling water and immediately plunge into the ice water. When cool, drain, place on absorbent towels, and refrigerate. Add the potatoes to the boiling water and cook until tender, about 10 minutes. Remove from the water and let cool to room temperature. Add the eggs to the boiling water and cook for 10 minutes. Drain, cool under cold running water, crack the eggs, and refrigerate until chilled.

2. Remove and discard the outer leaves of the lettuce. Tear the remaining leaves into pieces and place in a large bowl. Trim the stems from the arugula and toss with the lettuce. Refrigerate.

3. Cut the tomatoes in half, and sprinkle the cut sides with the minced garlic and then with salt. Set aside.

4. Lay the swordfish on a cutting board and slice it across the grain into 8 thin pieces. Sprinkle with salt and pepper, and set aside in the refrigerator until serving time.

5. When it's time for dinner, blend together the oil, lemon juice, tomato paste, salt, and ¼ teaspoon pepper. Pour half the dressing over the lettuce and arugula, toss to coat, and mound on plates or in individual salad bowls. Arrange a neat pile of the green beans on each serving of lettuce, placing it near the bottom edge of the plate. Place 2 potatoes next to each pile of beans. Place 6 olives next to the potatoes. Peel the hard-cooked eggs, cut them in half, and place 2 halves opposite the potatoes on each plate. Sprinkle the salads with the capers.

6. Place a heavy skillet over high heat. Add the tomatoes, cut side down, to the skillet and cook for 2 minutes. Remove from the skillet and arrange on the salad. Add the swordfish to the skillet, in batches if necessary, and cook, turning once, for about 1½ to 2 minutes, or until just opaque in the center. Arrange 2 pieces of swordfish in the center of each salad. Dress the salads with the remaining dressing, garnish with the basil leaves and anchovy fillets, and call your guests to the table.

SEARED SCALLOP SEVICHE

SERVES 4

*I*n this recipe really large scallops are pan-grilled in an intensely hot pan to quickly caramelize the surface of the scallops. The lemon marinade accomplishes the rest of the "cooking."

Choose a light pasta course to begin this dinner.

1½ pounds large sea scallops (about 12 to 16 scallops)
½ cup fresh lemon juice
2 teaspoons chopped fresh tarragon or 1 teaspoon dried
Salt to taste
¼ teaspoon ground white pepper
1½ pounds asparagus
1 egg yolk
2 tablespoons Pernod
½ cup olive oil
2 ripe tomatoes

1. Heat a nonstick skillet over high heat until nearly smoking hot. Add the scallops and quickly sear them, no more than 20 seconds on each side. Remove the scallops from the skillet, cut them in half crosswise, and place them in a bowl. Add the lemon juice, tarragon, salt, and pepper, and gently toss. Cover and refrigerate for 2 hours, occasionally stirring the scallops in the marinade.

2. Meanwhile, bring a large pot of salted water to the boil. Cut off the tough bottom inch or so of the asparagus; if using large asparagus, peel the stalks. Fill a large bowl with ice water. Add the asparagus to the boiling water and cook until barely tender, for 1 to 4 minutes, depending on the thickness of the asparagus, then remove from the boiling water and immediately plunge into the ice water. Drain on towels.

3. Place the egg yolk in a bowl. Drain the scallops and add the marinade to the yolk. Add the Pernod and mix well. Slowly beat in the oil until incorporated. Taste for salt and pepper and adjust as necessary. Refrigerate until ready to serve.

4. When it's time for dinner, slice the tomatoes and fan them on individual plates. Arrange a neat pile of asparagus spears across the plate. Place the scallops, seared side up, on top, drizzle with the dressing, and serve.

TOMATO AND PASTINA ASPIC
WITH SPICED CRAB

SERVES 5 TO 6

I especially like this crab and jellied mold because it's like dining on a salad of chilled August tomatoes and pasta. If you like crab cocktail, you'll go nuts for this dinner.

> 1 cup small pasta, such as pastina, riso, orzo, or small shells, or
>   2 cups cooked
> 1 tablespoon olive oil
> 1 28-ounce can whole tomatoes
> 1 tablespoon powdered gelatin
> ½ cup dry white wine
> 2½ cups chicken stock or canned low-sodium chicken broth
> 1 tablespoon minced garlic
> 1 teaspoon salt
> ½ teaspoon freshly ground black pepper
> 16 fresh basil leaves
> 1¼ pound crabmeat, flaked
> 2 tablespoons mayonnaise
> ½ teaspoon Old Bay Seasoning
> ¼ teaspoon curry powder

1. Cook the pasta until *al dente,* according to the package directions. Drain, toss with the oil, and refrigerate until chilled.

2. Drain the tomatoes, reserving ½ cup of the juices. Chop the tomatoes, combine with the ½ cup juice, and refrigerate. Oil a 6-cup ring mold and place in the refrigerator to chill.

3. Dissolve the gelatin in the white wine. Place the chicken broth, garlic, salt, and pepper in a small pan and bring to a boil over medium heat. Add the dissolved gelatin, boil for 1 minute, and remove from the heat. Measure out ¼ cup of the gelatin mixture and set aside. Add half the remaining gelatin mixture to the cold pasta and half to the tomatoes. Toss to combine and return both to the refrigerator.

4. Remove the chilled mold from the refrigerator. Pour the reserved ¼ cup gelatin mixture evenly over the bottom of the mold and arrange the basil leaves in this aspic. Refrigerate for 5 minutes to set slightly.   *(continued)*

16

5. Remove the mold from the refrigerator and add the tomatoes in an even layer. Carefully spoon the pasta mixture evenly over the tomatoes. Refrigerate until set, about 4 hours.

6. When it's time for dinner, unmold the tomato aspic onto a platter. Gently mix the crab with the mayonnaise, Old Bay Seasoning, and curry powder, and mound in the center of the aspic. Serve immediately.

Individual Eggplant Parmesan

*E*ggplants—the name comes from the small, white, egg-shaped variety—have been staples in Italy since the fifteenth century. Since I like to see the natural shapes of food on my plate, this recipe is for individual stacks of eggplant—it's prettier to eat this way and doesn't remind you of the ubiquitous Parmigiana. I serve this dish at room temperature, as if it were an antipasto, although you can also present it bubbling from the oven.

Use medium eggplants—the large ones tend to be bitter. Disgorging the slices in salt to draw out the moisture in the vegetable prevents the eggplant from absorbing an excessive amount of oil during cooking. (The specific amount of oil for cooking the slices will depend on how well the eggplant has given up its water.)

Serve with garlic bread and a Caesar salad.

> 4 pounds medium eggplants, peeled and cut lengthwise into ⅜-inch slices (about 4 to 5 eggplants)
> ¼ cup kosher salt
> 6 tablespoons unsalted butter
> 9 tablespoons all-purpose flour
> 2 cups milk
> ¼ teaspoon ground mace
> Salt and freshly ground black pepper to taste
> ¼ cup grated Parmesan cheese
> 2 28-ounce cans Italian plum tomatoes, seeded and chopped, with their juices
> 1 tablespoon minced garlic
> 1 tablespoon chopped fresh oregano or 2 teaspoons dried
> Olive oil, for frying
> 4 slices Fontina cheese (about 6 ounces total)

1. Layer the eggplant slices in a colander, sprinkling each layer with kosher salt. Place the colander on a plate and set aside to disgorge for 1 hour.

2. Meanwhile, melt the butter in a small saucepan over medium heat. Add the flour and cook for 2 minutes, stirring. Slowly add the milk, stirring constantly. Add the mace and salt and pepper, reduce the heat to low, and cook, stirring, for about 5 minutes, until the mixture is very thick. Remove from the heat and stir in the Parmesan cheese. Set this balsamella sauce aside.

3. Combine the tomatoes with their juices, the garlic, and oregano in a saucepan and cook over medium heat until thickened and reduced by about one quarter, about 1 hour. Add salt and pepper to taste. (This makes about 1¼ quarts sauce.)

4. Preheat the oven to 375°F.

5. Rinse the eggplant slices and pat dry. Heat about ¼ inch olive oil in a large skillet over medium heat. Spread the flour on a plate. Lightly dust the eggplant slices with the flour, shaking off the excess, and add as many slices to the pan as will fit in a single layer without crowding. Cook the eggplant for 1½ minutes on each side, or until lightly browned. Remove from the skillet and drain on towels. Set the cooked slices aside on a plate, and repeat with the remaining eggplant, adding more olive oil as needed.

6. Arrange 4 of the eggplant slices in a large baking pan. Spread each slice with 1 tablespoon of the balsamella and spoon on 1 tablespoon of the tomato sauce. Place another slice of eggplant on top and repeat the process, ending with eggplant. Cover the pan with foil, prick holes in the foil with the tip of a knife, and bake until bubbling hot, about 1 hour. Remove the foil, place a slice of Fontina on each stack of eggplant, and bake for another 20 minutes.

7. Remove the eggplant from the oven. Let cool to room temperature and spoon remaining tomato sauce over the eggplant before serving. (This dish can be prepared in advance and refrigerated for a day or two; bring to room temperature before serving.)

CHOPPED VEGETABLE SALAD

SERVES 4

*S*alad meals are popular in Los Angeles. First there was the chopped salad, originally served at the Brown Derby. This salad of chopped avocado, tomato, bacon, blue cheese, and iceberg lettuce gave way to many and varied chopped salads. This is my version, with a honey-mustard vinaigrette. I cut the veggies in different sizes so that they "fork" better.

Begin dinner with bowls of hot, creamy potato soup or a smoky bean soup.

1 bunch broccoli, florets only (reserve the stalks for another use)
¼ pound green beans, preferably haricots verts or Chinese long beans
¾ cup shelled peas
¼ pound snow peas
½ pound white mushrooms
2 tablespoons fresh lemon juice
½ head romaine lettuce
2 ripe tomatoes, cut into 16 chunks each
1 small zucchini, finely chopped
1 small yellow squash, finely chopped
1 small carrot, peeled and finely grated
8 ounces fresh mozzarella, preferably Italian bufala
1 pound cooked chicken, smoked chicken or turkey, ham, or cooked shrimp
¼ cup prepared mustard
2 tablespoons honey
5 tablespoons white wine vinegar
½ cup vegetable oil

1. Bring a large pot of salted water to a boil. Fill a large bowl with ice water. Plunge the broccoli florets into the boiling water, return to the boil, and blanch for 1 minute. Immediately remove the florets from the water and plunge into the ice water. When cool, drain the florets on absorbent towels, then place in a large bowl and refrigerate. Blanch the green beans for 2 minutes, the peas for 1 minute, and the snow peas for 30 seconds, refreshing each vegetable in the ice water and draining on towels. Cut the green beans into ¼-inch rounds. Cut the snow peas into ¼-inch-wide julienne strips. Add the beans, peas, and snow peas to the broccoli.

2. Slice the mushrooms fine, toss with the lemon juice, and add to the bowl of blanched vegetables.

3. Discard the tough outer romaine leaves, then rinse, dry, and cut the remaining leaves into 1-inch pieces. Add to the salad bowl.

4. Add the tomatoes, zucchini, yellow squash, and carrot to the salad bowl.

5. Chop the mozzarella and chicken (or turkey, ham, or shrimp), combine in a bowl, and refrigerate.

6. Combine the mustard, honey, and vinegar in a small bowl, then slowly beat in the oil. Set aside.

7. When it's time to serve dinner, add 2 tablespoons of the dressing to the mozzarella/chicken mixture and mix well. Add the remaining dressing to the bowl of vegetables and mix well. Mound the veggies on individual plates and divide the cheese and chicken mixture among the salads. Serve chilled.

Chef's Salad

The chef's salad was probably the invention of some fifties "Continental" restaurant (restaurant geographers are still trying to discover this unknown continent). Many Americans didn't consider what they ate to be a meal if it didn't include meat and potatoes, so someone had the idea of serving a complete meal on a bed of lettuce, and the chef's salad was born.

Its popularity led to the salad bars of the seventies and eighties. Although they now seem to be falling out of favor, the legacy they leave is the idea that a salad can be a whole meal comprised of all food groups—carbohydrate, starch, and protein—heaped on a pile of lettuce, whose flavors are united by the dressing.

GRAND AÏOLI

SERVES 4

*T*his is an all-vegetable dish named after the garlic and olive oil sauce all the different vegetables are dipped into. It's the dinner my friend, Ron Meyers, likes to serve best. In fact, the only time he manages to get dinner on the table at a reasonable hour is when he makes this. So if you're as busy as he is, you'll impress your middle-of-the-week dinner guests by miraculously producing this wonderful cooked-in-advance meal. If you like, serve cold poached chicken or slices of cold pot roast along with the vegetables.

A trick I learned from food scientist Harold McGee's *The Curious Cook* is that freezing egg yolks enables them to absorb more oil, so you can make a mayonnaise that is less eggy-tasting and more stable.

2 egg yolks
4 small turnips, peeled and quartered
4 small carrots, peeled
1 bunch celery, top trimmed
12 small new potatoes
1 cup plus 3 tablespoons extra virgin olive oil
2 medium onions (unpeeled)
1 small head broccoli, cut into large florets
3 tablespoons finely minced garlic
1 teaspoon fresh lemon juice
1 tablespoon boiling water
Salt to taste

1. Freeze the egg yolks, then defrost them.

2. Preheat the oven to 400°F.

3. Place the turnips, carrots, celery, and potatoes in a large pot, cover with salted water, and bring to a boil over high heat. Immediately remove from the heat and drain. Cut the celery in half lengthwise. Toss the vegetables in 3 tablespoons of the olive oil.

4. Place the turnips and onions in a roasting pan and bake for 15 minutes. Add the potatoes and bake for 10 more minutes. Add the carrots and bake 10 minutes longer. Add the broccoli and celery and bake until all the vegetables are tender, 20 to 25 minutes longer. Transfer the vegetables to a plate and let cool to room temperature.

5. Meanwhile, place the defrosted egg yolks, garlic, and lemon juice in a bowl and whisk together. Whisking steadily, add 1 tablespoon of the remaining 1 cup oil a drop at a time to start the mayonnaise. Then continue to add the oil in a slow, steady stream, whisking constantly, until all the oil is incorporated. Whisk in the boiling water. Taste for salt and add as desired. Refrigerate until ready to serve.

6. When it's time for dinner, arrange the vegetables on a serving platter and pour the aïoli into a bowl.

Oil and Vinegar

Dressings and vinaigrettes—these cool sauces go by many names—unify the various ingredients on the plate. I think all salad dressings should have a tartness—usually from either vinegar or lemon juice—to highlight the salad ingredients. And the oil used must complement it. Here's a guide to choosing the best combinations:

- Flavorless salad oils—soy, safflower, corn, peanut—combine with any vinegar to make a simple vinaigrette, but they are particularly suitable with herb vinegars such as tarragon. Choose a flavorless oil when you don't want to add an extra flavor to an ensemble of ingredients.

- Olive oils and wine vinegars—red, white, sherry—make dressings with a particular character. Use them to dress meats, fish, and poultry and spicy or pungent lettuces such as arugula, radicchio, endive, and chicory. Olive oils vary in their degree of flavor from fruity to bitter and you must taste each new brand before deciding how to use it best.

- Use cold-pressed nut oils, such as walnut and hazelnut, with fruit or balsamic vinegars. These dressings are good for fruit salads and chilled poultry, shellfish, or poached salmon salads.

POACHED EGGS ON BACON, SPINACH, AND TOMATO SALAD

SERVES 4

*B*egin dinner with this warm "BST" salad, and follow it with a chunky soup, like a minestrone. The spinach wilts ever so slightly under the warm ingredients; try to get tender, young leaves, which will wilt more than large older ones. Fried bread, one of the most satisfying things to eat, is even better when you use it to sop up runny egg yolks and a warm blue cheese dressing.

4 large beefsteak tomatoes
¼ cup olive oil
2 medium onions, finely diced (about 1½ cups)
2 tablespoons minced garlic
1 bunch spinach, trimmed and washed (about 6 to 7 cups
    cleaned leaves)
4 warm poached eggs
12 thick slices bacon, cut crosswise into ¼-inch strips
8 thin slices French bread
3 tablespoons red wine vinegar
8 ounces blue cheese, crumbled
Freshly ground black pepper to taste
Salt to taste

1. Bring a large pot of water to a boil. Core the tomatoes and cut an X through the skin at the bottom end. Plunge the tomatoes into the boiling water. As soon as the water returns to the boil, remove the tomatoes and plunge into a bowl of ice water; drain. Remove and discard the skins, which should peel off easily. Cut the tomatoes in half crosswise and squeeze out the seeds. Quarter each tomato half and set the tomatoes aside in a small bowl.

2. Heat 1 tablespoon of the oil in a small saucepan over medium heat. Add the onions and garlic and cook, stirring, until soft, about 5 minutes. Add the tomatoes, cook for 1 minute, and remove the pan from the heat. Set aside at room temperature until ready to serve.

3. When it's time for dinner, arrange the spinach on individual plates and place the tomatoes, with the onions and garlic, on top.

4. Heat the remaining 3 tablespoons olive oil in a skillet, add the bacon, and cook, stirring, for about 4 minutes, until fat is rendered. Add the bread

slices and cook until golden, about 1 minute, then turn and cook until golden on the other side. Arrange 2 slices of bread next to each poached egg. Pour the vinegar into the pan, stir in the cheese, and cook for 30 seconds. Add a grind of pepper, taste for salt, and add if necessary. Spoon the bacon, cheese, and dressing over the salads and serve immediately.

CHICKEN SALAD WITH CRISPY ONION WEDGES

SERVES 4

*T*his coffee-shop–style salad pleases on the most basic level. It has bacon, cheese, hard-cooked eggs, and a crispy onion cake. It may be that this should really be a sandwich. Anyway, serve whole wheat toast with it.

4 boneless, skinless chicken breast halves

Salt and freshly ground black pepper to taste

2 medium onions

¼ cup buttermilk

4 eggs

½ pound green beans

1 tablespoon tomato paste

1 tablespoon prepared mustard

3 tablespoons dry sherry

¼ cup sherry vinegar

⅓ cup olive oil

3 tablespoons all-purpose flour

¼ cup flavorless vegetable oil

1 small head romaine lettuce, inner leaves only, sliced crosswise into
    1-inch strips (about 4 cups sliced leaves)

2 ripe tomatoes

4 ounces blue cheese

8 slices bacon, cooked and drained

1. Preheat the broiler. Lay the chicken breasts on a work surface, press down with the palm of your hand, and slice each breast horizontally into 2 thin cutlets. Sprinkle with salt and pepper.   *(continued)*

2. Broil the chicken for about 2 minutes per side, or until done. Remove from the heat and set aside on a plate.

3. Peel the onion and halve it lengthwise. Cut the onion lengthwise into the thinnest slivers possible. Place the slivers in a bowl and pour in the buttermilk. Sprinkle with salt and toss to coat. Set aside for at least 10 or up to 30 minutes.

4. Fill a large pot with salted water and add the eggs. Bring to a boil and cook for 5 minutes. Remove the eggs and cool them under cold running water. Fill a large bowl with ice water. Add the green beans to the pot of boiling water and cook until crisp-tender, about 3 to 5 minutes. Drain and immediately plunge into the ice water. Drain, place on absorbent towels, and set aside. Peel the cooled eggs and set aside.

5. Combine the tomato paste and mustard in a small bowl. Add the sherry and sherry vinegar and mix until smooth. Slowly whisk in the olive oil. Set this dressing aside.

6. Heat half the vegetable oil in an 8-inch nonstick skillet over high heat. Meanwhile, place the flour in a medium bowl. Drain the onion slivers and add to the flour. Toss well. Add half the onions to the hot oil, spread them to the edges of the pan, and cook until golden on the bottom, about 2 minutes; press the onions into the oil with a spatula as they cook. Flip the onion cake and cook about 2 minutes longer. When crispy and golden on both sides, remove from the pan and drain on paper towels. Repeat with the remaining oil and onions.

7. To serve dinner, place the romaine and green beans in a bowl and toss with half the dressing. Mound on individual plates or in wide-rimmed soup bowls. Slice the tomatoes and arrange around the lettuce. Place a chicken breast on top of each mound of lettuce. Cut each egg in half and place the halves on either side of the chicken. Spoon the remaining dressing over the chicken breasts, then crumble the blue cheese over each salad and garnish with the bacon. Cut the onion cake into 4 wedges and place one on the side of each plate. Call the family to the table.

PICNIC FRIED CHICKEN

SERVES 3 TO 4

*T*he fried chicken I knew as a child was actually rolled in cornflakes and baked in the oven. It was good, but when it went on picnics, the cornflakes always fell off, exposing the flaccid skin of the chicken. I didn't much go in for flaccid skin on chickens then, and I still don't. When I make fried chicken, I remove the skin and soak the chicken in buttermilk—the acids tenderize the meat and add a slightly sour taste. Dredging the chicken in flour gives it a new skin. I fry it until golden, then bake it in the oven to eliminate most of the fat from the frying. (Be sure not to crowd your skillet, or the chicken will steam rather than fry.) My mother agrees that this is better chicken for picnics than her cornflake recipe, and probably no more fattening, even for the frying.

> 1 cup buttermilk
> 1 tablespoon freshly ground black pepper
> 1 teaspoon salt
> 2 pounds chicken pieces, skin removed
> ½ cup all-purpose flour
> Flavorless vegetable oil, for frying

1. Combine the buttermilk and pepper in a nonreactive bowl or baking dish. Add the chicken pieces and refrigerate for 3 hours, turning the pieces once.

2. Spread the flour on a plate. Remove the chicken from the buttermilk, pat dry, and dredge with the flour.

3. Preheat the oven to 375°F.

4. Fill a large heavy skillet with an inch of oil. When the oil is hot, add the chicken without crowding and fry, turning once, until golden on both sides. You may have to fry the chicken in batches. Drain on paper towels.

5. Place the chicken on a rack in a roasting pan and bake until well done, about 10 to 15 minutes.

6. Let the chicken cool to room temperature before packing into your picnic hamper, or cool and refrigerate until ready for dinner. It may also be served hot from the oven.

SMOKED CHICKEN SALAD WITH FRESH BEETS

SERVES 3 TO 4

I've made this dinner with smoked chicken and smoked turkey; they both work well. It's even good with smoked eel or smoked trout, because the sweetness of the apple, beets, and onions plays against the saltiness of any smoked item. Beets and apples are, themselves, terrific together.

1½ pounds beets (about 4 to 5 medium beets)
3 medium onions, roughly chopped
1 3- to 3½-pound smoked chicken, or 1½ pounds smoked chicken or
* turkey meat*
½ cup cider vinegar
⅔ cup vegetable oil
1 tablespoon chopped fresh dill
1 green apple, such as a Granny Smith

1. Trim the tops from the beets, leaving about 1 inch of the stems. Rinse the beets without breaking the skin. Place the beets in a pot, cover with cold water, cover the pot, and cook over medium heat until tender, about 35 minutes. Drain and let cool. When the beets are cool enough to handle, slip off their skins. Thinly slice the beets lengthwise and place in a bowl to cool.

2. While the beets are cooking, place the onions in a medium skillet (without oil), cover, and cook over medium heat, stirring occasionally, until the onions are dry and beginning to turn a golden color, about 25 minutes. Transfer to a bowl and let cool.

3. Remove the skin and meat from the chicken if using a whole bird. Discard the skin. Cut the leg meat into thin julienne strips, mix half with the onions, and toss well. Reserve the rest for garnishing. Cut each breast diagonally into 3 pieces. (Use the bones for making a smoked chicken broth.)

4. Beat the vinegar, oil, and dill together. Pour half the dressing over the beets.

5. When it's time for dinner, peel, core, and dice the apple, and add it to the chicken and onions. Arrange the beets on a platter and mound the chicken mixture on top. Fan the breast pieces around the mound and spoon the remaining dressing over the salad.

ROAST DUCK AND PEAR SALAD

SERVES 2 TO 3

*I*t's so easy to serve room-temperature duck that this recipe should inspire you to offer this tasty bird more often. Roast the bird early in the afternoon, then skin and bone it when it has cooled. Before serving, crisp the skin for garnish. If you refrigerate the meat before assembling the salad, simply pop it into a microwave or hot oven to take the chill off.

The strong nutmeg infusion in the dressing pinches you awake at the first bite of lettuce. Follow this clean-tasting salad with some pungent cheeses at room temperature. The wine should be red and robust.

> 1 5-pound duck
> ⅛ teaspoon freshly grated nutmeg
> 1 cup chicken stock, duck stock, or canned low-sodium chicken broth
> 2 tablespoons honey
> ½ cup malt vinegar
> ½ cup vegetable oil
> 1 firm ripe pear
> 1 small head red leaf lettuce, washed, dried, and torn into pieces

1. Preheat the oven to 425°F.

2. Place the duck on a rack in a roasting pan and roast for 10 minutes. Reduce the oven heat to 350°F and roast the duck 1½ hours longer. Drain off the fat as it collects in the pan during the roasting, and reserve 1 cup.

3. Remove the duck from the oven and let cool until you can comfortably handle it. Remove the skin, cut into ¼-inch-wide strips, and set aside. Remove all the meat from the duck. Cut the breast meat into ½-inch-wide strips about 2 inches long; cut the thigh and leg meat into slivers of approximately the same size. Set the meat aside.

4. Heat the reserved 1 cup duck fat in a heavy pan to 325°F, or until very hot, and fry the duck skin until crispy, about 3 minutes. Drain on paper towels.

5. Combine the nutmeg and stock in a small pot, bring to a boil over high heat, and cook until reduced by half, about 5 minutes. Pour into a large bowl, add the honey and vinegar, and let cool. Beat in the oil, and set this dressing aside until ready to serve.

6. When it's time for dinner, peel the pear and cut it into thin strips and add to the dressing. Add the lettuce and toss. Mound the lettuce on plates, arrange the duck meat on top of each serving, and sprinkle the strips of duck skin over the top.

TURKEY AND SWEET POTATO SALAD

SERVES 4

*T*his is a good dinner for turkey leftovers or for cutlets. It may seem like winter food, but it's really a warm-weather pleaser, too. Begin dinner with a bowl of littleneck or Manila clams steamed in white wine. Finish with ice cream sundaes.

6 tablespoons grainy mustard
2 soft-boiled eggs
½ cup heavy cream
2 tablespoons chopped fresh tarragon or 1 teaspoon dried
6 tablespoons olive oil
1 bunch watercress
1 head Boston lettuce
2 pounds sweet potatoes (about 2 large potatoes), peeled
¼ cup white wine vinegar
3 cups diced cooked turkey (about 1 pound)

1. Combine the mustard and eggs in a blender or food processor. Place the cream in a small saucepan; if using dried tarragon, add it to the cream. Bring the cream to a boil over medium heat. Remove from the heat and add, running the blender on medium, to the mustard/egg mixture. If using fresh tarragon, add it now. Slowly add the oil. Set the dressing aside.

2. Remove and discard any tough stems and discolored leaves from the watercress and place the leaves in cold water. Remove and discard the dark green outer leaves and root end of the Boston lettuce. Separate the lettuce leaves and wash them in the cold water with the watercress. Remove from the water, dry well, and refrigerate.

3. Cut the sweet potatoes into 1-inch pieces. Place in a pot, cover with salted water, bring to a boil over high heat, and cook 8 to 10 minutes, until soft. Drain and place in a bowl.

4. Pour the vinegar over the potatoes, cover, and let sit for 5 minutes. Add the turkey and half the dressing and mix well. Set aside at room temperature until ready to serve.

5. When it's time to serve dinner, toss the lettuce with the remaining dressing and mound it on individual plates. Arrange the turkey/potato mixture on the lettuce and serve immediately.

SPLIT PEA AND RIB SALAD

SERVES 4

*G*enerally, split peas are used only in soups and, sometimes, as a puree. You will be charmed, I have no doubt, by this eccentric "chili," using split peas as salad.

2 racks pork baby back ribs (about 1¾ pounds total)
1 teaspoon black peppercorns
2 tablespoons ketchup
¼ cup soy sauce
1 cup orange juice
1 cup split peas
1 teaspoon dried thyme
1 medium carrot, diced
1 medium onion, diced
2 celery stalks, thinly sliced
1 bunch sorrel, trimmed and chopped
1 head escarole lettuce
3 tablespoons olive oil
3 tablespoons fresh lemon juice
Warm tortillas, for serving
Sour cream, for serving

1. Place the ribs in a large pot and add the peppercorns, ketchup, soy sauce, orange juice, and water to cover. Cover and bring to a boil over high heat, then reduce the heat to low and simmer for 20 minutes, turning once. Remove the ribs and let cool. Boil the cooking liquid, uncovered, for about 10 minutes, or until it has reduced and is syrupy. You should have about 1 cup liquid. Pour through a strainer into a bowl and let cool.

2. Place the split peas in a pot and add the thyme and water to cover. Cover and cook over medium heat until the peas are tender but not mushy, about 25 minutes, adding more water a little at a time if necessary. Transfer the peas to a bowl and stir in the carrot, onion, celery, and sorrel. Let cool.

3. Meanwhile, preheat the oven to 350°F or heat a grill.

4. Cook the ribs, basting with the reduced cooking liquid, until they are browned and tender, about 30 minutes in the oven, 20 minutes on a grill. Transfer them to a work surface. When they are cool enough to handle, remove the meat from the bones. Trim and discard any excess cartilage from the meat. *(continued)*

Cool Dinners

5. Trim off and discard the outer leaves from the escarole and cut off any dark green tops, so that you have only light green, crisp leaves. Separate the leaves, rinse and dry, and place in a bowl.

6. When you want to serve dinner, add the oil and lemon juice to the escarole and toss well. Place a few leaves of escarole on each plate and mound some of the split pea salad on top. Garnish with the rib meat. Serve warm tortillas on another plate, and offer sour cream on the side.

Perfect Aspic

I always thought it ironic that the name the French gave to their classic beef and vegetable aspic, a chilled dish presented "en gelée," was "à la mode"—meaning up-to-date, stylish, and trendy—because for so many years it's been considered old-fashioned food and hardly anyone makes it anymore. But, like men's ties and women's hemlines, what goes around comes around, and I've recently rediscovered aspic. A cooked and chilled morsel of poultry, fish, or beef, even a macédoine of vegetables or a poached egg or fruit, is set in a mold and covered with clear, sparkling jelly. The preparation is easy, but you have to start early enough so the jelly has time to set. So start your aspic early in the day. (A bonus on summer days—you're out of the kitchen before the heat of the day has you yearning for a swimming pool.)

Here are some guidelines for preparing a perfect aspic:

• A strong, clear homemade broth makes the best jelly, especially one made with a calf's foot. To yield 4 cups of aspic, cook 2 split calf's feet in 7 cups of broth for 4 to 5 hours. Don't let the liquid boil, or the stock will be cloudy. Strain through cheesecloth before using. Much easier, and perfectly acceptable, however, is an aspic prepared from your own chicken stock or canned low-sodium chicken broth, with powdered gelatin added.

• Trim all traces of fat from the fish, poultry, or meat you are using.

• Completely chill all morsels of food before setting in the mold; chill the mold, too.

• Stir the jelly over a bowl of ice to thicken it.

• If the jelly thickens too much and starts to get lumpy while you are assembling the aspics, simply replace it over low heat for a minute, stirring until syrupy again.

TOURNEDOS OF BEEF À LA MODE

SERVES 4

*W*hat I truly like about this dish is the flavor of the broth after it cooks with the steak and vegetables. And there's no need to feel obliged to clarify the jelly so that it's perfectly clear. I use large café au lait cups as molds, but any 4- to 4½-inch diameter cup, mold, or ramekin will do.

4 5-ounce filet mignon steaks, trimmed of all fat
1 tablespoon vegetable oil
1 onion, diced
1 cup thinly sliced carrots
2 cups dry white wine
8 cups chicken stock or canned low-sodium chicken broth
1 teaspoon salt
¼ teaspoon freshly ground black pepper
3 bay leaves
2 tablespoons powdered gelatin
1 cup frozen peas, defrosted
¼ cup finely chopped fresh parsley
Sprigs of watercress, for garnish
Grated horseradish, for serving
Dijon mustard, for serving

1. Heat a heavy skillet over high heat. Lightly rub the steaks with the oil. When the skillet is smoking hot, add the steaks and brown for 1½ minutes on each side. Remove the steaks from the skillet, wipe the skillet dry, and add the onion, carrots, 1 cup of the wine, the broth, salt, pepper, and bay leaves. Bring to a boil over high heat, reduce the heat to medium, and add the steaks. Cook the steaks for about 6 minutes for medium rare, then remove from the broth. If necessary, trim the steaks so that they are slightly smaller in diameter than the aspic molds, reserving the trimmings. Refrigerate the steaks. Meanwhile, cook the broth and vegetables 25 minutes more.

2. Pour the cooking liquid through a strainer into a large measuring cup. Place the vegetables in a bowl and add the peas. If you have reserved trimmings from the steaks, coarsely chop them and add to the vegetables. Place the vegetables in the refrigerator to chill.

3. Pour the remaining 1 cup wine into a small bowl and dissolve the gelatin in it. Pour the wine into the broth. You should have 4 cups of liquid; if you don't, add enough cold water to make 4 cups. Set the measuring cup in a bowl of ice water, add the parsley, and stir until syrupy.   *(continued)*

4. Spoon 2 tablespoons of the liquid into each of four 4- to 4½-inch coffee cups or molds and refrigerate for 5 minutes, or until set.

5. When the jelly is set, divide chilled vegetables among the molds. Spoon enough jelly over the vegetables to cover and refrigerate for 10 minutes.

6. Place a steak in each coffee cup. Spoon the remaining jelly over the steaks, covering them, and refrigerate until completely set, at least 3 hours.

7. To serve, unmold the aspics onto a large platter. (To make unmolding easy, either dip the molds up to the rims in hot water for 10 seconds or wrap a warm damp towel around each one for 10 to 20 seconds.) Garnish with sprigs of watercress, and accompany with horseradish and mustard.

Steak Tartare

SERVES 4 TO 6

*T*here are only two things that I order from hotel room service, and one of them is steak tartare—it's failsafe, especially since you can personalize the recipe. All they have to do is get the grind right.

Begin this dinner with some clam chowder and serve a Caesar or plain green salad after the steak. I like crispy hot French fries with the tartare, but if you don't have time to prepare them, put out a bowl of potato chips.

You can use the tenderloin, which is among the leanest but also one of the least flavorful cuts. Top round, which I prefer, is extremely lean but with good flavor. Use only the freshest meat.

2 pounds beef tenderloin or top round
22 anchovy fillets
½ cup drained capers
2 tablespoons grated horseradish, preferably fresh
1½ tablespoons Dijon mustard
1½ tablespoons finely chopped fresh parsley
3 tablespoons finely minced onion
¾ teaspoon Tabasco sauce, or to taste
1½ teaspoons Worcestershire sauce
1 egg yolk
1½ tablespoons fresh lemon juice
¼ cup virgin olive oil

1. Trim all the fat and connective tissue from the meat: If using tenderloin, simply remove any exterior fat and use a sharp knife to remove the "silverskin" that covers the meat. If using top round, look for the natural divisions in the meat and separate the muscles. Remove any silverskin and other connective tissue. Cut the meat into 1-inch cubes. (Or ask your butcher to prepare the meat when you order it.)

2. Place four plates in the refrigerator to chill.

3. Fit a meat grinder with the coarse disc and grind the meat. Or finely chop the meat by hand; if you do this in batches, the chopped meat will be more uniform. Do not use a food processor—it will turn the meat to mush.

4. Reserve 4 to 6 anchovies (1 per serving) for garnish and finely chop the remaining anchovies with the capers. Place in a bowl. Add the horseradish, mustard, parsley, onion, and Tabasco and Worcestershire sauces, then add the egg yolk and lemon juice and mix well. Slowly beat in the oil until absorbed. Refrigerate until ready to serve the tartare.

5. When it's time to get dinner on the table, add the meat to the anchovy mixture and, using two forks, mix well. Mound on the chilled plates and use a fork to flatten each mound into a large hamburger-shaped round. Garnish with the reserved anchovies. Serve immediately with warm toast or good dark bread.

ROAST TENDERLOIN WITH GARLIC AND DATE COMPOTE

SERVES 4

*T*he garlic in the compote turns to a kind of candy when it absorbs the sugar from the dates. It's a great "condiment" that makes the meat seem like a wonderful gamey treat, almost more like venison than beef.

Accompany this dish with a pilaf of rice or couscous, and serve a tomato and lettuce salad afterward.

24 garlic cloves, roughly chopped
¼ cup vegetable oil
1½ cups chicken stock or canned low-sodium chicken broth
24 pitted dates
1 tablespoon Dijon mustard
2 pounds beef tenderloin, in 1 piece
Salt and freshly ground black pepper to taste

1. Preheat the oven to 450°F.

2. Combine the garlic and 2 tablespoons of the oil in a saucepan and cook over medium heat, stirring, for 2 minutes. Add the stock, cover, and cook for 5 minutes. Add the dates and cook for 5 minutes. Remove from the heat and stir in the mustard. Transfer to a bowl and let cool.

3. Rub the beef tenderloin with the remaining 2 tablespoons oil and sprinkle with salt and pepper. Place the tenderloin in a roasting pan, place in the oven, and reduce the oven temperature to 375°F. Roast for 15 minutes, turn, and roast 12 to 15 minutes longer, or until a meat thermometer reads 135°F for rare. Transfer the tenderloin to a plate and let cool for 1 hour before serving.

4. When it's time for dinner, cut the tenderloin on the diagonal into ¼-inch slices. Arrange overlapping slices in a circle on a large plate, and spoon the garlic and date compote onto the center of the plate.

Kettle Dinners

*C*ooking in a covered vessel over a hearth fire is how most meals were prepared until the early years of the nineteenth century. Early ovens were simple brick enclosures. The coals had to be continually raked out, and the food constantly monitored. Complicated dishes were beyond the scope of the average cook. Add to this the fact that the little meat available to most people consisted of tougher cuts that required a moist heat method of cooking to make them palatable. It's no wonder that today's so-called comfort food is usually boiled or braised. Cooking foods in liquid—a broth or stock—reminds us of simpler times.

A kettle and a hearth—what an incredible image of kitchen economy and harmony. Kettle dinners cook slowly and by themselves—no need for a watched pot. When dinner is ready, it can sit in the pot until you're ready to set the table.

Every country has its version of a boiled dinner. Japanese and Korean restaurants serve some of my favorites, the broth laced with star anise or garnished with shiso leaves. In France it's called pot au feu and restaurants have pretty much standardized the dish to consist of beef and/or chicken (usually both), with leeks, onions, carrots, and cabbage thrown in near the end.

Kettle dinners can take various guises. There are lots of soup dinners here—rich cheese and onion ones, a few fish chowders, and even a Thanksgiving chowder of turkey and cranberries. As a starter, these soups will feed twice as many as they would as a main course. Then, naturally, there are pot roasts and stews. Some stews, like the chilies, are based on beans. There's also a French bean dish called a potée, named after the kettle in which it's cooked. Gumbo, which takes its name from both the distinctive roux used to thicken it and the okra that is always included, can be endlessly varied. These dishes, with their cut-up pieces of meat, remind us that the kettle is democratic and just in its apportionment of victuals.

Kettle Dinners

CHEESE SOUP WITH CORN SPAETZLE

SERVES 2 TO 3

*7*o prevent the cheese from separating from the soup base, it's best to dissolve it in a small amount of the soup in a food processor or blender, then add it to the pot of soup. Cook the spaetzle separately so it stays light. Serve an assortment of smoked fish or deli meats along with some dense, dark pumpernickel bread, and that's dinner.

1 tablespoon vegetable oil or unsalted butter
2 medium onions, roughly chopped
2 cups fresh or frozen corn kernels
2 12-ounce bottles of beer
2 cups chicken stock, canned low-sodium chicken broth, or water
Salt
Freshly ground black pepper to taste
¼ cup yellow cornmeal
5 tablespoons all-purpose flour
¼ teaspoon baking powder
¼ teaspoon ground white pepper
⅛ teaspoon ground nutmeg
2 egg whites
1 pound sharp Cheddar cheese

1. Heat the oil over medium heat. Add the onions and cook, stirring occasionally, for 10 minutes. Add the corn and cook, stirring occasionally, for 5 minutes.

2. Add the beer, stock, and salt and pepper to taste, cover, raise the heat to high, and bring to a boil. Boil for 10 minutes.

3. Transfer the contents of the pot to a blender or food processor and process, in batches if necessary, to a coarse puree. Return the soup to the pot, cover, and set aside.

4. Combine the cornmeal, flour, baking powder, 1 teaspoon salt, the white pepper, and the nutmeg in a bowl. With an electric mixer set at medium speed, beat in the egg whites and beat until a rough dough forms. (The dough will be sticky.)

5. Bring a large pot of salted water to a boil. Drop small spoonfuls of batter into the water. As the spaetzle cooks, it will rise to the top. Cook 1 minute longer, about 3 to 4 minutes in all, remove with a slotted spoon, and drain on towels.

What's for Dinner?

6. When ready to serve dinner, heat the spaetzle in a low oven. Reheat the corn soup. Put the cheese in a blender or food processor. Add about a cup of the hot soup and process until smooth. Then stir the mixture into the hot soup. Pour the soup into a tureen. Arrange the spaetzle in individual soup bowls and ladle out the soup at the table.

ONION SOUP WITH GOAT CHEESE FLANS

SERVES 4

A terrific midnight meal for après theater or movie. The key to success is cooking the onions long enough to caramelize them, turning them a deep rich brown without burning them—the rest is easy. Offer copious quantities of the steaming soup in deep bowls, with plenty of delicious bread to dunk. The flans add a different touch and are more enticing than the melted cheese topping that most restaurants smother their onion soups with. Serve an endive and walnut salad, and end with strong coffee and bittersweet chocolate truffles.

2 tablespoons vegetable oil or unsalted butter
1 pound soup bones
4 pounds yellow onions, roughly chopped
6 eggs
3 egg yolks
¼ pound goat cheese, crumbled
1½ cups milk
2 tablespoons minced garlic
7 cups chicken stock, canned low-sodium chicken broth, or water
¼ teaspoon ground mace
4 bay leaves
Salt and freshly ground black pepper to taste

1. Preheat the oven to 325°F. Lightly butter four 4-ounce ramekins.

2. Heat the oil in a heavy pot over medium-low heat. Add the bones and onions and cook, stirring occasionally, for 1 hour, or until the onions are a deep golden brown. *(continued)*

Kettle Dinners

3. While the onions are cooking, prepare the flans: Beat the eggs, yolks, and cheese together lightly. Heat the milk until scalded and stir into the eggs and cheese. Fill the prepared ramekins with the egg/cheese mixture and place in a baking pan. Add hot water to come halfway up the sides of the ramekins, and bake for 45 minutes, or until the flans are set. Remove the ramekins from the water and set aside.

4. Add the garlic to the caramelized onions and cook for 5 minutes. Add the stock, mace, bay leaves, and salt and pepper, increase the heat to high, and simmer for 20 minutes. Remove the soup bones and discard.

5. Run a knife around the inside of each ramekin and turn out the flans. Place one in each soup bowl. Pour the soup into a tureen and ladle it out at the table.

NOTE: The soup may be prepared in advance and reheated. The flans may be made up to 2 hours in advance and left, covered, at room temperature. (The heat from the soup will rewarm them sufficiently.)

POTATO, LEEK, AND COD SOUP

SERVES 4

*I*f you can, use waxy, less starchy potatoes such as yellow Finnish, Kennebecs, red rose, or white rose in this soup to avoid a mealy texture.

I learned a funny thing about codfish—they're lazy and spend a lot of time resting on the ocean floor. That's why they're so white. They lack the dark muscles found in more active fish, which use them for high-speed swimming and quick movements, either toward prey or away from predator.

1 pound salt cod
1 quart milk
2 tablespoons unsalted butter or margarine
1½ cups finely sliced leeks, white part only (about 3 large leeks)
1 tablespoon all-purpose flour
1½ pounds waxy potatoes, peeled and thinly sliced
½ teaspoon ground white pepper
½ cup sour cream
1 tablespoon finely chopped fresh dill

1. Soak the salt cod overnight, in water to cover, changing the water at least once.

2. Drain the cod and place in a pot with the milk. Cover and simmer over medium heat, for 8 minutes. Remove the cod from the pot, pour the milk through a strainer, and set aside. Flake the fish and discard any skin and bones.

3. Melt the butter in a large pot over low heat. Add the leeks and cook, stirring occasionally, until soft, about 5 minutes. Sprinkle the flour over the leeks, stir well, and add the reserved milk, the potatoes, and pepper. Cover, increase the heat to medium, and simmer for 15 minutes. Add the cod and remove the pot from the heat. The soup can be prepared ahead to this point and refrigerated.

4. When it's time to get dinner on the table, place the sour cream in a small bowl. If necessary, reheat the soup to piping hot. Stir ½ cup of the soup into the sour cream, then stir this mixture into the soup. (Do not heat the soup again or the sour cream will curdle.) Pour the soup into a tureen, sprinkle with the dill, and serve.

CIOPPINO

SERVES 4

*T*his tomato seafood soup is native to San Francisco, although it seems at once Spanish, Portuguese, and Italian in temperament. As with all good fish stews, the ingredient list will change according to the fish selection in the market. Some cooks use only shellfish, others use a combination of fish and shellfish. Authenticity, as always, is not nearly as important as a good-tasting result.

Use overripe tomatoes for the base and season with lots of garlic. And ask your fishmonger for the fish bones (from non-oily fish). This stew should cook at a frenetic boil to help emulsify the liquid and olive oil.

2 1-pound live lobsters
1 pound fish bones
¼ cup olive oil
1 large onion, roughly chopped
24 plum tomatoes, preferably overripe, halved
6 or more garlic cloves (to taste), coarsely minced
2 cups dry white wine
2 sprigs fresh thyme or 1 teaspoon dried
1 teaspoon salt, or to taste
¼ teaspoon cayenne pepper, or to taste
8 tiny new potatoes
1½ pounds assorted firm-fleshed fish fillets, such as halibut, bass,
   bluefish, swordfish, or mahi mahi, cut into ½-inch chunks
Garlic Sauce (recipe follows)
Grated Parmesan or Romano cheese, for serving

1. Preheat the oven to 350°F.

2. Cook the lobsters in a large pot of boiling water for 5 minutes. Drain and cool. Remove the meat from the shells, reserving the shells, cut into 1-inch chunks, and refrigerate.

3. Place the lobster shells and fish bones in a roasting pan and roast for 30 minutes.

4. Meanwhile, heat the oil in a large stockpot over medium heat. Add the onion and cook, stirring, for 10 minutes, or until softened. Add the tomatoes and garlic, cover, and cook another 10 minutes.

5. Add the lobster shells and fish bones to the tomatoes. Add the wine, thyme, salt, pepper, and 3 cups water, increase the heat to high, cover, and bring to a boil. Reduce the heat to low and gently simmer, uncovered, for 2 hours.

6. Pour the soup through a strainer with large holes, pressing against the solids to extract as much of the tomato pulp and meat remaining on the fish bones as possible. Or pass the soup through a food mill.

7. Pour the soup into a clean pot, cover, and bring to a boil over medium heat. Add the potatoes and cook until soft, about 15 minutes. Add the fish and cook for 10 minutes. Add the lobster meat and cook 1 minute longer.

8. Divide the fish, lobster meat, and potatoes among four large soup bowls. Ladle the soup into the bowls, and offer the Garlic Sauce and grated cheese as accompaniment.

GARLIC SAUCE

MAKES 1 CUP

4 garlic cloves, peeled
1 egg yolk
2 tablespoons fresh lemon juice
¼ cup fresh bread crumbs
¼ teaspoon salt
⅓ cup olive oil

Place the garlic, egg yolk, lemon juice, bread crumbs, and salt in a blender or food processor and process until smooth. With the motor running, add the oil a drop or two at a time and process until incorporated.

SEAFOOD CHOWDER

SERVES 4

*T*his is a white dish, and you might want to keep the theme throughout with an endive, goat cheese, and pine nut salad as a starter and white chocolate mousse or vanilla pudding for dessert. Serve the soup spooned over cooked rice, and this becomes an "à la king" presentation.

6 tablespoons unsalted butter
½ small onion, diced (about ⅓ cup)
1 small carrot, diced (about ⅓ cup)
1 large celery stalk, diced (about ½ cup)
5 tablespoons all-purpose flour
3 cups bottled clam juice
¾ cup dry white wine
4 sprigs fresh thyme, leaves only, or 1 teaspoon dried
⅛ teaspoon ground nutmeg
Salt to taste
¼ teaspoon ground white pepper, or to taste
1 medium potato, peeled and diced (about 1 cup)
4 jumbo shrimp
4 large scallops
8 clams
8 mussels, scrubbed and debearded
4 ounces skinless salmon fillet, cut into chunks
4 ounces skinless halibut fillet, cut into chunks
2 cups milk

1. Melt 5 tablespoons of the butter in a 3-quart pot over low heat. Add the onion, carrot, and celery and cook, stirring occasionally, for about 5 minutes. Stir in the flour and cook, stirring for 1 minute.

2. Add the clam juice, 2 cups water, the wine, thyme, nutmeg, salt, and pepper and bring to a boil over high heat. Reduce the heat to low and simmer for about 1½ hours, skimming off the foam.

3. Add the potato and cook for 20 minutes, or until the potato is tender and the cooking liquid has reduced to about 3 cups.

4. Transfer the soup to a clean pot and add the shrimp, scallops, clams, mussels, salmon, halibut, and milk. Bring to a boil over medium heat and immediately remove from the heat. Stir in the remaining 1 tablespoon butter, taste for salt and pepper and add as desired. Serve piping hot.

SERVES 6

*T*his New England–inspired soup is as warming after a fall football afternoon as it is welcome after a 4th of July fireworks display. The bacon adds a subtle smokiness to the shrimp and chicken.

Serve this in large bowls, with plenty of bread for soaking up the last drops of soup.

¼ pound bacon, cut into ¼-inch dice

1 cup dry white wine

1½ pounds boneless, skinless chicken breasts, cut into 1-inch-wide
* strips*

12 jumbo shrimp, peeled and deveined

5 cups fish stock, chicken stock, or canned low-sodium chicken broth

1 tablespoon finely minced garlic

2 teaspoons finely minced onion or shallots

1 teaspoon celery seed

1 teaspoon aniseed or fennel seed

3 sprigs fresh tarragon, leaves removed and chopped, or
* 1 tablespoon dried*

2 cups broccoli florets

12 shucked oysters (optional)

¾ cup milk

Salt and freshly ground black pepper to taste

2 cups cooked rice (optional)

2 tablespoons unsalted butter

1. Set a large heavy pot or Dutch oven over low heat, add the bacon, and cook, stirring, for 2 minutes, without browning. Add the white wine, increase the heat to high, bring to a boil, and cook for 1 minute to burn off the alcohol.

2. Add the chicken, shrimp, stock, garlic, onion or shallots, celery seed, and aniseed; if using dried tarragon, add it now. Bring to a boil, then reduce the heat to medium, cover, and cook 3 minutes. Add the broccoli and cook, uncovered, for 2 minutes. Add the oysters, if desired, and the milk. Taste the soup for salt and pepper and add as desired.

3. To serve, using a slotted spoon, transfer the bacon, chicken, shrimp, and broccoli to individual soup bowls. If serving rice, add it to the bowls. Return the broth to a boil and stir in the butter until melted. Remove from the heat and, if using fresh tarragon, add it to the soup. Serve the soup in a tureen, and ladle it into the garnished bowls at the table.

Kettle Dinners

MULLIGATAWNY SOUP

SERVES 4

*M*ulligatawny, the soup of chicken, apples, and lentils, was almost a cliché in Continental restaurants a few years ago. Here chicken thighs cooked in the soup rather than the usual little bits of chicken added as garnish turn it into dinner. Serve hot basmati or Texmati rice to spoon into the soup to give it even more texture and substance. A plate of sliced papaya and avocado with some lemon juice and walnut oil spooned over will complement the mulligatawny perfectly.

2 tablespoons unsalted butter
8 chicken thighs or about 2½ pounds chicken pieces
2 medium onions, finely diced
2 celery stalks, finely diced
1 medium carrot, finely diced
2 tablespoons curry powder
3 cups chicken stock, canned low-sodium chicken broth, or water
2 cups unfiltered apple cider
Salt to taste
Cayenne pepper to taste
⅓ cup dried lentils
¾ pound potatoes, peeled and diced
1 teaspoon dried dill
1 cup chopped peeled apples (about 2 small apples)
1 cup plain yogurt
12 sprigs cilantro (fresh coriander)

1. Melt the butter in a soup pot over medium heat. Add the chicken, onions, celery, and carrot, sprinkle with the curry powder, and mix well. Cook, stirring occasionally, for 15 minutes.

2. Add the stock, cider, salt, cayenne pepper, and lentils. Cover, reduce the heat to low, and cook for 20 minutes. Add the potatoes and dill and cook 20 minutes longer. (The soup can be prepared in advance to this point, cooled, and refrigerated.)

3. When it's time to put dinner on the table, reheat the soup if necessary. Add the apples, then remove from the heat and whisk in the yogurt. Pour the soup into a tureen, garnish with cilantro, and serve immediately.

CHICKEN AND MUSSELS IN A POT

SERVES 4 TO 5

I guess that I'm approaching middle age, because I've grown so fond of boiled chicken dinners. As my tastes change (and mature?), I seem to crave crispy less and smooth more—and that includes the skin of a boiled chicken.

1 stewing hen (4 to 5 pounds)
4 cups chicken stock or canned low-sodium chicken broth
1 teaspoon saffron threads or ¼ teaspoon powdered saffron
1 teaspoon fennel seed
1 tablespoon minced shallots or onion
1 tablespoon minced garlic
2 tablespoons Pernod (optional)
Salt to taste
1½ pounds small new potatoes
24 mussels, scrubbed and debearded
2 sprigs fresh tarragon, leaves only, or 1 teaspoon dried

1. Place all the ingredients except the potatoes, mussels, and tarragon in a pot just large enough to hold the chicken. Cover, and bring to a gentle boil over medium heat. Reduce the heat to low and cook at a slow simmer for 45 minutes.

2. Add the potatoes and simmer 30 minutes longer.

3. Transfer the chicken to a work surface. Skim the fat off the surface of the cooking liquid, and add the mussels to the pot; if using dried tarragon, add it now. Cover the pot and simmer over medium heat until the mussels open, about 7 minutes. If using fresh tarragon, add it now.

4. Cut the chicken into serving pieces and arrange in wide soup bowls. Place the mussels around the chicken, and spoon a little of the broth into the bowls. Transfer the potatoes to a bowl and serve on the side. Serve the remaining broth in a tureen.

Kettle Dinners

POACHED CAPON IN SWEET AND SPICY WINE SAUCE

SERVES 4 TO 5

*S*ince I always have to ask my market to order capon for me, I'm guessing that most everyone has forgotten this well-flavored bird, a neutered rooster. Capon is best cooked at a slow simmer to break down the tough connective tissue and bring out its succulent texture. It should be basted frequently with the pan juices.

Serve boiled new potatoes so you can crush them into the gravy on your plate. Serve lots of vegetables, too, such as spinach, zucchini, or squash.

> 1 capon or large stewing hen (about 5 pounds)
> 1 parsnip, peeled and finely shredded
> 1 tablespoon black peppercorns
> 4 bay leaves
> 1 large carrot, roughly chopped
> 1 onion, roughly chopped
> 1 celery stalk, roughly chopped
> 1 bottle muscat, Sauternes, or other sweet white wine
> ½ cup sour cream
> Freshly ground black pepper to taste

1. Remove the giblets from the capon and rinse it inside and out. Toss the shredded parsnip with 2 teaspoons salt and stuff into the cavity of the capon. Tie the capon legs together and fold the wings under. Place the peppercorns, bay leaves, carrots, onion, and celery in a pot just large enough to hold the capon and place the capon on top. Pour in the wine, and sprinkle the capon with salt. Cover and bring to a simmer over medium heat. Cook for 1½ hours, or until the capon is tender.

2. Remove the capon from the pot. Strain the poaching liquid and keep warm. Discard the solids.

3. To serve, scoop the parsnip out of the capon and arrange on a serving platter. Carve the capon and place on the bed of parsnip. Pour the sour cream into a small bowl and slowly beat in the reserved hot cooking liquid. Spoon the sauce over the bird and sprinkle the capon and parsnip generously with pepper.

TURKEY POT ROAST WITH
LEEKS AND CREAMY BARLEY

SERVES 3 TO 4

*W*hite meat is drier to begin with, and lacks the succor of dark, and when you cook a whole turkey, the breast overcooks when the dark meat is just right. So, cook a breast rather than a whole bird to control the way the white meat comes out.

1 tablespoon vegetable oil
1 turkey breast half (about 3½ pounds)
1 onion, studded with 2 cloves
1 tablespoon minced garlic
3 bay leaves
1 tablespoon fresh thyme or 1 teaspoon dried
¾ cup pearl barley
½ teaspoon salt, or to taste
½ teaspoon ground white pepper
2 tablespoons unsalted butter
5 large leeks, white part only, thinly sliced (about 3½ cups)
⅓ cup heavy cream

1. Heat the oil in a large Dutch oven or roasting pan. Add the turkey, skin side down, and cook over high heat until the skin is golden, about 7 minutes. Remove the turkey and pour off the oil.

2. Return the pot to the heat and add 3 cups water, the onion, garlic, bay leaves, thyme, barley, salt, and pepper. Replace the turkey, skin side up. Cover, reduce the heat to low, and simmer for 1 hour.

3. Meanwhile, heat the butter in a large skillet over low heat. Add the leeks, cover, and cook for 20 minutes, stirring occasionally, or until the leeks are tender. Remove from the heat and set aside; keep warm.

4. Transfer the turkey to a cutting board. Remove the onion and bay leaves from the pot and discard. Add the cream and cook for 3 minutes, or until the barley mixture thickens.

5. To serve, carefully remove the turkey from the bones. Cut the meat against the grain into thin diagonal slices. Pour the barley mixture onto a large platter. Fan the turkey slices around the barley and pile the leeks in the center.

TURKEY AND CRANBERRY CHOWDER

SERVES 3 TO 4

*H*ere is a soup version of a traditional feast dinner, complete with vegetables and meat—even the cranberries are included. Of course it would be easiest to do after Thanksgiving when you're likely to have a turkey carcass. You can keep fresh cranberries in the freezer until you want to make this dinner.

1 turkey carcass
4 bay leaves
1 teaspoon black peppercorns
4 tablespoons margarine or unsalted butter
1 carrot, diced
1 celery stalk, diced
1 medium onion, diced
¼ cup all-purpose flour
5 cups chicken stock or canned low-sodium chicken broth
1 teaspoon salt, or to taste
1 medium potato, peeled and diced
1½ pounds raw or cooked turkey (or whatever meat is left on the
    carcass), diced
2 tablespoons sugar
¼ cup white wine vinegar
½ cup sour cream
½ cup fresh or frozen cranberries

1. Break up the turkey carcass, wrap the bones, bay leaves, and pepper-corns in cheesecloth, and set aside.

2. Melt the butter in a large pot. Add the carrot, celery, and onion and cook over medium heat, stirring occasionally, for 5 minutes.

3. Stir in the flour, then slowly add the broth and 5 cups water. Add the wrapped turkey carcass and the salt, cover, and bring to a boil. Remove the lid and simmer for 45 minutes. Remove and discard the turkey carcass. Add the potato and cook for 10 minutes, then add the turkey. Cook 10 minutes more if using raw turkey, or 2 minutes more for cooked.

4. Meanwhile, combine the sugar and vinegar in a small heavy saucepan, and cook over medium-low heat until all the liquid has evaporated and the sugar is a dark golden brown. Immediately add the cranberries. Lower the heat,

cover, and cook for 5 minutes, or until the cranberries just begin to fall apart. Pour into a serving bowl.

5. Place the sour cream in a small bowl. Stir about 1 cup of the hot soup into the sour cream, then stir this mixture into the soup. (Do not reheat the soup after adding the sour cream, or it will curdle.) Strain the soup into a tureen, reserving the solids. Garnish each soup bowl with a mixture of the diced vegetables and turkey. Ladle the soup out at the table and pass the cranberry compote.

Roux

Roux is a mixture of cooked flour and butter used to thicken soups, gravies, and sauces. There are a few different methods for making a roux. The simplest is to combine equal amounts of the flour and butter and cook gently for 5 minutes on top of the stove. The result will be a blond roux; you can also make a blond roux by cooking the flour/butter mixture in a 350°F oven, stirring occasionally, for about 15 minutes. Cooking the roux is essential to eliminate the raw flavor of the flour. A blond roux should add very little flavor of its own to a sauce, gravy, or soup.

A brown roux is cooked until the flour is a deep brown. I make it by first toasting flour in a 350°F oven until it's a medium golden color. It's important to shake the pan as the surface of the flour browns so that all the flour toasts evenly. Because this can be a fairly long process, I usually toast a few cups of flour so I have some on hand and can quickly prepare a brown roux by simply adding melted butter to the flour. The toasted flour adds not only a rich color to brown sauces, but a distinctive flavor to a soup, gravy, or sauce.

The general rule of thumb is to thicken 1 cup of sauce with 2 tablespoons roux. However, the darker the roux, the less thickening ability it has. So you may need to add a bit more—how much more depends on your particular roux. Soups usually need about half the amount of roux used to thicken sauces. Soups and sauces are always tastier if they are just thickened lightly with a roux or other thickener and then simmered until the liquid is reduced by approximately one third and the desired texture attained.

SMOKED CHICKEN AND SHRIMP GUMBO

SERVES 6 TO 8

*T*he more you cook, the better your gumbos will be—not because you're more practiced but because you'll have more odds and ends of ingredients to throw in the pot. Absolute musts are okra and rice. The rest is up to you. Some good combinations are sausage and duck, turkey and sausage, steak and lobster, or, as in this case, shrimp and smoked chicken. Ham hocks or bacon or oysters can be added to almost any gumbo with happy results. The unique flavor of a real gumbo comes from the dark roux used to thicken it. Cajuns burn their roux, Creoles use a blond one; I prefer one that is quite dark, but not black. Many versions are also thickened with okra and filé powder (ground sassafras leaves), both of which I use here.

½ cup all-purpose flour
2½ quarts poultry, fish, and/or meat stock
1 tablespoon tomato paste
1 medium onion, roughly chopped (about 1 cup)
1 celery stalk, roughly diced
2 sprigs fresh thyme or ½ teaspoon dried
1 teaspoon cayenne pepper
2 bay leaves
Salt to taste
4 tablespoons melted butter
2 tablespoons gumbo filé powder, plus additional, for serving
1 to 1½ pounds jumbo shrimp
1 3-pound smoked chicken or 1½ pounds smoked chicken meat,
  diced
Gumbo Rice (recipe follows)
16 okra, trimmed and cut into ¼-inch rounds
Tabasco sauce, for serving

1. Preheat the oven to 350°F.

2. Place the flour in a plate or medium ovenproof skillet and toast in the oven until a deep golden color, about 45 minutes. Check the flour frequently and stir it every 10 minutes so it browns evenly.

3. Meanwhile, combine the stock(s), tomato paste, onion, celery, thyme, cayenne, bay leaves, and salt in a heavy 3-quart pot and bring to a boil over high heat. Reduce the heat to low and simmer, gently, uncovered, for 30 minutes.

4. When the flour is a dark golden color, whisk in the melted butter until completely blended. The mixture will darken dramatically in color. Transfer this roux to a heavy pot or Dutch oven and cook over very low heat for 5 minutes. Stir in the hot stock, raise the heat to medium, and simmer, uncovered, for 1 hour, or until lightly thickened. Skim the liquid frequently as it reduces. Stir in the gumbo filé powder, and strain into a clean pot. (The gumbo can be made in advance to this point and refrigerated for up to 5 days, or frozen for up to 6 months.)

5. Meanwhile, peel and devein the shrimp, reserving the shells, and roughly chop the meat. Refrigerate the shrimp until needed. Place the shells on a double thickness of cheesecloth and set aside. If using a whole smoked chicken, remove the meat from the bones. Dice the meat and refrigerate until needed. Discard the skin and add the bones to the shrimp shells.

6. Tie up the shells and bones in the cheesecloth, add to the gumbo, and simmer for 30 minutes. (Meanwhile, prepare the Gumbo Rice.)

7. Add shrimp, chicken, and okra to gumbo and cook for 15 minutes.

8. To serve, strain the gumbo into a soup tureen. Spoon some rice into each soup bowl and top with the shrimp, chicken, and okra. Ladle out the gumbo broth at the table and pass extra gumbo filé and a bottle of Tabasco.

GUMBO RICE
MAKES 1½ CUPS

1 tablespoon unsalted butter
2 tablespoons finely minced onions
½ cup long-grain rice
¾ cup chicken stock or canned low-sodium chicken broth
1 teaspoon cayenne pepper
1 teaspoon gumbo filé powder

1. Preheat the oven to 350°.

2. Place the stock in a small pot and bring to a boil over high heat.

3. Meanwhile, melt the butter over low heat, in a small ovenproof pot with a lid. Add the onion and cook for about 2 minutes. Add the rice and toss to coat with the butter.

4. Add the boiling stock, gumbo filé, and cayenne pepper to the rice. Cover and transfer to the oven for 15 to 20 minutes, until the rice is tender and the liquid has been absorbed.

Kettle Dinners

About Stews

Stews, like pot roasts, are braised foods. A hot liquid is used to cook a solid ingredient, such as a large cut of meat. The usual candidates for this moist-heat cooking method include flavorful cuts that require long cooking to become tender—rump roast, chuck roast, bottom round, brisket, or shoulder of beef, lamb, veal, or pork. Braising, which prevents the meat from drying out or burning, is pretty simple. An initial browning of the meat concentrates the juices, results in a dark rather than a light stew, and contributes its own special flavor. Red meat for Irish stew, Yankee pot roast, or beef Burgundy, for example, should be browned over high heat. Be sure to cook the meat until it is very dark—much of the color "dissolves" into the braising liquid and the meat becomes lighter during stewing. (After browning, pour out any grease that accumulated before adding the cooking liquid.)

Browning white meats such as veal, pork, and rabbit imparts a toasty flavor that goes particularly well with tomatoey stews. For pale-colored cream stews, such as blanquettes and fricassees, the ingredients should remain white, so don't brown the meat first.

Cook your stews in a heavy pot with a tight-fitting lid so the liquid doesn't evaporate, and add aromatic vegetables—onions, carrots, and celery—to round out flavors during the long cooking. When the meat is tender, remove it from the stew, strain the cooking liquid over the meat, and discard the vegetables—their flavors have been absorbed into the braising liquid. Separately cook new vegetables, then cook the meat and vegetables in the sauce for a few minutes before serving to integrate the flavors. Each ingredient should have a strong flavor but act as counterpoint to the others, while the mellow flavor of the long-cooked sauce unites all the ingredients like the bass line of a fugue.

Although they "cook by themselves," stews do take a long time. So, cook a good quantity of any stew you make, and then freeze some of the meat and sauce separately in meal-size batches. Kitchen mythology tells us that stews are always better the second day—well, when properly frozen and defrosted, they're better after the second *month*. But don't freeze leftover stew vegetables, because they lose flavor. Defrost the meat and gravy separately, then reheat together and add freshly cooked vegetables before serving. Use different vegetables and add fresh herbs to create variations on your original stew so that no one feels that he's being served leftovers.

BOILED BEEF DINNER

SERVES 6

*T*his boiled beef dinner can be made from a tough, less expensive cut of meat such as shoulder blade, shin, or brisket—or, to save some time, use sirloin tips, a relatively economical choice that's well flavored. The collagen in the meat's connective tissues of these tougher cuts dissolves into gelatin, flavoring the broth and giving it body. If your butcher can get it for you, add a split calf's foot to the pot; it contributes its own special flavor and makes for a healthier brew. Offer a platter of meat and vegetables and serve the broth separately. Eat all of it in soup plates. The customary mustard, horseradish, and gherkins accompaniments spice the dish up wonderfully. I start the more strongly flavored beef in cold water to extract its flavors for the broth, and add the chicken to hot liquid to retain the flavor in the meat. The result is a rich broth and a tasty chicken.

1 calf's foot, split (optional)
1 pound sirloin tips
8 medium carrots, thinly sliced (about 4 cups)
2 medium yellow onions, finely diced (about 1½ cups)
1 small bunch celery, thinly sliced (about 3 cups)
½ tablespoon black peppercorns
6 bay leaves
3 sprigs fresh thyme or ½ teaspoon dried
1 tablespoon salt
1 4-pound boiling chicken, cut into 8 pieces
1 tablespoon unsalted butter
2 large leeks, white part only, cut into ¼-inch slices
Prepared horseradish, for serving
Dijon mustard, for serving
Gherkins, for serving (optional)

1. Place the calf's foot and beef in a 6-quart pot, cover with cold water, and bring to a boil over high heat. Immediately drain the meat and rinse out the pot. This step will eliminate much of the "scum" that meats produce when boiled.

2. Return the meat to the pot and add 2 cups of the carrots, 1 cup of the onions, 2 cups of the celery, the peppercorns, bay leaves, thyme, and salt. Add 10 cups cold water, cover, and bring to a boil over high heat. Reduce the heat to low and simmer, uncovered, for 45 minutes. Add the chicken and cook 45 minutes longer. *(continued)*

Kettle Dinners

3. Transfer the meat and chicken to a platter. Pour the cooking liquid through a fine strainer into a large pot, discarding the solids, and keep warm.

4. Melt the butter in a large pan over medium heat. Add the leeks and the remaining carrots, onion, and celery. Cover and cook gently until the vegetables are soft, about 10 minutes.

5. Reheat the broth until boiling. Arrange the cooked vegetables, beef, and chicken on a large serving platter. Pour the broth into a tureen and serve the meal steaming hot. Offer horseradish, mustard, and, if desired, gherkins as accompaniments.

NOTE: When you're boiling or poaching and your aim is to retain flavor in the food itself, placing it in boiling liquid seals in flavor. But when you want to extract flavor from an ingredient to obtain a more flavorful broth, starting the cooking in cold liquid allows the flavors to melt into the broth.

LA POTÉE AUVERGNATE

SERVES 5 TO 6

*T*his dish is a regional pot au feu, or boiled dinner. I used to have it all the time in Paris at a small restaurant called La Potée. There it contained sausage, pork, beans, cabbage, and lots of garlic. Garlic is magical with dried beans, so cook whole cloves. And a strong herbing of the kettle avoids a boring porridge of a dish. If you prefer, use sage or additional thyme in place of the rosemary. Remember that when you cook fresh herbs for a long time, they mellow, so don't be stingy with them here.

If you're on a diet that restricts fat, trim the pork well before cooking. Then, about midway through the cooking, pull out the bacon and separate the layer of fat from the meat. Discard the fat and replace the bacon in the pot.

2 garlic sausages
6 ounces slab bacon, cut into 5 or 6 pieces
1 medium onion, diced (about ¾ cup)
24 garlic cloves, peeled
1 calf's foot, split (optional)
1 pound pork stew meat
½ cup dried Great Northern beans
4½ to 5½ cups chicken stock, canned low-sodium chicken broth,
*   or water*
2 sprigs fresh rosemary
3 sprigs fresh thyme
4 bay leaves
Freshly ground black pepper to taste
2 medium potatoes
1 teaspoon salt, or to taste
12 ounces boneless smoked pork, cut into 1-inch cubes
1 small head green cabbage, cut into eighths and cored

1. Prick the sausages and place them in a 2-quart heavy pot with the bacon. Cook over medium heat for 10 minutes to render some of the fat. Remove the sausages and set aside. Pour off excess fat from the pot.

2. Add the onions, garlic, calf's foot, and pork stew meat, cover, and cook for 10 minutes. Add the beans and enough broth to just cover all the ingredients. Then add the rosemary, thyme, bay leaves, and pepper. Cover, bring to a boil, and transfer the pot to the oven. Turn the oven on to 350°F and cook for 1 hour, until the beans are barely soft. Check from time to time and add broth or water if the beans start to dry out.

3. Meanwhile, cut the sausages into 1-inch pieces and quarter the potatoes.

4. When the beans are just tender, skim off the fat and add the smoked pork, cabbage, sausages, potatoes, and salt. Cover, replace the pot in the oven, and cook for 35 more minutes.

5. Fish the bay leaves out of the pot and discard. Serve the potée in the pot in which you cooked it.

NOTE: To completely defat the dish, remove the meat from the potée and refrigerate the meat and potée separately until chilled. The fat will congeal on the surface of the stew, and you will be able to remove most of it. Then return the meat to the pot, reheat, and serve.

BRAISED OXTAILS, POTATOES, AND CARROTS

SERVES 3 TO 4SERVES 3 TO 4

Oxtails make great soups because they are gelatinous and flavorful. The shy and dainty among us miss out on the best part of this dish—picking up the pieces of oxtail with your hands and sucking out every morsel of goodness. Perhaps you don't want to serve it to folks with whom you're not on intimate terms.

I like to drink beer with oxtails because it seems to cut their richness.

3 pounds oxtails
3 tablespoons flavorless vegetable oil
1 medium onion, finely minced (about 1 cup)
1 cup dry white wine
2 cups sliced carrots (about 5 carrots)
1 cup peeled, seeded, and chopped tomatoes
2 cups chicken stock or canned low-sodium chicken broth
8 small new potatoes, cut into 1-inch chunks

1. Preheat the oven to 325°F.

2. Pat the oxtails dry with paper towels. Heat the oil in a large heavy skillet over high heat. Add the oxtails in batches and brown well on all sides, about 10 minutes; do not crowd the pan or the oxtails will not brown. Place the oxtails in a 3-quart casserole and set aside.

3. Discard the fat in the skillet and place the skillet over low heat. Add the onion and cook until softened, about 5 minutes, stirring to dissolve and scrape up the browned residue on the bottom of the pan. Add the wine, increase the heat to high, and simmer until it has reduced by half.

4. Scrape the onion/wine mixture over the oxtails, add the carrots and tomatoes, cover tightly, and bake for 1 hour. Meanwhile, bring the stock to a boil.

5. Add the stock and potatoes to the oxtails, cover, and cook 30 minutes longer.

6. Spoon the grease off the top of the liquid in the casserole. Place the oxtails, potatoes, and carrots in individual soup bowls, and spoon the liquid over.

What's for Dinner?

CORNED BEEF AND BRUSSELS SPROUTS WITH POTATO DUMPLINGS

SERVES 6 TO 8

*F*or kids, the kitchen is a dangerous place, home to treacherous appliances and gadgets like the pressure cooker. We kids knew the pressure cooker would explode: It was marked with clear warnings of this possibility, and it was probable that you'd be disfigured while preparing supper. The only meal worth the risk was a boiled corned beef dinner. So, awed by mother's heroism, we promised ourselves to eat even the dreaded cabbage, and to not complain about the jiggly fat on the meat.

I like to make my corned beef with Brussels sprouts instead of cabbage, but if you want to remain more traditional, go right ahead. It would be pretentious, not to mention wasteful, to serve a first course with this dinner. Everyone should eat as much of it as they possibly can and then spend the rest of the evening complaining of overeating. The next day everyone can complain that there isn't enough leftover beef for sandwiches.

> *4 to 5 pounds corned beef (in 1 piece)*
> *1 pound potatoes*
> *½ cup all-purpose flour*
> *2 teaspoons salt*
> *1 teaspoon ground white pepper*
> *¼ teaspoon ground mace*
> *1 teaspoon baking powder*
> *3 eggs*
> *12 white boiling onions*
> *24 Brussels sprouts or 1 small green cabbage, cut into 8 wedges*
>   *and cored*
> *12 small carrots, peeled*
> *2 tablespoons prepared horseradish*
> *2 tablespoons grainy mustard*
> *½ cup vegetable oil*

1. Place the corned beef in a large pot and add cold water to cover by 2 inches. Cover and bring to a boil over high heat. Reduce the heat to low and cook until tender, about 45 minutes per pound (about 4 hours for a 5-pound corned beef). Or use a pressure cooker, and cook according to the manufacturer's instructions.   *(continued)*

2. Meanwhile, bake the potatoes in a microwave or conventional oven until soft. Scoop out the flesh, place in a bowl, and mash. Add the flour, salt, pepper, mace, and baking powder and mix well. Add the eggs and mix until incorporated. Cover and set aside. The dumpling mixture can be made up to 30 minutes before cooking.

3. Peel the onions and cut an X in the root ends. Remove the outer leaves from the Brussels sprouts and cut an X in the root ends.

4. When the corned beef is done, remove from the pot, cover, and keep warm. Add the onions, sprouts or cabbage, and carrots to the pot and simmer, covered, until tender, 15 to 20 minutes. Transfer to a bowl with some of the cooking liquid, cover, and keep warm.

5. Drop large tablespoons of the potato batter into the pot, in batches if necessary, and cook, covered, for about 10 minutes, until cooked through. Transfer the dumplings to a bowl with some of the cooking liquid and keep warm.

6. Combine the horseradish and mustard in a small bowl. Remove ⅓ cup of the hot cooking liquid from the pot, strain, and add to the horseradish mixture. Beat in the oil. Transfer the sauce to a sauceboat.

7. Place the corned beef on a cutting board and trim off any exterior fat. Slice the meat on the diagonal across the grain and place on a serving platter. Arrange the vegetables and dumplings around the meat. Serve the cooking liquid separately and pass the mustard and horseradish sauce.

Dinners My Grandmother Wouldn't Recognize

*G*randma food is special. For one thing, it doesn't taste like your mother's. Also, it's very curious to eat the same food that your mother and father ate when they were kids. Going to Grandma's is like going to the Museum of the History of Your Family.

My grandmother Pearl was an intuitive cook, if not a particularly fastidious one. We might have found a bit of gristle in the ground meat filling for stuffed cabbage, and there often were bones in the gefilte fish dumplings. Her measuring cups were simply some coffee cups that lived in the canisters of flour and sugar—so when she shared a recipe for, say, coffee cake, her "cup of flour" was not your cup of flour and the recipe wouldn't work. But her food was magical. She could throw things together in a seemingly haphazard way, with splendid results, and she was capable of incredibly delicious spur-of-the-moment improvisations. Everything always came out right, but none of her dishes tasted exactly the same each time. She never spoiled a dish by adding too many things to the recipe. She always said that ingredients should marry, never fight, and her food, although it sometimes tended toward the improvisatory, was in fact straightforward and well conceived.

Grandmother Helen was, quite simply, a good cook. Her cooking had a certain timidity that came from having followed written recipes throughout her life, although by the time she had grandchildren the recipes had long since been committed to memory. She could prepare flawless favorites—chicken soup, especially, and potato pudding—that tasted exactly the same every time. Her cooking was organized. She never seemed to burn anything or to make a mistake that she had to disguise at the eleventh hour. We loved her food for its steadfastness.

The recipes in this chapter are my versions of the Polish and Russian Jewish dishes of my immigrant grandmothers. I've tried to capture the essence of their cooking, while at the same time changing ingredients or using some they would never have dreamed of.

Although this cuisine has a reputation for heaviness, I've modernized the ingredients somewhat to fit my present lifestyle and all our dietary concerns.

The fish recipes are not for fish that have recently become prevalent in the markets, such as Hawaiian deep sea fish and fresh tuna. Those you'll find in other chapters. My grandmothers cooked river fish like whitefish, pike, carp, and salmon.

This is a cuisine heavy on grains, and I've improvised a few recipes using my favorites—buckwheat and barley. Who would have guessed that these two cereals would ever be considered chic?

There's the ubiquitous brisket, too, but I cook it Texas-style—I think my grandmas would have liked it. And no grandma chapter would be complete without two of the once-dreaded childhood dishes—tongue and liver. But people's tastes change.

PEARL'S PICKLED BLUEFISH

SERVES 4

*M*y grandmother used to add raisins and bitter almonds to this dish, and the result was truly satisfying. But you can't buy bitter almonds anymore because they are a source of cyanide. And the raisins don't make sense without the almond flavor. So the focus is now on coriander, dill, and mustard.

Served with potato salad, cucumber salad, chilled asparagus, and sliced garden tomatoes, this chilled dish makes an easy, yet elegant warm-weather dinner. Whitefish, halibut, and cod fillets are also delicious prepared this way.

4 6-ounce bluefish fillets
2 medium onions, thinly sliced
1 tablespoon prepared mustard
2 teaspoons coriander seeds
1 teaspoon minced garlic
2 tablespoons chopped fresh dill
1 cup dry white wine
¼ cup white wine vinegar
Salt and freshly ground black pepper to taste
2 tablespoons grainy mustard
2 tablespoons mayonnaise

1. Preheat the oven to 375°F.

2. Arrange the fish in a baking dish just large enough to hold the fillets comfortably, spread the onions over the top, and set aside.

3. Combine the mustard, coriander, garlic, dill, wine, vinegar, ¼ cup water, and salt and pepper in a small pan and bring to a boil over high heat. Pour over the bluefish and onions. Cover and bake for 5 minutes.

4. Let cool to room temperature, and refrigerate.

5. When it's time for dinner, mix the mustard and mayonnaise together and place in a small serving bowl. Transfer the onions to a serving platter, arrange the bluefish fillets around the onions, and spoon some of the liquid over the fish and onions.

HERBED WHITEFISH ROULADES
IN HORSERADISH BROTH

SERVES 4

*K*nowing that our grandmother's eyesight wasn't great, we searched carefully for the toothpicks she used to keep her *rouladen* rolled. But this was always an elegant dish, even though it was a regular family dinner.

Horseradish is one of those assertive flavors that taste stronger when released in a broth. For your vegetables, serve carrots and peas—they're sweet and can go right into the broth if you like.

12 small new potatoes
3 tablespoons chopped fresh parsley
1 tablespoon chopped fresh tarragon or 1 teaspoon dried
3 tablespoons finely minced fresh chives
1 teaspoon celery seed
3 tablespoons unsalted butter, at room temperature
4 7-ounce skinless whitefish fillets
Salt and white pepper to taste
½ cup dry white wine
½ cup heavy cream
1 tablespoon prepared horseradish

1. Place the potatoes in a large pot, add salted water to cover, and bring to a boil. Boil 7 minutes; drain and set aside.

2. Place the parsley, tarragon, chives, celery seed, and butter in a food processor and pulse until incorporated.

3. Lay the fillets on a work surface, skinned side up, and sprinkle with salt and pepper. Spread the herbed butter on the fillets and roll them up jelly-roll fashion. Secure each roll with string.

4. Combine the wine, cream, and horseradish in a large shallow pan, cover, and bring to a boil over medium heat. Add the fish and the parboiled potatoes, cover, reduce the heat to low, and simmer for 8 minutes.

5. Remove the fish and potatoes from the pan, cut the strings and discard, and transfer the fish and potatoes to wide soup bowls. Spoon the cooking liquid over the top and serve immediately.

BAKED WHITEFISH WITH FIDDLEHEAD FERNS

SERVES 4

*F*erns are such primitive, prehistoric-looking vegetables—yes, vegetables—that you want to eat them just to be cool. Then you realize that they have a marvelous flavor and texture, sort of okra meets asparagus. Look for them in the market fresh after the spring rains in the northern forests; they're also available frozen. If you can't find any, use okra or asparagus instead—my grandmother did.

1 medium onion, finely diced
¾ pound fiddlehead ferns or asparagus
4 tablespoons unsalted butter
Salt and ground white pepper to taste
½ cup dry white wine
3 tablespoons Dijon mustard
4 7-ounce whitefish fillets
½ teaspoon celery seed
1 tablespoon Pernod

1. Preheat the oven to 375°F.

2. Place the onion and fiddleheads in a baking dish. Add 1 tablespoon of the butter and sprinkle with salt and pepper. Bake for 20 minutes. Remove from the oven and keep warm.

3. Meanwhile, combine the wine and mustard in a 3-inch deep baking dish just large enough to hold the whitefish fillets in one layer. Add the whitefish, sprinkle with salt and pepper, the celery seed, and the Pernod, and bake for 20 minutes.

4. To serve, arrange a bed of the onions and fiddleheads on a platter. Remove the fish from the baking dish and place on top. Swirl the remaining 3 tablespoons butter into the fish cooking liquid until melted and incorporated, and pour over the fish. Serve immediately.

WHITEFISH AND PIKE DUMPLINGS
IN CHILLED SORREL SOUP

SERVES 4

*G*efilte fish is a Jewish fish dumpling. My grandmother wrapped her dumplings in pieces of whitefish skin, then cooked them with the roe, which I thought had a funny texture and squeaked when you chewed them. I always assumed that gefilte fish took a fair amount of culinary finesse. Well, it doesn't, I found out, when we tested this recipe. My version is meant to be a chilled dinner, not a starter. The dumplings get their unique texture from cracker crumbs. They are cooked, then cooled and served in a sour sorrel soup. Start dinner with crudités of cucumbers, radishes, peppers, tomatoes, and spring onions.

1 pound skinless whitefish fillets
1 pound skinless pike fillets
2 carrots, roughly chopped
2 onions, 1 quartered and 1 finely diced
½ cup finely crushed crackers, such as unsalted saltines or
    Carr's water biscuits
2 eggs
4 cups chicken stock or canned low-sodium chicken broth
Salt and ground white pepper
2 teaspoons vegetable oil
1 tablespoon minced garlic
3 tablespoons malt vinegar
1 tightly packed cup sorrel leaves (center ribs and stems removed),
    roughly chopped
8 small new potatoes
½ cup sour cream

1. Grind the whitefish, pike, carrots, and the quartered onion together in a meat grinder fitted with the fine disc. Place in a bowl, add the crushed crackers, eggs, ½ cup of the chicken stock, ½ teaspoon salt, and ¼ teaspoon pepper, and mix well. Cover and refrigerate for 30 minutes.

2. Meanwhile, heat the oil in a large pot over medium heat. Add the diced onion and the garlic and cook until the onion is soft, about 5 minutes. Add the malt vinegar and remaining 3½ cups chicken stock, increase the heat to high, and bring to a boil. Reduce the heat to low, add the sorrel, and let simmer while you shape the dumplings.

3. Moisten your hands with water and form 12 egg-shaped dumplings from the fish mixture.

4. Carefully drop the dumplings into the soup, add the potatoes, cover, and simmer for 20 minutes.

5. Remove from the heat, remove the dumplings from the soup, and place them in a large bowl. Combine the sour cream with ½ cup of the hot soup, then pour the thinned sour cream into the soup. Pour the soup over the dumplings and let cool slightly, then refrigerate to chill completely before serving, at least 3 hours.

6. When it's time for dinner, remove the dumplings from the soup and divide among four soup bowls. Taste the soup for salt and pepper and add as needed. Spoon the chilled soup around the dumplings and serve.

SALMON AND WHITEFISH STRUDEL

SERVES 6

I love the fact that so many of the grandma fish recipes have nothing to do with the kind of fish cooking that we're used to today. It's not a cookery based on simply grilled fish scented with oils and herb jus, but rather it combines earthy ingredients—in this case buckwheat and cabbage—as if the fish were just a more delicate meat.

1 medium head green cabbage, shredded (about 6 cups)
5 tablespoons kosher salt
2 tablespoons unsalted butter
1 teaspoon dried dill
1 medium onion, diced (about ¾ cup)
1 cup toasted buckwheat groats
Salt and freshly ground black pepper to taste
1¼ pounds skinless salmon fillets
1¼ pounds skinless whitefish fillets
6 sheets frozen filo dough, thawed
8 tablespoons melted unsalted butter or margarine

1. Place the cabbage in a colander, toss with the kosher salt, and set aside on a plate to degorge for 30 minutes. Rinse and squeeze dry.   *(continued)*

2. Heat 1 tablespoon of the butter in a large skillet. Add the cabbage and dill, cover, and cook over medium heat, stirring occasionally, for 7 minutes. Remove from the heat and set aside.

3. Heat the remaining 1 tablespoon butter in another skillet. Add the onion and cook over medium heat, stirring, for 2 minutes, to soften. Add the buckwheat, 2½ cups water, and salt and pepper to taste, cover and cook for 1 minute. Remove from the heat and let stand until all the liquid is absorbed, about 5 minutes.

4. Meanwhile, cut the salmon and whitefish into strips ½ inch thick and 2 inches long. Sprinkle with salt and pepper and set aside.

5. Preheat the oven to 350°F.

6. Lay 1 sheet of the filo lengthwise on a work surface and brush lightly with melted butter. Place a second sheet on top and brush with more butter. Repeat with a third sheet. Starting on the part of the sheet closest to you, arrange strips of salmon lengthwise in a single row, the thick end of each piece next to the thin end of its neighbor. Next, arrange a lengthwise strip of cabbage next to the salmon, then a strip of kasha, and finish with a single lengthwise row of whitefish. The bottom two thirds of the filo sheets should be covered. Brush the uncovered third of the filo with butter and roll up tightly, jelly-roll style. Make a second roll with the remaining filo and other ingredients.

7. Place the rolls, seam side down, on a baking sheet and tie the ends with a string. Brush the surface with melted butter, place the rolls in the oven, and bake for 25 minutes. Cover the roulades with foil during the last 10 minutes if the filo begins to darken too much.

8. To serve, cut off the tied ends and cut each strudel into 3 pieces. Arrange the pieces on plates and offer the remaining melted butter on the side.

HELEN'S ROAST CHICKEN
WITH HERB STUFFING

SERVES 4

*R*oast chicken is a simple meal, less pretentious than a fancy dish of cut-up chicken in sauce, yet it's a more formal ritual. Someone carves, the others politely request white or dark and hope for the best.

Roasters are more flavorful than fryers, but are older and tougher. Roast the bird slowly for falling-apart tender meat. This moist stuffing won't drink up all the juices from the bird as it cooks. I like to make too much stuffing and I cook the excess in a covered casserole.

¼ cup olive oil or 4 tablespoons unsalted butter
2 medium onions, finely diced, (about 1½ cups)
4 celery stalks, thinly sliced (about 1½ cups)
4 cups stale bread, roughly diced into ½-inch pieces
4 cups chicken stock or canned low-sodium chicken broth
2 tablespoons fresh thyme or 1 teaspoon dried
2 tablespoons chopped fresh sage or 1 teaspoon dried
Salt and freshly ground black pepper
1 4½- to 5-pound roasting chicken
¼ cup all-purpose flour
1 cup dry white wine

1. Heat the olive oil or butter in a large pot over medium heat. Add the onions and cook for 5 minutes, stirring occasionally. Add the celery and cook, stirring occasionally, for 10 minutes. Stir in the bread, ½ cup of the chicken stock, the thyme, half the sage, 1 teaspoon salt, and 1 teaspoon pepper and cook for 5 minutes, mixing well. Scrape the stuffing mixture into a large bowl, cover, and refrigerate to chill completely.

2. Preheat the oven to 425°F.

3. Fill the cavity of the chicken with the chilled stuffing, pressing in as much as you can. (Any leftover can be cooked along with the chicken in a covered baking dish.) Truss the bird and sprinkle with salt and pepper.

4. Place the bird on its side in a large roasting pan. Place in the oven and immediately lower the temperature to 350°F. Roast for 15 minutes. Turn on the other side and cook for another 15 minutes. Turn the bird breast up, cover with a lid or aluminum foil, and roast for 45 minutes. Remove the lid or foil and cook 15 minutes longer, or until the thigh moves easily in its joint.

(continued)

5. Remove the bird from the roasting pan and set aside on a serving platter. Place the roasting pan over medium heat, stir in the flour, and cook for 2 minutes, stirring with a wooden spoon. Add the wine and the remaining 3½ cups broth and cook for about 10 minutes, scraping up any residue on the bottom of the pan, until the gravy has reduced by about half. Remove from the heat, add the remaining sage, and season to taste with salt and pepper.

6. Pour gravy into a sauceboat, untruss the bird, and serve immediately.

ROAST CHICKEN WITH KASHA AND BOWTIES

SERVES 4

*I*t seems that no one eats kasha anymore except for Russians and Eastern European Jews. Kasha—buckwheat groats—has a distinctively earthy, toasty flavor. Mixed with bowtie pasta, it's a traditional side dish. With the addition of chicken it becomes dinner.

1 4- to 5-pound roasting chicken
1 tablespoon dried thyme
Salt to taste
Ground white pepper to taste
2 medium onions, finely chopped (about 1½ cups)
1 cup buckwheat groats
2½ cups chicken stock, canned low-sodium chicken broth, or water,
  or a combination
1 cup bowtie pasta (farfalle)
1 tablespoon vegetable oil
½ cup sour cream or plain yogurt
2 tablespoons chopped fresh dill
1 tablespoon prepared horseradish

1. Preheat the oven to 350°F.

2. Remove the backbone from the chicken; with a sharp knife, cut down along either side of the backbone from neck to tail and remove it. Lay the

chicken flat on a work surface, skin side up, and lay a large roasting pan over it. Press down on the roasting pan to flatten the chicken. Carefully loosen the skin of the chicken without detaching it and rub the meat with the thyme. Sprinkle both sides of the chicken with salt and pepper.

3. Place the chicken skin side up in a roasting pan and roast for 10 minutes. Remove the chicken from the pan and smash it flat with a mallet. Return to the pan and roast for 20 minutes.

4. Remove the chicken from the roasting pan and pour off all but 2 tablespoons of the fat. Add the onions to the pan, replace the chicken, and roast for 30 minutes.

5. Remove the chicken from the pan and stir in the buckwheat and chicken broth. Add ½ teaspoon salt, or to taste. Replace the chicken on top of the buckwheat and onions and bake for 30 minutes.

6. Meanwhile, bring a large pot of salted water to the boil and cook the bowtie pasta for 5 minutes, or until tender. Drain, toss with the oil, cover, and set aside. Combine the sour cream, dill, and horseradish and set aside.

7. To serve dinner, remove the chicken from the roasting pan and place on a serving platter. Add the bowties to the kasha, mix well, and mound in a serving dish. Serve the sour cream on the side.

CHICKEN FRICASSEE

SERVES 3 TO 4

*T*his is not the elegant French version of the dish. When I was growing up, we went out to French restaurants for that. I always thought of this as down-home New York soul cooking.

2 tablespoons unsalted butter

1 tablespoon flavorless vegetable oil

3½ pounds chicken pieces

Salt and ground white pepper

1 cup chicken stock or canned low-sodium chicken broth

1 teaspoon finely minced garlic

¾ teaspoon ground nutmeg

1 cup heavy cream

1 pound button mushrooms, trimmed

1. Preheat the oven to 375°F.

2. Heat the butter and oil in a Dutch oven over low heat. Season the chicken pieces with salt and pepper and cook, turning once, for about 7 minutes; do not brown the chicken.

3. Remove the chicken from the Dutch oven and drain off the fat. Replace the leg and thigh pieces and add the stock, garlic, nutmeg, 1 teaspoon salt, and ¼ teaspoon pepper. Bring to a boil, cover, and transfer to the oven. Bake for 15 minutes. Add the breasts, mushrooms, and cream, cover, and bake for another 15 minutes.

4. Transfer the chicken and mushrooms to a serving platter, cover, and place in the turned-off oven to keep warm. Place the Dutch oven over high heat and boil the sauce until it has reduced and is thick enough to coat the back of a spoon.

5. To serve, pour any juices that have accumulated around the chicken into the sauce. Spoon the sauce over the chicken and mushrooms.

ROASTED TURKEY THIGHS

SERVES 3 TO 4

*C*ooks of my mother's generation always wanted white meat. The grand-mothers always wanted dark meat. And no one was lucky enough to be able to buy turkey parts the way we can today. Turkey was seasonal—you found it in the fall and you cooked the whole thing.

2 turkey thighs
2 tablespoons chopped fresh sage
Salt and freshly ground black pepper to taste
1 small head red cabbage
3 tablespoons kosher salt
4 tablespoons melted unsalted butter or margarine
1½ pounds sweet potatoes or yams (about 2 large)
2½ cups chicken stock or canned low-sodium chicken broth
½ cup white wine vinegar
1 teaspoon chopped fresh rosemary
3 tablespoons walnut or olive oil

1. With your fingers, carefully loosen the turkey skin from the thighs without detaching it, and rub the sage evenly over the turkey meat. Sprinkle the thighs with salt and pepper and refrigerate for at least 1 hour or up to a day.

2. Cut the cabbage in half lengthwise and cut out and discard the core. Lay the halves cut side down on a work surface and shred the cabbage as fine as you can. (You should have about 8 cups.) Place the cabbage in a colander, add the kosher salt, and toss well to mix. Set the cabbage aside to degorge for 1 hour.

3. Preheat the oven to 350°F.

4. Rinse the cabbage and drain well. Spread the cabbage over the bottom of a roasting pan and place the turkey on top. Brush the turkey with 2 tablespoons of the melted butter, cover the pan, and roast for 1 hour.

5. Meanwhile, scrub the sweet potatoes, cut them into 2-inch chunks, and toss with the remaining 2 tablespoons melted butter.

6. Add the sweet potatoes to the roasting pan and roast 50 minutes longer, or until the potatoes are soft and the turkey is cooked through.

(continued)

Dinners My Grandmother Wouldn't Recognize

7. While the turkey is roasting, combine the stock and vinegar in a 1-quart pot, bring to a boil over medium heat, and boil for 5 minutes, or until reduced by one third. Add the rosemary and salt and pepper to taste, remove from the heat, and set aside in a small bowl until ready to serve dinner.

8. Remove the turkey from the bones and arrange the meat in the center of a platter. Mound the cabbage on one side of the turkey and pile the sweet potatoes on the other. Whisk the oil into the reduced chicken broth and pour over the turkey. Serve immediately.

VEAL AND CARROT TSIMMES
WITH WHEAT DUMPLINGS

SERVES 6

*T*simmes is a stew. (It's also Yiddish slang for a fuss, a to-do, as in "What's the big tsimmes?") In this case, it's a stew of veal and carrots melted together. It should be a bit sloppy, and vaguely sweet. The slower and longer it cooks, the better it tastes.

2 pounds veal stew meat
4 bay leaves
½ teaspoon dried thyme
Salt and freshly ground black pepper
5 cups chicken stock or canned low-sodium broth
3 cups thinly sliced carrots
5 tablespoons unsalted butter or margarine
4 onions, finely diced (about 3 cups)
1 cup whole wheat flour
⅓ cup cooked bulgur
2 eggs
½ teaspoon baking powder
¼ teaspoon white pepper
5 tablespoons all-purpose flour
2 cups milk

1. Place the veal, bay leaves, thyme, salt and black pepper to taste, and stock to cover in a large pot, cover, and bring to a boil over high heat. Reduce the heat to low and simmer for 40 minutes. Add the carrots and cook 20 minutes more.

2. Meanwhile, heat 1 tablespoon of the butter in a skillet over medium heat. Add 2 cups of the onions and cook, stirring from time to time, for about 10 minutes, or until softened. Transfer the onions to a bowl and add the whole wheat flour, bulgur, eggs, baking powder, ¼ teaspoon salt, and the white pepper. Mix until well blended, cover, and set aside.

3. Remove the veal from the heat and strain the contents of the pot through a large strainer into a bowl. Discard the bay leaves. Set the meat and carrots aside, and reserve the cooking liquid. (The tsimmes can be prepared to this point up to a day in advance and refrigerated, but do not prepare the dumpling batter until shortly before serving.)

4. Rinse out the pot, place it over medium heat, and add the remaining 4 tablespoons butter. Add the remaining onions and cook for 3 minutes, stirring frequently. Add the flour and stir until the onions are well coated. Stir in the reserved cooking liquid and the milk, add the veal and carrots, and cook for 20 minutes.

5. When it's time for dinner, cook the dumplings: Drop tablespoon-size dollops of batter into the pot, cover, and cook for 10 minutes.

6. Serve the tsimmes straight from the pot.

VEAL SHORT RIBS WITH
MUSHROOMS AND NOODLES

SERVES 3 TO 4

*I*f my grandmother had thought about it, she might have made something like this dish. It's a creamy mélange of textures and flavors. Make the ribs easier to eat by removing the meat from the bones before serving, then carefully trim off the offending connective tissue, leaving the really terrific succulent bits of meat found between the ribs.

2 tablespoons flavorless vegetable oil
2½ pounds veal short ribs
2 onions, diced (about 1½ cups)
2 tablespoons tomato paste
3 cups chicken stock or canned low-sodium chicken broth
½ teaspoon dried thyme
3 bay leaves
1 teaspoon salt, or to taste
½ teaspoon black peppercorns
1½ pounds small white mushrooms
6 ounces egg noodles
2 tablespoons chopped fresh parsley

1. Heat the oil in a Dutch oven over high heat. Add the ribs and brown on both sides. Remove the ribs and pour off the fat.

2. Reduce the heat to medium, add the onions and tomato paste, and cook for 1 minute. Add the chicken stock, thyme, bay, salt, and peppercorns. Replace the ribs, cover, and place in the oven. Turn on the oven to 350°F and cook for 1½ hours.

3. Remove the ribs from the cooking liquid and let cool. Strain the liquid into a saucepan, skim off the fat, and set aside.

4. When the ribs are cool enough to handle, remove the meat from the bones and trim off and discard all the exterior layers of fat. Set the meat aside.

5. When it's time to get dinner on the table, cook the egg noodles in boiling salted water according to the package directions. Meanwhile, add the mushrooms and trimmed meat to the reserved cooking liquid and cook over high heat for 5 minutes.

6. Drain the cooked noodles and place them in soup bowls. Spoon the meat, mushrooms, and gravy over the noodles, and sprinkle with the parsley.

SERVES 4

*B*arley is one of the oldest cultivated grains. There are records of its plantings in Mesopotamia as early as 7000 B.C., but wheat supplanted it as the grain of choice during Roman times. Now barley is a staple only in the Middle East—and at my grandmother's house, where it was used at least once a month to make the mushroom barley soup we all adored.

I love barley for its texture as much as its flavor. If you don't already cook with this healthy grain, you should try it. Pearl barley is best because of its tiny size.

Cook the short ribs first, then add the other ingredients to the kettle and cook until done. Serve a cucumber and tomato salad before the soup and ribs.

1 tablespoon flavorless vegetable oil or chicken fat
3 pounds beef short ribs
2 medium onions, diced
2 tablespoons minced garlic
6 cups chicken stock, canned low-sodium chicken broth, or water
Salt and freshly ground black pepper to taste
¾ cup pearl barley
6 celery stalks, finely sliced
2 pounds small white mushrooms
1 teaspoon dried dill

1. Heat the oil in a 3-quart pot over medium heat, add the ribs, and brown them on all sides, about 10 minutes. Add the onions and garlic and cook for 5 minutes, stirring occasionally.

2. Add the broth and salt and pepper, cover, reduce the heat to low, and cook for 30 minutes.

3. Add the barley and celery, cover, and cook for 1 hour, or until the barley is soft.

4. Add the mushrooms and dill and cook for 10 minutes.

5. Remove the ribs from the soup and arrange them on a platter. Pour the soup into a tureen and ladle it out at the table.

BARBECUED BRISKET

SERVES 4 TO 6

*I*n my family, just about every occasion involving food is an opportunity to serve beef brisket. My aunt Soretta gives hers a burnt ketchup coating. My grandmother Pearl's brisket was cooked with lots of onions. She browned the onions in chicken fat to get that dark caramelized flavor, then added lots of carrots and celery to the braise for their aromatic sweetness.

When I moved to California, I learned to prepare brisket for Texas-style barbecue. First the meat is braised, then finished on a slow grill. The braising liquid is reduced to a glaze and slathered on the meat.

1 cup dry white wine
3 cups apple cider
¼ cup honey
2 tablespoons Dijon mustard
¼ cup soy sauce
2 tablespoons brown sugar
1 tablespoon minced garlic
1 tablespoon minced fresh ginger
1 tablespoon coriander seeds
2 sprigs fresh thyme
1 small brisket of beef (about 2½ pounds)

1. Combine all the ingredients except the brisket in a Dutch oven or heavy roasting pan. Add the brisket, cover tightly, and place in the oven. Turn on the oven to 350°F and cook for 1 hour.

2. Remove the brisket from the cooking liquid and set aside, covered. Transfer the liquid to a medium pot and cook over medium heat until reduced to a glaze and thick enough to coat the back of a spoon.

3. Light about 12 charcoal briquettes in a covered grill and add a small piece of mesquite or other wood, placing the charcoal and wood to one side of the grill. Place the brisket on the grill rack so that it is not directly over the coals. Paint it with some of the glaze and cover the grill. Smoke the brisket for 1 hour, turning the meat and coating it with glaze every 15 minutes. Add a small amount of additional charcoal or wood, if the fire seems to get too cold.

4. Remove the brisket from the grill, slice the meat thinly against the grain, and serve. Heat any remaining glaze to a boil and offer on the side.

CALF'S LIVER IN HORSERADISH SAUCE

SERVES 4

*M*y family's recipe for liver was always made with beef liver. It cooked most of the afternoon, it seemed, while I remained outdoors. I wished I could have remained outdoors during dinner, too, or been invited to a friend's house, but it never worked out that way.

Calf's liver is mild and best when cooked quickly over high heat to medium rare. The horseradish, onion, and shallots give a tart piquancy that rounds out the flavor and makes it taste more like well-aged beef than the childhood nightmare that I remember.

> *1¼ pounds calf's liver, cut into 8 thin slices*
> *Salt and freshly ground black pepper to taste*
> *Flour, for dusting*
> *2 tablespoons peanut oil*
> *1 tablespoon prepared horseradish*
> *1 tablespoon finely minced onion or shallots*
> *2 tablespoons distilled white vinegar*
> *3 tablespoons dry white wine*
> *3 tablespoons unsalted butter*

1. Pat the liver dry. Sprinkle lightly with salt and pepper, then dredge in flour, shaking off the excess.

2. Heat 1 tablespoon of the oil in a large skillet over high heat. When the oil is hot, place 4 slices of liver in the skillet, without crowding, and cook for 1 minute on each side, or longer if you like your liver well done. Remove the liver and set aside in a warm place. Heat the remaining 1 tablespoon oil and cook the remaining liver.

3. Wipe the skillet clean with a paper towel and replace it over high heat. Add the horseradish, onion, vinegar, wine, and a pinch of salt. Cook until most of the liquid has evaporated. Remove from the heat and whisk in the butter.

4. Arrange the liver on a platter and spoon the sauce over the top. Serve immediately.

BRAISED TONGUE AND SAUERKRAUT

SERVES 6

*A*u Pied de Cochon is a popular bistro at the edge of Les Halles, Paris's former central market. Making a slight detour on my way home from work, I would pass right by and stop in for a late-night supper of braised tongue. This was my first experience with the fresh variety. My grandmother always prepared a smoked or pickled one.

Since the meat is so rich, I prefer pairing tongue with an astringent or tart flavor that cleanses the palate—in this recipe, sauerkraut. Serve it with the plainest cooked vegetables and either mashed or boiled potatoes. It might be poor manners, but you should mash up everything on your plate with the gravy.

1 onion, cut in half
1 carrot, cut into chunks
1 celery stalk, cut into 4 pieces
2 cloves
1 garlic bulb, cut in half crosswise
2 tablespoons salt, or to taste
1 teaspoon black peppercorns
6 bay leaves
1 fresh, smoked, or pickled tongue (about 4 pounds)
4 cups sauerkraut
12 small new potatoes
2 tablespoons chopped fresh dill
Grainy mustard, for serving

1. Place the onion, carrot, celery, cloves, garlic, salt, peppercorns, and bay leaves on a large square of cheesecloth or a kitchen towel and tie into a bundle. Place in a large pot, add the tongue, and cover with cold water. Cover, place over high heat, and bring to a boil. Reduce the heat to low and simmer gently for 2 hours. Check the pot periodically to make sure the tongue is completely covered, and add more water if necessary.

2. Add the sauerkraut and simmer for 1 hour. Remove the tongue from the pot and set aside on a plate to cool. Drain the sauerkraut and discard the vegetables and herbs and spices.

3. Make a shallow incision down the top of the tongue and carefully peel the outer layer off the entire tongue. Trim any cartilage or vein from the base.

4. Place the sauerkraut and tongue in a roasting pan. Bury the potatoes in the sauerkraut, cover the pan, and place in the oven. Turn on the oven to 350°F and cook for 1 hour.

5. Transfer the tongue to a carving board and, starting at the tip, cut it into thin slices. Place the sauerkraut on a platter, arrange the sliced tongue on top, and arrange the potatoes around. Sprinkle with the chopped dill and offer mustard on the side.

Fifties Favorites and Other Funky Dinners

*I*n postwar, pre–Julia Child America, the premier source of new recipes was not, as today's foodies would like to think, the late great James Beard—it was the sides of boxes and the backs of jars. If you can define the spirit of an era by the kind of food that was popular, then these were the tuna-noodle-casserole, chicken-fried-in-corn-flakes, icebox-cake years.

People had a lot more time to prepare meals than they do in today's two-income society, but what excited and provoked the American cook most was not a free-range chicken or edible flowers, it was the new convenience foods and the recipes that grew up around them. This was modern technology, better than nature. In every such recipe, at least one main ingredient was a prepared food, like the can of fruit salad added to a gelatin mold, or the canned cream of mushroom soup added to a chicken dish.

The source of all these ideas was the large food manufacturers. You could sell more dehydrated onion soup, they figured, if you showed people how to make at least two other recipes using it.

I recently surveyed supermarket shelves and found a quantity of tips and recipes unmatched in any cookbook. You can still find a good recipe for bridge mix on cereal boxes, numerous recipes for cookies on the chocolate chip bags, and even a tamale recipe on the back of a box of cornmeal. There are even interesting suggestions that use unfamiliar in-gredients on boxes of the so-called new grains, such as couscous and quinoa.

The following group of dinners is not meant to be fancy versions of box-top recipes or imitations of the food we knew as kids. There's no recipe here for lobster noodle casserole with caviar or shepherd's pie with veni-son, no matter how delicious they may sound to some readers. These dishes are not presented tongue-in-cheek, either—the recipes upon which these dinners are based are already kitschy enough.

Fifties Favorites and Other Funky Dinners

The originals were meant to please and nourish in a healthful, balanced manner. The sad reality is that they promoted the misconception that technology produces more healthful food than nature, and thereby reinforced unnutritious eating habits. I've tried to resurrect them only because I think that, in fact, these new versions will do exactly that—please and nourish in a simple, honest fashion. These are mostly unsophisticated meals that don't depend on fancy techniques or ingredients.

SERVES 4

*C*hildren are always admonished to eat their vegetables. I snuck cauliflower into this basic recipe and it seems logical since cauliflower with cheese is so appealing. Begin dinner with a large salad or a vegetable soup.

½ cup sun-dried tomatoes
4 tablespoons unsalted butter or margarine
2 onions, roughly diced (about 1½ cups)
2 cups small cauliflower florets
3 tablespoons all-purpose flour
3½ cups milk
½ teaspoon salt, or to taste
½ teaspoon ground white pepper
3 bay leaves
¼ teaspoon ground nutmeg
½ pound elbow macaroni
4 ounces Gouda cheese, grated
12 ounces sharp Cheddar cheese, grated

1. Pour enough boiling water to cover over the tomatoes and let soften for 2 minutes. Drain, chop, and set aside.

2. Heat the butter in a large skillet over medium heat. Add the onions and cauliflower, cover, and cook, stirring, for 5 minutes. Stir in the flour and cook for 2 minutes. Stir in the milk, and add the salt, pepper, bay leaves, nutmeg, and tomatoes. Reduce the heat to low, cover, and cook for 10 minutes, stirring occasionally.

3. Meanwhile, cook the macaroni in boiling salted water according to the package instructions. Drain and transfer to a large bowl.

4. Remove the bay leaves from the cauliflower mixture and pour the contents of the skillet over the macaroni. Add the Gouda and half the Cheddar cheese. Mix well and transfer to a buttered ovenproof casserole or baking dish.

5. Cover the casserole and place in the oven. Turn on the oven to 350°F and bake for 25 minutes. Sprinkle the surface with the remaining Cheddar cheese and bake uncovered for 10 minutes, or until the top browns lightly. Serve immediately.

Upper Crusts

My dictionary defines *crust* as a hard outer layer. According to this definition, planets have crusts, but in a word association game most of us probably think of bread or pie. Crusts wrap food, forming a barrier that you have to break through before getting to the good stuff, like a well-wrapped gift.

The crusts that form in cooking are pleasing because they add a contrasting element to a dish, a textural counterpoint and an intriguing, nearly burnt, flavor. Think of a marshmallow toasted on a stick over the campfire and you'll get the picture.

Poultry has skin that forms a natural crust and acts like a basting bag, holding in the juices while the bird becomes golden and crispy on the outside. Ask your butcher to leave the skin on a fresh ham—it roasts better and the skin forms an appealing crust called crackling. Large roasted cuts of red meat form crusts that seal all the juices inside. (This is why poking the roast with a thermometer during cooking is a bad idea—it breaks the crust and allows the juices to run out.)

Small pieces of seafood, poultry, and meat cook too quickly to form a crust, so we often dust them in flour or cornstarch to help form one and keep them moist. Onion rings and other deep-fried foods have an added crust—they're dipped in bread crumbs and egg or a batter. Properly fried foods should be crisp and not at all greasy—the crust is intended to isolate the food from the frying fat.

Cheese, when it melts, forms a good crusty topping. The fat runs out and turns golden, leaving the milk solids to become all gooey and stringy—my favorite part of a pizza.

But a crust is special because there's never a lot of it in proportion to what it's covering. And maybe because it reminds us of a time when we were young and were allowed to save the best thing on our plate for last.

TUNA, NOODLE, AND CHEESE CASSEROLE

SERVES 6

I prefer stronger flavors and food with more texture, so I plead guilty to making this quintessential kids' favorite an adult dinner with the addition of dried mushrooms and Gruyère cheese. But this still pleases on a basic level.

2 ounces dried mushrooms, preferably black Chinese or Polish
2 cups milk
2 tablespoons unsalted butter or margarine
2 tablespoons all-purpose flour
2 cups chicken stock or canned low-sodium chicken broth
2 teaspoons Old Bay Seasoning (see Note)
½ teaspoon salt
¼ teaspoon freshly ground black pepper
8 ounces penne or ziti
1 6¾-ounce can tuna, drained and flaked, or 7 ounces fresh tuna,
  chopped
¼ pound Gruyère or Swiss cheese, grated

1. Soak the mushrooms in the milk for 1 hour.

2. Drain the mushrooms, reserving the milk, and chop coarsely.

3. Preheat the oven to 325°F. Generously grease a 9- by 12-inch baking dish with butter.

4. Melt the butter in a medium pot over low heat. Add the mushrooms and cook for 2 minutes. Whisk in the flour, then the reserved milk, the chicken broth, Old Bay Seasoning, and salt and pepper. Increase the heat to medium and cook until the sauce is thickened, about 3 minutes. Remove from the heat and set aside.

5. Meanwhile, cook the pasta in boiling salted water according to the package directions until just al dente. Drain and transfer to a bowl.

6. Add the tuna to the pasta. Pour in the mushroom sauce, add about two thirds of the grated cheese, and mix well. Spread the tuna/pasta mixture evenly in the prepared baking dish, cover with aluminum foil, and bake until bubbling, about 45 minutes. Uncover, sprinkle with the remaining cheese, and bake for 15 minutes longer. Serve immediately.

NOTE: You can substitute a mixture of paprika, ground mace, cayenne, and celery salt for this favorite Chesapeake Bay seasoning.

COD CAKES IN CREAM SAUCE

SERVES 4

*F*ish sticks and frozen fish croquettes are almost the only form in which kids eat fish, because then it doesn't seem like fish. Cod is a lean, bland fish. It's pretty flaky and tends to fall apart when you cook it, so I grind it and form it into patties. Serve the cod cakes with spaghetti and begin with a well-dressed wedge of iceberg lettuce. A big glass of milk is the only thing to drink with this dinner.

2 to 3 tablespoons unsalted butter
1 small onion, finely diced (about ½ cup)
1 celery stalk, finely diced (about ½ cup)
1 small carrot, peeled and finely diced (about ¼ cup)
¼ cup milk
1 small potato, baked and (flesh only) mashed (about ⅓ cup)
½ cup dried bread crumbs
2 eggs
¼ teaspoon nutmeg, preferably freshly grated
½ teaspoon salt, or to taste
½ teaspoon freshly ground black pepper
1½ pounds skinless cod fillets, ground or finely chopped
1 cup dry white wine
1 cup chicken stock or canned low-sodium chicken broth
2 sprigs fresh thyme or ¼ teaspoon dried
½ cup heavy cream
2 tablespoons finely chopped fresh parsley

1. Melt 1 tablespoon of the butter in a medium skillet over medium heat. Add the onion, celery, and carrot, cover, and cook until soft, about 5 minutes. Add the milk and mashed potato and mix well. Transfer the contents of the skillet to a large bowl.

2. Add the bread crumbs, eggs, nutmeg, salt, and pepper and mix well. Add the fish and mix well. Form the mixture into 8 patties, place on a plate, cover, and refrigerate for at least 30 minutes, or up to 2 hours.

3. Preheat the oven to 350°F.

4. Combine the white wine, stock, and thyme in a saucepan, bring to a boil over medium heat, and boil until reduced by half, about 15 minutes. Add the cream and cook until the sauce is thick enough to coat the back of a spoon. Remove from the heat, cover, and keep warm.

5. Meanwhile, heat 1 tablespoon butter in a large skillet over medium heat. Add the cod cakes to the skillet without crowding. (You may have to cook them in batches, adding more butter as necessary.) Cook until golden on both sides, about 3 minutes total. Drain on paper towels and place in a baking dish. When all the cod cakes have been fried, transfer the dish to the oven and bake for 8 to 10 minutes, or until cooked through. Transfer to a platter.

6. Add the parsley to the cream sauce, spoon over the cod cakes, and serve immediately.

COD LOAF WITH WARM TARTAR SAUCE

SERVES 5 TO 6

*M*y grandfather had a lamp and gift shop in downtown Utica, New York, and when we'd go to visit, we'd have lunch at a cafeteria called The Home Dairy. On Fridays there were always fish dishes on the menu, and this cod loaf is similar to one I remember being served.

2½ pounds skinless codfish fillets
1 medium potato, baked
4 tablespoons unsalted butter
½ cup finely diced onion
½ cup finely diced carrots
½ cup finely diced celery
3 egg yolks
¼ teaspoon ground mace
¼ teaspoon curry powder
1 teaspoon salt
½ teaspoon ground white pepper
6 sweet gherkin pickles
2 tablespoons capers, drained
1 tablespoon prepared horseradish
2 tablespoons chopped fresh parsley
2 tablespoons fresh lemon juice
¼ cup mayonnaise

1. Preheat the oven to 350°F. Lightly grease a 1-quart baking dish or loaf pan.   *(continued)*

Fifties Favorites and Other Funky Dinners

2. Line the bottom and sides of the prepared baking dish with the cod fillets, making a single uniform layer and trimming off any pieces that overlap or hang over the sides. You should have about 1 pound of trimmings. Refrigerate the baking dish.

3. Cut the cod trimmings into ½-inch cubes and place in a bowl. Scoop out the inside of the baked potato and add it to the bowl. Pass the fish and potato through a meat grinder fitted with the coarse disc, or place in a food processor and pulse until coarsely ground. Replace in the bowl.

4. Heat 2 tablespoons of the butter in a medium pan over medium heat. Add the onion, carrots, and celery, cover, and cook for 15 minutes. Add the vegetables to the cod/potato mixture, then add the egg yolks, mace, curry powder, salt, and pepper and mix well.

5. Fill the lined baking dish with the vegetable/cod mixture, and smooth the top. Cover with foil and place the dish on a baking pan to catch any juices that bubble over. Bake for 45 minutes, or until puffy.

6. While the loaf is baking, prepare the sauce: place the pickles and capers in a food processor and pulse until finely chopped. Scrape into a small saucepan and add the horseradish, parsley, and lemon juice. Heat over medium heat until warm. Swirl in the remaining 2 tablespoons butter, whisk in the mayonnaise, and remove from the heat.

7. To serve dinner, unmold the cod loaf onto a platter and stir any juices that have accumulated into the sauce. Spoon the sauce over the loaf.

NOTE: If you prefer to prepare individual portions, halve the fillets lengthwise and cut into 5 or 6 long strips, reserving about 1 pound fish for the filling. Butter a baking sheet and form the strips of cod into circles on the sheet. Spoon some filling into the center of each. Bake for 25 minutes.

CHICKEN AND FRESH NOODLES

SERVES 4

9 hadn't thought about this dish in years, until Heidi, the barely-out-of-her-teens cashier at my restaurant, came into the kitchen toward the end of her shift and made a special request for some chicken and noodles. She seemed to need the fortification that only a familiar dinner can provide.

This recipe is the real thing, well worth the effort. Roasting a chicken and then making a good gravy isn't difficult, but it isn't fast either. So if you want to comfort the family in a big way, you're going to have to spend a little time on their behalf. It will certainly be appreciated when you serve a dish that is so much more flavorful than the version that comes out of cans and boxes.

1 4-pound roasting chicken, with giblets
Salt and freshly ground black pepper
1 cup plus 2 tablespoons unbleached all-purpose flour
4 cups chicken stock or canned low-sodium chicken broth
2 branches fresh thyme or 1 teaspoon dried
2 bay leaves
Pinch of ground mace
1 cup whole wheat flour
3 eggs
1 tablespoon vegetable oil
2 tablespoons chopped fresh parsley

1. Preheat the oven to 350°F.

2. Remove the giblets from the chicken and set aside. Rinse the chicken, pat dry with paper towels, and sprinkle inside and out with salt and pepper. Place in a roasting pan, and roast for 1¼ hours.

3. Transfer the chicken to a plate. Pour off all but 2 tablespoons fat from the roasting pan, place the pan over medium heat, and stir in 2 tablespoons of the flour. Cook, stirring, for 2 minutes, then add the broth and stir, scraping up any browned bits that have stuck to the bottom of the roasting pan. Pour the liquid into a large saucepan, add the thyme, bay leaves, mace, and reserved giblets, cover, and bring to a simmer over medium heat.

4. Meanwhile, as soon as the chicken is cool enough to handle, cut off the breast meat, leaving each breast whole. Cut off the legs and thighs and remove the meat from the bones. Shred the dark meat, place on a plate, cover, and set aside.   *(continued)*

5. Cut up the chicken carcass with a large knife and add the bones and skin to the pan of stock. Simmer, uncovered, until the liquid has reduced to the consistency of a sauce, about 30 minutes. Skim any fat and impurities that rise to the surface as the broth cooks.

6. Meanwhile, make the noodles: Combine the remaining 1 cup all-purpose flour, the whole wheat flour, eggs, oil, and ½ teaspoon salt. Mix together in a mixer or by hand and then knead the dough for 5 minutes, or until no longer sticky. Roll out the dough as thin as possible, using a pasta machine or by hand, and cut into noodles about 2 inches long and about ¾ inch wide. Dust with flour and set aside on a plate.

7. When it's time to serve dinner, bring a large pot of salted water to a boil. Add the noodles and cook just until tender, about 4 minutes; drain. Meanwhile, place the reserved chicken meat in a large skillet. Strain the sauce over the chicken, and discard the bones. Cover and place over low heat to reheat. Place the noodles in a large serving bowl or tureen and arrange the chicken on top. Pour the sauce over everything, sprinkle with the parsley, and serve immediately.

Spaghetti and Better Meatballs

SERVES 4 TO 5

I had in mind the cooking of central Asia when I created this recipe, rich in lamb, goat, and yogurt. The result is lamb meatballs, with a sauce of yogurt, mint, dill, and cilantro, but ground beef works equally well.

Meatballs, in order to be good, have to have something added to the meat to give it more flavor and a lighter texture. Unfortunately, we have come to see this as adulteration rather than part of cooking, thanks to food companies that try to stretch a more expensive ingredient with a less expensive one—a filler or extender—for the sake of higher profits rather than a better product. Ingredients should work toward making a dish more satisfying and healthy. I add couscous to my meatballs and don't feel in the least that I'm cheating. In fact, I'd almost prefer a couscous ball with a little meat to hold it together—but then there would be no need for the pasta.

Dinner needs some vegetables so the family gets its complement of food groups. Serve broccoli sautéed in garlic and olive oil or some roasted red peppers.

3 to 5 tablespoons olive oil, plus additional for the tomatoes
1 medium onion, finely diced (about ¾ cup)
1 cup cooked couscous
1 pound ground lamb
1 teaspoon ground cumin
Salt and freshly ground black pepper
1 tablespoon all-purpose flour
1½ cups chicken stock or canned low-sodium chicken broth
½ pound spaghetti
2 tomatoes, halved crosswise
½ cup sour cream or yogurt
½ tablespoon chopped cilantro (fresh coriander)
1 tablespoon chopped fresh mint
2 tablespoons chopped fresh dill

1. Heat 1 tablespoon of the oil over medium heat. Add the onion and cook, stirring, for 5 minutes. Transfer to a bowl and add the couscous, lamb, cumin, 1 teaspoon salt, and ½ teaspoon pepper, and mix well. Form into meatballs, using a generous tablespoon of the mixture for each one. You should have about 32 meatballs.

2. Heat 2 tablespoons oil in a large deep skillet over medium heat. Add just enough of the meatballs to fit without crowding the pan and cook for about 5 minutes, shaking the pan, until browned on all sides. Drain on paper towels. Repeat with the remaining meatballs, adding more oil as necessary.

3. Stir the flour into the fat remaining in the pan, mixing to form a paste, and cook for 2 minutes. Stir in the chicken stock, add the meatballs, cover, and simmer for 20 minutes.

4. Meanwhile, heat the broiler.

5. Cook the spaghetti according to the package directions; drain. Meanwhile, brush the cut sides of the tomatoes with olive oil, sprinkle with salt and pepper, and broil for 3 to 5 minutes.

6. Remove the meatballs from the sauce and keep warm. Skim any fat from the surface of the sauce and strain the sauce into a bowl. Stir in the sour cream, cilantro, mint, and dill, and mix well. Divide the spaghetti among four soup bowls. Place a broiled tomato in the center of each serving, arrange the meatballs on top, and spoon the sauce over.

COCOA JOES ON A BUN

SERVES 4

We never had sloppy Joes at our house, but if we had, I'm sure my mother would have added a little instant coffee, her favorite secret ingredient. This more baroque version adds instant coffee, cocoa powder, cumin, and cinnamon. I also prefer my Joes made with flank steak rather than with ground beef. This is, in fact, a dish that you'll want to feed the kids—it's not at all like the mixture of ground meat and orange reddish fat they serve up at school. Coleslaw and potato salad are natural side dishes.

1¾ pounds flank steak
2 teaspoons flavorless vegetable oil
1 onion, roughly diced
2 teaspoons cocoa powder
1 teaspoon instant coffee powder
1 teaspoon ground cumin
⅛ teaspoon ground cinnamon
3 tablespoons tomato paste
1 teaspoon minced garlic
Chopped red onion, for serving
Sliced tomatoes, for serving
Mayonnaise and ketchup, for serving
4 hamburger buns

1. Cut the flank steak into 1-inch pieces and set aside.

2. Heat the oil in a Dutch oven or ovenproof casserole over medium heat. Add the onion and cook, stirring, for 3 minutes, or until soft. Add the cocoa powder, coffee, cumin, cinnamon, tomato paste, garlic, and 1½ cups water and mix well. Add the flank steak, cover, place in the oven, and turn the oven on to 350°F. Cook until the flank steak is very tender and almost falling apart, about 1½ hours.

3. Using a slotted spoon, transfer the meat to a bowl. Then, using two forks, shred the meat. Replace the meat in the pot and mix well. (The meat can be prepared ahead and refrigerated; reheat to serve.)

4. When it's time to put dinner on the table, place some chopped red onion in a small bowl. Put the sliced tomatoes on a plate. Put mayonnaise and ketchup on the table. Toast the buns, and reheat the meat if necessary. Scrape the meat into a large serving bowl, and serve immediately.

*C*heese steak authenticity means traveling to Philadelphia, going to the South End, and finding the stand with the longest line out front. But if you can't have authentic, have this—great, gooey, open-faced sandwiches.

1 1-pound loaf French or Italian bread
3 tablespoons unsalted butter
¼ cup olive oil
2 tablespoons minced garlic
1 1¾-pound beef skirt steak
1 small onion, finely minced (about ½ cup)
1 tablespoon all-purpose flour
½ cup milk
¼ pound sharp Cheddar cheese, grated

1. Preheat the oven to 425°F. Slice the bread open along one side and open it flat like a book.

2. Combine the butter, 3 tablespoons of the oil, and the garlic in a small saucepan, and heat over low heat for 5 minutes. Pour evenly over the bread. Close the loaf and wrap in foil.

3. Heat the remaining 1 tablespoon oil in a heavy skillet over high heat. Add the steak and sear well on both sides. Lower the heat to medium, add the onion, and cook for 4 minutes for medium-rare steak, or longer if desired. Transfer the steak to a plate and keep warm. Sprinkle the flour over the onion in the skillet and mix well. Stir in the milk and cook for 1 minute, or until thickened. Reduce the heat to low, stir in the cheese, and heat just until the cheese is melted. Remove from the heat and keep warm.

4. Meanwhile, place the bread in the oven and bake until heated through, about 5 to 7 minutes.

5. Cut the bread into 4 pieces. Place on individual plates and open out each piece of bread. Thinly slice the steak on the bias, against the grain, and arrange on the bread. Stir any juices from the steak into the cheese mixture and spoon over the sandwiches. Serve immediately.

FOUR BURGERS

*T*he hamburgers of my early youth were dense, well-cooked meat patties—the burgers that couldn't be juicy because then they might taste like meat. They were cooked in a covered skillet or under the broiler. In the summer they were cooked out of doors, and any charm that may have been added by the flavor of an open fire was negated by the strong taste of lighter fluid. City people thought lighter fluid was the most important ingredient of a good picnic.

When I was a bit older, we used to hang out at a 15-cent burger stand. The burgers were thin and dry and garnished with a slice of sweet pickle. The bun was too large for the patty and needed a lot of ketchup on it to make it moist and give it any flavor.

In college I learned to love rare burgers and took to adding an appalling mishmash of ketchup, mayonnaise, mustard, onion, tomato, and relish. After graduating I moved into an apartment and discovered Julia Child hamburgers, ones that were garnished with elegant sauces. I guess you'd have to say my taste for hamburgers is indefatigable.

SPICED HAMBURGERS

SERVES 4

*T*he fact that herbs and spices could change the way food tasted was the astounding culinary discovery of my childhood.

> 1 tablespoon olive oil
> 1 small onion, finely minced
> 1 tablespoon finely minced garlic
> 1 teaspoon freshly ground black pepper
> ½ teaspoon ground nutmeg
> 1 teaspoon ground coriander
> 1½ pounds ground beef
> 4 hamburger buns, toasted
> 4 thin slices red onion
> 4 slices tomato
> Ketchup, mustard, and mayonnaise, for serving

1. Combine the oil and onion in a small skillet over medium heat and cook, stirring, for about 4 minutes, or until the onion softens. Add the garlic, pepper, nutmeg, and coriander and cook for a minute longer.

What's for Dinner?

2. Scrape the onion mixture into a bowl, add the beef, and mix well. Form into 4 patties about ¾ to 1 inch thick. Place on a plate, cover, and refrigerate for 20 minutes.

3. Place a large heavy skillet over high heat. When it is nearly smoking hot, add the hamburger patties and cook for 3 minutes. Turn and cook to the desired doneness, about 3 minutes for very rare, up to 6 minutes for medium.

4. Place the burgers on the hamburger buns and garnish each with a slice of onion and tomato. Offer ketchup, mustard, and mayonnaise and encourage mass slathering.

Achieving Hamburger Perfection

Hamburgers should not be prepared with lean meat because they become dry and dense in texture when cooked. Meat ground for burgers should be only moderately lean, with about 12 to 14 percent fat. If you want to season the ground meat with herbs or spices, do so not more than 30 minutes before cooking, or the flavor will "bleed" out. Form patties that are about ¾ to 1 inch thick. Chill them for 20 minutes after you make them, then cook them straight from the refrigerator. They will retain their juices better and will be easier to both char and cook rare or medium rare.

When cooking your burgers, use intense heat. Cook them on the stove in a smoking skillet with no fat added, or place under a preheated broiler, close enough to the heat that they cook rapidly. When cooking on a grill, make sure that the coals are red hot; lightly oil the burgers first so that the drippings will flame and char the surface of the meat. No matter how you cook them, turn them only once—it is important that ground meats form a good crust on both sides so that the juices remain inside. When properly cooked, even a medium-well burger can be juicy.

If you're going to melt cheese over the patties under a broiler, do so a minute before they have reached desired doneness. If you're cooking in a skillet or on a grill, you will have to place a lid over the patties, which will speed up the cooking, so make sure that the burgers are still rare when you add the cheese.

OPEN-FACED HAMBURGERS AU POIVRE

SERVES 4

*O*ne of the ways that Americans were introduced to French sauces was by being served them on hamburgers. This is the classic Dijonnais recipe.

1½ pounds ground beef
2 tablespoons coarsely ground black pepper
⅓ cup red wine
3 tablespoons Dijon mustard
1 tablespoon chopped fresh tarragon or 1 teaspoon dried
1 tablespoon green peppercorns
⅔ cup heavy cream
2 English muffins, split and toasted

1. Form the ground beef into 4 patties about ¾ to 1 inch thick. Press the coarse black pepper into both sides of each patty. Place the patties on a plate, cover, and refrigerate for 20 minutes.

2. Combine the red wine and mustard in a saucepan; if using dried tarragon, add it now. Simmer over medium heat until reduced by half, about 8 minutes.

3. Add the green peppercorns and cream and simmer until the liquid has reduced to the consistency of a sauce. Remove from the heat; if using fresh tarragon, add it now.

4. Place a large heavy skillet over high heat. When it is nearly smoking hot, add the hamburger patties and cook for 3 minutes. Turn the patties and cook to the desired doneness, about 3 minutes for very rare, up to 6 minutes for medium.

5. Place the burgers on buns and generously spoon the sauce over.

LAMB CHEESEBURGERS

SERVES 6

*B*acon is ground with the lamb to give these patties a sausage-like texture. They make the tastiest of all cheeseburgers.

2 pounds lamb stew meat
¼ pound bacon, coarsely chopped

½ cup crumbled Roquefort or blue cheese
6 hamburger buns
Mustard and mayonnaise, for serving

1. Pass the lamb and bacon through a meat grinder fitted with the medium disc. Mix well and form into 4 patties. Refrigerate, covered, for 20 minutes.

2. Heat a large heavy skillet over high heat until almost smoking hot. Add the patties, reduce the heat to medium, and cook for 3 minutes. Turn and cook for 4 minutes. Place a heaping tablespoon of the cheese on each patty, cover, and cook 1 to 2 minutes longer, or until the cheese is melting.

3. Place the patties on the hamburger buns and serve immediately. Offer mustard and mayonnaise.

TURKEY BURGERS WITH MUSHROOMS

SERVES 6

*7*hese burgers are cooked in a skillet, but if you prefer to cook them on a grill or under a broiler, you can sauté the mushrooms separately in butter.

¼ pound bacon, coarsely chopped
2 pounds ground turkey
1 teaspoon chopped fresh sage or ½ teaspoon dried
1 tablespoon unsalted butter
1 pound white mushrooms, thinly sliced
Salt and freshly ground black pepper to taste
6 hamburger buns, toasted
Mayonnaise, for serving

1. Place the bacon in a food processor and process until smooth. Add the ground turkey and sage and pulse just until well mixed. Form the mixture into 4 patties. Refrigerate, covered, for 20 minutes.

2. Heat the butter in a medium skillet over medium heat. Add the patties and cook for 4 minutes. Turn, add the mushrooms, and season with salt and pepper. Cook, stirring occasionally, for 5 minutes.

3. Place the patties on the hamburger buns, and garnish with the sautéed mushrooms. Serve immediately, and offer mayonnaise.

POT ROAST AND SWEET BAKED CARROTS

SERVES 6

*K*ids love either mushy or crunchy textures, or flavors that seem to melt together. They have nothing to complain about with this dinner—the meat is cooked for a long time until tender, the flavors all marry together, and the carrots become so sweet that everyone forgets that they don't really like them.

2 tablespoons flavorless vegetable oil
1 2-pound beef chuck roast or eye-of-round roast
1 medium onion, roughly chopped, plus 1 (peeled) onion stuck with
   3 cloves
2 tablespoons instant coffee powder
1 tablespoon tomato paste
2½ cups chicken stock, canned low-sodium chicken broth, or water
3 bay leaves
Salt
½ teaspoon black peppercorns
3 cups thinly sliced carrots (about 10 carrots)
2 tablespoons unsalted butter or margarine

1. Preheat the oven to 325°F.

2. Heat the oil in a Dutch oven or ovenproof casserole over high heat. Add the beef roast and brown well on all sides. Remove the roast and pour off the oil.

3. Place the pot over medium heat, add the chopped onion, and cook, stirring, until softened, about 3 minutes. Stir in the instant coffee and tomato paste, then add the broth, 1½ teaspoons salt, bay leaves, and the peppercorns and bring to a boil. Return the roast to the pot, add the whole onion, cover, and transfer to the oven. Cook for 2½ hours, or until very tender.

4. Meanwhile, place the carrots in a baking dish. Season with salt and pepper to taste and dot with the butter. Cover and bake for 45 minutes.

5. Remove the meat from the pot. Skim the fat off the cooking liquid and strain. Arrange a bed of the carrots on a serving platter. Slice the pot roast and arrange the slices on the carrots. Spoon some of the cooking juices over the meat and serve.

SAUSAGES AND PEPPERS WITH APPLES

SERVES 4 TO 6

*M*arylouise Oates prepares this family recipe for company. A dish like this one disarms the guest and makes conversation easy, because everyone feels as comfortable as if they were at home. I put in some apples—a simple but unexpected addition that gives the dish another dimension.

> 2 medium onions
> 3 red bell peppers
> 3 medium Red Delicious apples
> 8 to 12 assorted fresh sausages, such as spicy Italian, bratwurst,
>   and turkey
> 1 tablespoon chopped fresh sage or 1 teaspoon dried
> ½ teaspoon ground coriander
> ¼ teaspoon ground mace
> 1 teaspoon salt, or to taste
> Freshly ground black pepper to taste
> 2 tablespoons chopped fresh parsley
> ½ cup dry white wine

1. Peel the onions, cut in half lengthwise, and slice lengthwise into thin slices. Halve the peppers lengthwise, remove the seeds and stems, and cut lengthwise into thin slivers. Peel the apples, halve them lengthwise, and remove the cores. Cut lengthwise into thin slices.

2. Prick the sausages (except turkey sausages) with a fork. Place all the sausages in a large skillet over medium heat and brown on all sides, about 5 to 6 minutes. Remove from the skillet and drain on paper towels. Pour off and reserve the fat remaining in the skillet.

3. Replace the skillet on the stove, and add the apples and 2 teaspoons of the reserved fat. Cook for 5 minutes, stirring occasionally. Transfer the apples to a bowl. Add another teaspoon of the fat to the skillet, add the onions and peppers, and cook, stirring occasionally, for 5 minutes. Add to the apples. (The sausages and apple mixture can be prepared several hours ahead and set aside at room temperature.)

4. When it's time to get dinner on the table, preheat the oven to 375°F.

5. Place the onion, peppers, and apple mixture in a baking dish or ovenproof casserole, add the sage, coriander, mace, salt, and pepper, and mix well. Arrange the sausages on top and pour in the wine. Bake for 30 minutes, or until cooked and everything is piping hot. Serve immediately.

Fifties Favorites and Other Funky Dinners

The Versatile Potato

Spanish explorers in the fifteenth and sixteenth centuries brought back to Europe natural treasures from Central and South America. Of all of them—tomatoes, corn, peppers both red and sweet, vanilla, gold—the potato took root like no other, both in the staple diet and in cooks' imaginations. It can be baked, boiled, roasted, and fried; mashed, sliced, cooked in cream or in broth; made into pancakes and savory puddings. Imagine a Briton sitting down to table sans spuds. Or a Frenchman eating *biftec* without *pommes frites.*

Potatoes have been an important food in Britain and Ireland since the early seventeenth century. In France, where the fried potato is king, the potato was scorned until the eighteenth-century economist and agronomist A. A. Parmentier convinced Louis XVI to wear a potato flower and serve the tuber at court. His fame has been secured by the number of French potato dishes that bear his name. The potato came to the United States in about 1710 via Ireland.

Potatoes fall roughly into two categories: dry, mealy ones, such as russets and Idahoes, and waxy ones, such as new potatoes and yellow Finns. The mealy ones have more starch and are best for baking, mashing, and frying; the waxy varieties—higher in moisture and lower in starch—are best for cutting into slices and using in salads, where they absorb less mayonnaise or oil than the mealy variety.

In general, freshly dug, or early crop, potatoes of either kind have a high sugar content and are preferable for salads; luckily they come to market in the late spring and summer months, just in time for potato salad weather. (Mature, or main crop, potatoes and ones that have been stored a while after having been dug have less moisture and much, if not all, of their sugar has turned to starch.)

To minimize the amount of water they soak up during cooking, boil potatoes for salad in their jackets and then peel them. While they're still warm, douse them with vinegar, then let them cool; this helps firm them so that they won't crumble in the salad.

SAUSAGE AND POTATO SALAD

SERVES 6

*T*he juices of several kinds of sausage ooze into this potato salad. Use sausages that are freshly made if you can find them. Polish kielbasa, Moroccan merguez, Mexican chorizo, hot or sweet Italian sausage, German bratwurst, even frankfurters are all possible choices.

> *2 pounds small waxy potatoes*
> *2 tablespoons white wine vinegar*
> *1 tablespoon flavorless vegetable oil*
> *1 medium onion, diced (about ¾ cup)*
> *4 hard-cooked eggs, finely chopped*
> *3 celery stalks, thinly sliced*
> *3 tablespoons chopped sweet pickles (optional)*
> *3 to 4 tablespoons mayonnaise*
> *½ teaspoon freshly ground black pepper*
> *Salt to taste*
> *8 to 12 assorted fresh sausages, such as spicy Italian, bratwurst,*
> *   and kielbasa*
> *Several kinds of mustard, for serving*

1. Place the potatoes in a pot and cover with salted water. Bring to a boil over high heat and cook until the potatoes are soft. Drain, peel, and cut into chunks. Place in a bowl, pour the vinegar over, cover, and let cool.

2. Heat the oil in a skillet, over medium heat. Add the onion and cook, stirring, until soft, about 5 minutes. Add the onion to the potatoes.

3. Add the eggs, celery, and pickles to the potatoes and toss well. Stir in enough of the mayonnaise to bind the ingredients, then add the pepper and salt and mix well. Refrigerate for at least 2 hours or up to a day.

4. When it's time for dinner, prick the sausages gently with a fork. Place them in a skillet and cook over medium heat until browned on all sides and cooked through, about 12 to 15 minutes, depending on the type of sausage. Drain on paper towels, then place on a plate to catch the juices and slice.

5. Mound the potato salad on plates and place the sausages on top. Serve a variety of mustards on the side.

SAUSAGE MEAT LOAF WITH DUXELLES GRAVY

SERVES 5 TO 6

*S*ausage meat added to a meat loaf tends to toughen the mixture, so I cook bread crumbs, milk, and Marsala together (called a *panade* in old-fashioned French cookery) to lighten the texture.

4 hot Italian sausages
1 pound ground beef
2 tablespoons tomato paste
1 teaspoon salt, or to taste
¾ cup fresh bread crumbs
½ cup milk
½ cup Marsala wine
3 eggs
½ pound white mushrooms
1 tablespoon all-purpose flour
1 cup chicken stock or canned low-sodium chicken broth

1. Remove the casings from the sausage and place the meat in a large bowl. Add the beef, tomato paste, and ½ teaspoon of the salt, mix well, and refrigerate.

2. Combine the bread crumbs, milk, and Marsala in a small skillet, place over medium heat, and cook, stirring, until the mixture forms a sticky mass, about 3 minutes. Scrape into a bowl and cool.

3. Add the bread crumb mixture to the meat and mix well. Add the eggs and mix well. Press the mixture into a 9- by 5-inch loaf pan, cover with foil, and place on a baking sheet to catch any juices that may bubble over. Place in the oven, turn the oven on to 350°F, and bake for 1 hour.

4. Meanwhile, puree the mushrooms in a food processor. Scrape the pureed mushrooms into a saucepan and cook over medium heat, stirring occasionally, until all the moisture has evaporated from the mushrooms, about 15 minutes. Stir in the flour and cook a minute longer. Stir in the stock and cook until the gravy is thick enough to coat the back of a spoon.

5. When it's time to get dinner on the table, pour any liquid that has accumulated around the meat loaf into the mushroom gravy. Turn out the meat loaf onto a work surface and slice into serving pieces. Arrange the slices on a platter and spoon gravy over. Serve the remaining gravy on the side, and accompany the meat loaf with your favorite mashed potatoes.

FRANKS AND BAKED BEANS

SERVES 10 TO 12

I actually use a variety of sausages in this dish because I like the different flavors they impart to the beans. If you stick to using just one favorite, though, spice up the beans by adding more mustard and ketchup to them. And make a lot—they freeze really well.

For cookouts, bring the cooked beans in a heavy copper pot and reheat them on the side of the fire. Grill your franks or sausages, slice them and add to the pot of beans, and let sit for 15 minutes on the side of the fire before serving.

3 cups (1½ pounds) dried white beans
½ cup molasses
2 tablespoons dry mustard
½ cup ketchup
¼ teaspoon ground cloves
½ teaspoon freshly ground black pepper
2 ham hocks
2 teaspoons salt, or to taste
20 franks, or franks and assorted sausages

1. Soak the beans in water to cover for 3 hours to soften them slightly. Drain. Preheat the oven to 275°F.

2. Place the beans in a heavy casserole, add the molasses, mustard, ketchup, cloves, and pepper, and mix well. Add the ham hocks and enough water to cover the beans by 2 inches. Cover the casserole and bake for 2 hours.

3. Add the salt, and add more water if the beans are getting too dry. Bake 6 hours more, checking the beans every hour or so and adding water if necessary.

4. Meanwhile, about 30 minutes before serving dinner, grill the franks and sausages and cut them into ¾-inch rounds. Add them to the beans for the final 20 minutes of cooking. Serve hot.

Fifties Favorites and Other Funky Dinners

PORK BAKED WITH BEANS

SERVES 8 TO 10

*I*t's hard to decide which is the tastier of the two ingredients, the pork or the beans. For a robust flavor and more color, brown the pork well and soften the onions before adding the beans and moistening the pot.

1 tablespoon vegetable oil
1 5-pound boneless pork shoulder
4 medium onions, roughly chopped (about 3 cups)
¼ cup tomato paste
2 cups dried red kidney beans
1 tablespoon minced garlic
1 teaspoon ground coriander
½ teaspoon cayenne pepper
4 bay leaves
1 teaspoon salt, or to taste

1. Heat the oil in a large heavy pot or Dutch oven over medium heat. Add the pork and brown on all sides. Remove the pork and pour off the fat. Add the onions and tomato paste and cook, stirring, for 5 minutes. Replace the pork, cover, and place in the oven. Turn on the oven to 300°F and cook for 1 hour.

2. Add the beans, garlic, coriander, cayenne, bay leaves, and 4 cups water to the pork. Cover and bring to a boil over high heat, then return the pot to the oven for 2½ hours. Check from time to time to make sure that the beans have not dried out, and add water ½ cup at a time as necessary. After 2 hours, stir in the salt.

3. To serve dinner, remove the pork from the casserole and slice it. Fish out the bay leaves from the pot and discard them. Pour the beans into a large serving bowl or deep platter and arrange the meat on top.

MAPLE SYRUP SHOULDER OF PORK

SERVES 4 TO 5

*7*he shoulder and butt roasts of pork are the most succulent because of all the internal fat marbling. This is a slow-roasting dish, giving you meat that is juicy and meltingly tender, and a kitchen filled with a delicious aroma of caramelizing maple syrup. Boil some sauerkraut to serve with the pork and you won't want to leave the kitchen—I do some of my best dreaming in a kitchen full of wonderful cooking smells.

> *1½ cups chicken stock or canned low-sodium chicken broth*
> *1 cup maple syrup*
> *1 2½- to 3-pound boneless pork shoulder roast, rolled and tied*
> *2 teaspoons kosher salt*
> *½ teaspoon ground white pepper*
> *2 teaspoons ground coriander*

1. Mix the broth and maple syrup together. Place the roast in a large glass or ceramic bowl, pour the maple syrup marinade over, and sprinkle with the salt, pepper, and coriander. Cover and refrigerate at least 12 hours, or up to 2 days, turning once or twice in the marinade.

2. Preheat the oven to 450°F.

3. Remove the pork from the marinade, reserving the marinade, and place on a rack in a roasting pan. Roast for 20 minutes, then reduce the oven temperature to 350°F and baste the roast with the maple syrup marinade. Roast, basting every 15 minutes, until the roast is cooked to medium (160°F on a meat thermometer), about 1¼ hours longer. If the basting liquid begins to burn on the bottom of the pan, add a little water to the pan.

4. Remove the pork from the pan. Add any remaining marinade to the pan and stir to dissolve the drippings on the bottom of the pan. Pour the liquid into a small saucepan and cook over medium heat until the liquid has reduced to the consistency of a thin sauce. Pour into a sauceboat.

5. To serve, slice the pork into ¼-inch-thick slices and arrange on a platter. Pass the sauce separately, and accompany with mashed potatoes and sauerkraut.

Dinners Without Meat

*I*f you were brought up in the fifties the way I was, a meal wasn't a meal if there was not some form of animal flesh involved. Mothers claimed instinctive knowledge that a diet ignoring meat was insidiously wrong. Protein metabolized into muscle and made you grow tall, straight-backed, and strong; it built taut, healthy, young American bodies. Vegetarianism was un-American and as subversive as—nudism!

To some degree or another, people have always thought, and certainly the idea has not died, that a food's intrinsic essence transfers to the eater. We say that someone is so adorable you could eat him up, implying that it's not simply enough to witness adorableness, you must make it part of your being. It's a "you are what you eat" mentality, and many of us allow or forbid ourselves certain foods, thereby hoping to deliver or withhold certain magical or healthful qualities. Like primitive man we still imbue the food we eat with a moral imperative. Meat eaters often see vegetarians, especially males, as wimps, and vegetarianism often elicits anger and hostility on the part of meat eaters.

Well, it turns out that Mother was wrong. We need protein, yes. Yet there are great sources of it other than animal flesh—the dairy choices and, especially, legumes and grains. And, although there's no such thing as unhealthful food, there are, indeed, unhealthful diets. And the meat-heavy model, lacking in vegetable and grain options, is one.

Meatless dinners are benign, soothing affairs. You may fight over the drumstick or the end cut of the roast beef, but not over a vegetable, an egg, or a piece of cheese. Sitting down to a meatless dinner is like taking a little vacation. The change of diet, if you're not a vegetarian, is a release and a relief.

I tried to make the recipes in this chapter hearty and robust. Meatless main courses often suffer from the cook's timidity about using a bold stroke of imagination. This is not punishment food. One powerful ingredient can ground a recipe. The garlic stew with poached eggs is a perfect example of how garlic can be a more than adequate substitute for white meat. There are egg recipes with new hashes—zucchini, crab, and sweet potato with salt cod. There are ethnic favorites, too, like blintzes and a frittata. And I've put a vegetarian twist on some old favorites such as stuffed cabbage and stuffed peppers.

Of course, there are other vegetarian recipes throughout the book too. Vegetable Chili (page 175), Macaroni and Cheese and Cauliflower (page 89), and Chick-pea Polenta with Tomato Sauce (page 168) are just a few of the meatless recipes in other chapters.

The Soothing Egg

Eggs, decidedly feminine food, never make an aggressive meal. They soothe stomach and nerves and seem somehow healing and nurturing. Alas, like so much else today, they're also considered a no-no by many people. If you do need to restrict them in your diet, purge them from dishes where they are hidden and useless. Don't use them to bind a meat loaf, for instance, or to thicken a salad dressing. Make your own mayonnaise or hollandaise-type sauces using yolks that you have frozen and defrosted—a single yolk, once having been frozen, will do the same job as five fresh ones! Have cereal for breakfast on work days—you don't need nurturing in the morning, you need it at the end of a hard day. Save your eggs for a nice meal, one that is the focus of your day.

ZUCCHINI HASH WITH POACHED EGGS

SERVES 2

*T*hese substantial zucchini pancakes are held together with the starch from a potato plus just a little flour. Use a nonstick pan to make the hash cakes, and you won't need to cook with a lot of butter. Zucchini hash pleases the palate the same way fried zucchini sticks do: crunchy, with a smooth center.

1½ pounds zucchini, shredded (about 5¾ cups)
1 tablespoon kosher salt
1 medium potato (about ½ pound), peeled and grated
1 tablespoon all-purpose flour
½ teaspoon salt, or more to taste
½ teaspoon ground white pepper
3 tablespoons unsalted butter
1 small onion, finely minced
2 tablespoons Dijon mustard
¼ cup milk
¼ cup plain yogurt
Cayenne pepper to taste
4 eggs
About ¼ cup sour cream

1. Place the zucchini in a colander, add the kosher salt, and toss well. Set aside to degorge for 30 minutes.

2. Preheat the oven to 350°F.

3. Squeeze the water out of the zucchini and pat dry with a towel. Combine the zucchini, grated potato, flour, salt and white pepper. Form into 4 patties.

4. Melt ½ tablespoon of the butter in a nonstick skillet and place a zucchini patty in the pan. Cook over medium-high heat until the hash cake holds together and is golden on the bottom, about 5 to 7 minutes. Flip and cook on the other side for 5 minutes. Place on a baking sheet and repeat with the remaining patties, using ½ tablespoon more butter to cook each one. Place in the oven to keep warm while you prepare the sauce.

5. Heat the remaining 1 tablespoon butter in a saucepan over medium heat. Add the onion and cook until soft, about 3 minutes. Stir in the mustard, then the milk, and cook for 1 minute. Remove from the heat and stir in the yogurt. Add cayenne pepper and salt if desired.   *(continued)*

6. Meanwhile, poach the eggs.

7. To serve, pour a pool of sauce onto a warm platter. Place the hash cakes on the sauce and arrange a poached egg on each patty. Garnish each with a dollop of sour cream.

The Allure of Garlic

The molecules that give garlic its strong pungency are activated only when they come in contact with air—that is, when the clove is cut into or crushed. These flavor molecules quickly break down when heated, though, and cooked garlic—whether blanched, sautéed, or roasted—is a different ingredient from raw.

The flavor of roasted garlic is unique. It is more civilized than raw, blanched, or sautéed garlic, because it pairs so well with so many other ingredients. It sweetens the taste of green, grassy broccoli in a salad, for instance. Cooked for a long time in soup it becomes mild and tastes more like a nut than a garlic clove. A paste of roasted garlic is wonderful spread on sandwiches or brushed on meat, poultry, or seafood before grilling or broiling.

The California garlic that you find in the markets during the summer is the freshest and strongest in flavor. September marks the end of the 10-week annual harvest. During the winter months, look for garlic imported from South America, which is the most flavorful at that time.

There is some evidence that garlic "lightens" the blood and helps lower cholesterol. This is an added incentive for those on whom the allure of garlic is lost. For us ailophiles, though, that's simply a nice adjunct to our happy addiction to the marvelous bulb.

GARLIC STEW

SERVES 6

*T*his vegetable dish runs the risk of seeming like a side dish or a pasta sauce, but garlic elevates it to main-course status. The runny yolks of poached eggs provide extra "sauce." All in all, a satisfying blend.

Serve salad, a cheese course, and a fruit dessert.

> ¼ cup olive oil
> 1 pound garlic (about 8 medium bulbs), separated into cloves
>   and peeled
> 2 medium onions, diced (about 2 cups)
> 3 tablespoons all-purpose flour
> 4 cups water, or chicken stock, or canned low-sodium chicken broth
> 1 lemon, cut in half
> 4 bay leaves
> 4 sprigs fresh thyme or ½ teaspoon dried
> 1 cup finely diced green beans
> 1 cup finely diced zucchini or yellow crookneck squash
> 1 cup small cauliflower florets
> 1 quart milk
> 1 cup fresh or frozen corn kernels
> 12 eggs
> Salt and freshly ground black pepper to taste
> 12 slices French bread

1. Heat 3 tablespoons of the olive oil in a 2-quart pot over medium heat. Add the garlic and cook, stirring occasionally, for 7 to 10 minutes, or until the cloves start to turn golden. Add the onions and cook until soft, about 5 minutes. Stir in the flour and cook for a minute. Add the water (or stock), lemon, bay leaves, and thyme, increase the heat to high, and bring to a boil. Lower the heat to medium and simmer, uncovered, for 30 minutes.

2. Meanwhile, heat the remaining 1 tablespoon oil in a medium skillet. Add the green beans, squash, cauliflower, and corn, cover, and cook over medium heat until the vegetables soften slightly, about 5 minutes.

3. Remove the lemon and bay leaves from the garlic stew, and stir in the milk. Add the vegetables, cover, and cook for 5 minutes. Add salt and pepper.

4. Meanwhile, poach the eggs.

5. Spoon the stew into soup bowls, arrange 2 slices of bread in the center of each serving, and top each slice with a poached egg. Serve piping hot.

Dinners Without Meat

LATIN AMERICAN OMELETTES

SERVES 4

*T*hese flat Spanish-style omelettes are finished in the oven, then turned out onto warm tortillas. A big corn salad, with some thinly sliced ham or prosciutto if you like, starts the dinner off right.

16 tomatillos
2 tablespoons olive oil
1 jalapeño pepper, or more to taste, seeded
1 teaspoon salt
1 small red onion, finely minced (about ½ cup)
4 tablespoons plus 2 teaspoons unsalted butter or margarine
2 cups diced onions (about 2 medium onions)
1 cup drained canned tomatoes, seeded and chopped
1 large avocado, diced
¼ cup chopped cilantro (fresh coriander)
12 eggs, lightly beaten
4 10-inch flour tortillas
Sour cream, for serving

1. Remove and discard the papery husks from the tomatillos and cut into quarters.

2. Combine the tomatillos, oil, jalapeño pepper, and salt in a small pot, cover, and cook over medium heat for 12 minutes. Transfer to a food processor or blender and puree. Pass the puree through a strainer into a bowl. Stir in the red onion and place the salsa in the refrigerator to chill.

3. Preheat the oven to 300°F.

4. Melt 2 tablespoons of the butter in a skillet over medium heat. Add the diced onions and cook for 10 minutes, stirring, until softened. Add the tomatoes, avocado, and cilantro and cook for a minute, to warm through. Remove from the heat.

5. Melt 2 teaspoons of the butter in an 8-inch skillet. Add one quarter of the onion/tomato mixture and one quarter (about a generous ½ cup) of the eggs. Swirl to distribute the onion mixture, cover, and cook just until the eggs are set, about 5 minutes. Turn the omelette onto a lightly buttered baking pan. Repeat with the rest of the eggs and onion mixture. Transfer the baking sheet to the oven and cook for 2 to 3 minutes.

6. While the omelettes are in the oven, heat the tortillas by placing them directly over a gas flame for about 20 seconds on each side, or heat briefly under a hot broiler, turning once. Place a tortilla on each plate.

7. Place an omelette on each tortilla. Put a dollop of sour cream and a spoonful of salsa on each omelette, and serve.

MUSHROOM, MACARONI, AND SPINACH FRITTATA

SERVES 3

*7*he chewy texture of the macaroni joins the light, puffy baked eggs and gives us a wonderful excuse for dolloping salty tapenade on top. With the frittata, serve a vegetable soup and a salad—something simple like home-grown tomatoes, arugula, and roasted peppers. If you have a kettle barbe-cue, light a fire and let it burn down. Place skillet on grill, put the lid on, and cook the frittata in the collecting smoke. You won't believe the flavor.

2 tablespoons olive oil
1 small onion, finely diced
1 tablespoon minced garlic
1½ cups sliced white mushrooms
½ cup cooked small macaroni shells or ¼ cup uncooked shells
2 cups chopped spinach
12 eggs
½ teaspoon salt, or to taste
½ teaspoon freshly ground black pepper, or to taste
Tapenade (recipe follows)

1. Preheat the oven to 350°F.

2. Heat 1 tablespoon of the oil in a large skillet over medium heat. Add the onion and garlic and cook for 1 minute. Add the mushrooms and cook, stirring, until all the moisture has evaporated, about 5 minutes. Stir in the macaroni, increase the heat to high, and add the spinach. Cook, stirring, until the spinach wilts. Transfer to a bowl.   *(continued)*

3. Lightly beat the eggs with the salt and pepper and stir into the spinach mixture.

4. Heat the remaining 1 tablespoon olive oil in a 12-inch skillet over medium-high heat. Add the frittata mixture and cook for 1 minute. Immediately transfer the skillet to the oven and cook until the frittata is barely set, about 15 minutes.

5. To serve, slide the frittata onto a serving plate. Pass the Tapenade.

TAPENADE

2 tablespoons chopped fresh parsley
½ cup pitted Niçoise or Kalamata olives
8 anchovies
1 tablespoon fresh lemon juice
3 tablespoons olive oil

Combine all the ingredients in a food processor and process to a paste.

CRAB HASH AND POACHED EGGS

SERVES 4

*T*hese pancakes are crisp yet creamy inside. The runny yolks make a sauce unnecessary, although no one will complain if you offer mayonnaise and ketchup. If you can find it, add some of the Maryland spice mixture called Old Bay Seasoning to both the hash mixture and your mayonnaise. Begin the dinner with steamed asparagus or tomato soup.

1½ pounds lump crabmeat
1½ pounds potatoes (about 3 medium potatoes)
1 tablespoon all-purpose flour
½ cup finely minced fresh chives
2 teaspoons chopped fresh thyme or 1 tablespoon dried
Salt and ground white pepper to taste
½ teaspoon Old Bay Seasoning (optional)
¼ cup milk
4 tablespoons unsalted butter or margarine
8 eggs

1. Place the crabmeat in a bowl and pick through it, removing and discarding any bits of shell.

2. Shred the potatoes on the shredding blade of a food processor, or coarsely grate them by hand. Add the potatoes, flour, chives, thyme, salt and pepper, and Old Bay Seasoning, if desired, to the crabmeat and mix well. Add the milk and mix well.

3. Preheat the oven to 375°F.

4. Melt 1 tablespoon of butter in an 8-inch nonstick frying pan over medium heat. Add one quarter of the hash mixture, shaping it into a 2-inch-thick cake in the pan. Cook, without stirring or moving the hash, for 3 minutes. Flip the hash cake, lower the heat to low, and cook for 5 minutes. Transfer to a baking sheet, and repeat with the remaining hash mixture and butter.

5. Place the hash cakes in the oven for 7 to 10 minutes to finish cooking.

6. Meanwhile, poach the eggs.

7. To serve dinner, place a hash cake on each plate and top with 2 poached eggs.

BATATA AND BACALAO CAKES
WITH POACHED EGGS

SERVES 4

*B*eginning in the sixteenth century, cod from the banks of eastern Canada and potatoes from Peru and the Caribbean were responsible for feeding much of Europe's population. The European explorers who brought the potato back to the Old World called it its Caribbean Indian name, *batata.* Tons of cod, variously called *bacalao* or *baccalà,* were fished, salted on board, and transported to Europe. But there's no evidence that the two foods were ever combined into marvelous hash patties like these. If you prefer, you can make the hash cakes with smoked whitefish instead of cod. It's more familiar to many people, and the results are just as delicious as the original.

1½ pounds salt cod
1 large sweet potato (about 1 pound)
½ teaspoon ground white pepper
¼ teaspoon ground mace
3 tablespoons all-purpose flour
11 eggs
4 tablespoons unsalted butter or margarine
¼ cup sour cream
Garlic and Red Pepper Sauce (recipe follows)

1. Soak the salt cod overnight in water to cover, changing the water twice. Drain.

2. Place the cod in a pot of cold water to cover, bring to a boil, and immediately drain. Place in a bowl and mash.

3. Shred the potato on the shredding blade of a food processor, or coarsely grate it by hand. Add the potato to the cod and mix well. Add the pepper, mace, flour, and 3 of the eggs and mix well. Form into 8 patties.

4. Preheat the oven to 250°F.

5. Melt 2 tablespoons of the butter in a large nonstick frying pan over medium heat. Add only enough of the patties to fit without crowding and cook, without moving the cakes, for 5 minutes. Flip the cakes, lower the heat to low, and cook for another 5 minutes. Drain on paper towels, then transfer the cakes to the oven to keep warm, and repeat with the remaining patties, using additional butter as needed.

6. Meanwhile, poach the remaining 8 eggs.

7. To serve, place 2 hash cakes on each plate, and top each cake with a poached egg. Place a small dollop of the sour cream on each egg. Serve the garlic sauce on the side.

GARLIC AND RED PEPPER SAUCE

MAKES 1 CUP

1 red bell pepper
2 tablespoons olive oil
2 tablespoons minced garlic
2 tablespoons minced shallots
½ teaspoon ground cumin
1 cup chicken stock or canned low-sodium chicken broth
½ cup heavy cream
4 tablespoons unsalted butter, cut into pieces
Salt and freshly ground white pepper to taste

1. If you have a gas range, place the pepper directly over a high flame; if you have an electric range, preheat the broiler. Cook the pepper, turning, so that the skin blackens completely on all sides. Place in a paper bag, close the top, and let rest 5 minutes. Hold the pepper under cold running water, and rub until all the blackened skin is removed. Slice the pepper in half, remove the stem and seeds, and finely chop.

2. Heat the oil in a small saucepan over medium heat, and cook the garlic, shallots, and cumin, without coloring, for about 2 minutes. Add the stock and cook until reduced by half. Add the cream and chopped pepper and reduce until thick enough to coat the back of a spoon. Remove from the heat and whisk in the butter. Taste for salt and pepper and add as desired.

Dinners Without Meat

BLINTZES

*B*lintzes are simply eggy crêpes. They are cooked on one side, then removed from the skillet, placed cooked side up, filled and rolled. When the filled blintz is cooked, the edges become golden with crisp patches. Blintzes should be thin, dense, and a little chewy. They freeze well, both unstuffed and stuffed.

Aim to cook the blintz "skins" with a scant amount of butter. The more seasoned the pan, the easier it is to accomplish. But when cooking stuffed blintzes, don't skimp—extra butter makes them that much more delicious.

1 cup all-purpose flour
1 teaspoon salt
4 eggs
1 egg white
1¾ cups milk
3 tablespoons melted butter, plus additional for cooking the blintzes

1. Place the flour and salt in a bowl.

2. Beat two eggs, white, and milk together in another bowl. Slowly add the egg mixture to the flour, stirring with a whisk until incorporated. Stir in the melted butter. Cover and set aside to rest, for 1 hour before using.

3. Melt about ¼ teaspoon butter in an 8-inch crêpe pan or nonstick skillet. Lift the skillet off the heat, add 2 tablespoons of the batter, and quickly tilt the skillet all around so the batter covers the bottom. Replace the skillet on the heat and cook until the surface looks dry and the edges of the blintz begin to pull away from the sides of the pan. Turn the skillet upside down and let the blintz fall out of the pan onto a towel. Repeat with the remaining batter.

4. Stack the blintz skins between squares of wax paper or plastic wrap when cool. They can be kept up to a day at room temperature, covered.

POTATO AND LEEK BLINTZES

SERVES 4

*F*riends of ours prepare a Russian-style Easter feast. The Lenten half of the meal consists of pickled and fresh fish, smoked salmon and caviar, cucumber salad, little potato blintzes, and buckwheat blinis. The second half is breaking Lent—with suckling pig and the fixings. It's quite a feast—two dinners at one sitting, really.

Blintzes accompanied by salmon caviar and smoked trout and garnished with horseradish-and-dill-flavored yogurt are a great dish, Lenten feast or no. Instead of serving the suckling pig course, begin dinner with a few different marinated vegetable dishes—cucumber salad, roasted peppers with lemon, asparagus vinaigrette. And finish with a rich dessert, like Nesselrode pie.

4 tablespoons unsalted butter or margarine
2 cups thinly sliced leeks (about 1¼ pounds)
¼ cup milk
2 medium potatoes (about 1 pound), baked
Salt and ground white pepper to taste
Nutmeg, preferably freshly grated, to taste
2 eggs
12 Blintzes (page 126)
¾ cup plain yogurt
2 tablespoons prepared horseradish
2 teaspoons freshly chopped dill
¼ cup salmon roe
4 smoked trout or whitefish, skinned, boned, and cut into thin strips

1. Heat 2 tablespoons of the butter or margarine in a skillet. Add the leeks and cook, stirring occasionally, for 5 minutes. Add the milk and cook for 1 to 2 minutes longer. Transfer the leeks to a bowl.

2. Scoop the flesh out of the baked potatoes and add it to the leeks. Mash together until almost smooth; a few lumps are fine. Season with salt and pepper and nutmeg, then add the eggs and mix well.

3. Lay a blintz skin, cooked side up, on a work surface. Spoon 2 heaping tablespoons of the potato mixture across the lower part of the blintz. Roll the crêpe blintz over once, fold over the sides, and roll the blintz over again. You will have a thick cigar-shaped roll. Repeat with the remaining blintzes and filling, placing them seam side down on a plate as they are finished.

(continued)

4. Combine the yogurt, horseradish, and dill and place in a serving bowl. Refrigerate.

5. Heat the remaining 2 tablespoons butter in a large skillet over medium-low heat. Add the blintzes seam side down and cook for 2 to 3 minutes, or until golden on the bottom. Turn them and cook until golden on both sides.

6. Place the blintzes on a platter, spoon some caviar on each one, and garnish with the smoked fish. Serve the yogurt on the side.

The Dairy Restaurant

The quintessential dairy meal developed in large cities after the great wave of immigrations from Eastern Europe at the end of the nineteenth century. Only a few remain today, remnants from a time when Manhattan's Lower East Side had a large immigrant Jewish population. Because Jewish (and Muslim) dietary laws forbid mixing dairy and meat, kosher restaurants are exclusively one or the other and dairy meant anything other than meat or poultry—fish and vegetables—and there was butter on the table instead of rendered chicken fat.

CHEESE AND APPLE BLINTZES

SERVES 4

7his is the most familiar blintz of all. It's fabulous as a summer dinner, especially if you start with a chilled beet, cabbage, or sorrel borscht. I've served these at three in the morning after an evening on the town.

5 to 6 tablespoons unsalted butter or margarine
1 medium onion, diced (about ¾ cup)
1 cup crumbled goat cheese
1 cup ricotta cheese
2 eggs
1 tablespoon fresh thyme or 1 teaspoon dried
Salt and ground white pepper to taste
12 Blintzes (page 126)
3 tart apples, such as Granny Smiths, peeled and diced
Pinch of ground mace
Pinch of ground cloves
½ cup plain yogurt

1. Heat 1 tablespoon of butter or margarine over medium heat. Add the onion and cook, stirring occasionally, for 5 minutes. Transfer to a bowl.

2. Add both the cheeses and the eggs to the onions and mash together until mostly smooth. Add the thyme and salt and pepper.

3. Lay a blintz skin, cooked side up, on a work surface. Spoon 2 heaping tablespoons of the cheese mixture across the lower part of the blintz. Roll the crêpe over once, fold over the sides, and roll the blintz over again. You will have a thick cigar-shaped roll. Repeat with the remaining blintzes and filling, placing them seam side down on a plate as they are finished.

4. Melt 2 tablespoons of the butter in a skillet over medium heat. Add the apples, mace, and cloves, and cook, stirring occasionally, until soft, about 7 minutes. Remove from the heat and keep warm.

5. Heat 1 tablespoon butter in a skillet over medium-low heat. Add 4 of the blintzes seam side down and cook for 2 to 3 minutes, or until golden on the bottom. Turn them and cook until golden on both sides. Remove from the skillet and keep warm in a low oven while you cook the remaining blintzes, adding more butter as necessary.

6. Place the blintzes on a platter and spoon the apples over them. Serve the yogurt on the side.

CHILE PEPPERS STUFFED WITH CHEESE AND CORN PUDDING

SERVES 4

*P*oblano chile peppers are green and mildly hot, although if allowed to darken on the vine they develop a louder spice. They are known as ancho chilies when they are dried. If you can't find them, use red or golden bell peppers (green bells don't work well in this dish), and add a small amount of red pepper flakes to the tomato coulis. Start dinner with chilled shrimp or crab mayonnaise and serve something chocolate for dessert.

8 poblano chile peppers or small red or yellow bell peppers
2 tablespoons olive oil, plus more for brushing
2 medium onions, finely minced
2 tablespoons finely minced garlic
1 cup fresh corn kernels
¾ cup ricotta cheese
1 cup grated Gouda cheese
3 eggs
¼ teaspoon ground mace
1 teaspoon chopped fresh rosemary
Salt and freshly ground black pepper to taste
1½ cups peeled and seeded tomatoes, drained (about 4 tomatoes)
2 tablespoons finely chopped fresh parsley

1. Roast and carefully peel the peppers (see page 203). Make an incision in one side of each pepper and remove and discard the seeds; try not to tear the peppers completely open. Set aside. Preheat the oven to 375°F.

2. Heat the oil in a small skillet over medium heat. Add the onions and garlic and cook, stirring, for 5 minutes, or until the onions are soft. Add the corn and cook for 3 minutes. Scrape into a bowl, and add the ricotta, Gouda, eggs, mace, rosemary, and salt and pepper. Mix well.

3. Spoon some of the ricotta mixture into each pepper. Brush the peppers with a little oil, place on a baking sheet, slit sides up, and bake for 30 to 35 minutes, or until the filling is set.

4. Meanwhile, chop the tomatoes. Place them in a saucepan and cook over medium heat for 5 minutes. Remove from the heat and stir in the parsley.

5. To serve, spoon the tomato coulis onto a platter and arrange the peppers on top.

SERVES 3 TO 4

*R*aclette is a cheese similar to Gruyère or Emmenthaler. You will often see huge wheels of it—about 20 pounds each—nestled at the side of a hearth in cafés throughout Switzerland. As the cheese warms and melts in the heat of the fire, you scrape off the softest part and eat it with potatoes and bread. Here I've added vegetables to create a complete dinner. If you're a person whose taste tends towards pastel colors and background music, beware of this cheese—its aroma is strong and tends to linger. This is most definitely red wine or dark beer kind of food.

1 bunch celery
⅓ cup olive oil
2 heads Belgian endive, halved lengthwise
2 large leeks, white part only, halved lengthwise
1 cup water, chicken stock, or canned low-sodium chicken broth
1 teaspoon salt
Freshly ground black pepper to taste
¼ cup balsamic vinegar
12 small new potatoes
1 pound raclette cheese, cut into 2-inch cubes
Dijon or hot mustard, for serving

1. Trim the top third from the celery and reserve for another use; cut the celery lengthwise into quarters.

2. Heat 3 tablespoons of the oil in a large skillet over medium-high heat. Add the endive, cut side up, and cook until browned, about 4 minutes. Turn and brown on the other side. Remove from the pan and set aside. Add the leeks, and cook them for 4 minutes on each side; remove and set aside. Add the celery and cook for 10 minutes, turning occasionally.

3. Return all the vegetables to the skillet and add the water (or stock), salt, and pepper. Cover and cook until tender, about 3 minutes for the endive, 5 minutes for the leeks, and 7 minutes for the celery, removing each vegetable as it is done.

4. Add the vinegar to the liquid remaining in the skillet and simmer until reduced by half. Pour into a small bowl and cool to room temperature. Then beat the remaining olive oil into the cooled sauce and set aside.

5. Meanwhile, bring a pot of salted water to the boil. Add the potatoes and cook until soft, about 12 minutes. Drain.   *(continued)*

Dinners Without Meat

6. Preheat the oven to 275°F.

7. Arrange the vegetables on an ovenproof serving platter. Scatter the cubes of cheese among the vegetables, and place in the oven for about 10 minutes, or until the cheese softens. Spoon the vinegar sauce over the vegetables and serve immediately. Offer mustard on the side.

MARKET VEGETABLE DINNER

SERVES 4

*T*his was my favorite dinner after returning from the beach in the summer. I'd stop at the outdoor vegetable market on First Avenue in New York City and fill a basket with vegetables, some to cook and others to add raw. It was always a slightly different meal.

Begin cooking as soon as you walk in the door. Cook the vegetables a couple at a time in a wok or large cast iron skillet over very high heat. You want them only lightly cooked, still crisp-tender, so keep the temperature as high as possible and don't crowd the pan. When all the veggies are cooked, place them in the refrigerator to chill while you take a cool shower to wash off sand and suntan lotion. When you return to the kitchen, add the lettuce, tomatoes, avocados, and vinaigrette—I never wait for the cooked vegetables to chill completely before assembling and serving the salad. (If you're in the mood, add diced ham or cooked bacon, chicken, or turkey to the salad.) The saltwater taffy I buy at the beach is dessert.

¼ cup lentils

2 teaspoons flavorless vegetable oil

1 large onion, halved lengthwise and cut lengthwise into slivers

1 red bell pepper, cored, seeded, and cut into rounds

1 small zucchini, cut into ¼-inch-thick rounds

½ pound large white mushrooms, halved

½ cup small cauliflower florets

1 ear white corn, kernels removed

1 head Boston lettuce

1 tablespoon Dijon mustard

⅓ cup sherry vinegar

½ cup olive oil

1 avocado, cut into large dice

1 large tomato, cut into large dice

2 hard-cooked eggs, cut into quarters (optional)

⅓ pound Swiss cheese, cut into ¼-inch dice (optional)

1. Bring a pot of salted water to the boil. Cook the lentils until soft, but not mushy, about 15 minutes. Drain and put into a large salad bowl.

2. Meanwhile, place a wok or large cast-iron skillet over high heat and add 1 teaspoon of the vegetable oil. When the oil is nearly smoking hot, add the onion and quickly spread it out across the bottom and sides of the wok. Cook for 1½ minutes without stirring, then stir and cook for another minute. Scrape into the salad bowl. Replace the wok on the stove.

3. Add ½ teaspoon of the oil to the wok. When it is nearly smoking hot, add the pepper and zucchini. Cook, stirring frequently, for about 2 minutes. Add to the onions and mix well. Replace the wok on the stove.

4. Add the remaining ½ teaspoon oil to the wok. When it's almost smoking hot, add the mushrooms and cauliflower. Place a lid on the wok and cook for 1 minute. Remove the lid and cook, stirring frequently, for 1 to 2 minutes. Add to the salad and mix. Replace the wok on the stove.

5. When the wok is hot again, add the corn. Cook for 1 minute without stirring, then cook for 30 seconds, stirring constantly. Add to the salad, mix well, and refrigerate for 20 minutes.

6. Wash and dry the lettuce and tear the leaves into pieces. Refrigerate.

7. Combine the mustard and vinegar in a small bowl and beat in the olive oil. Set aside.

8. When ready to serve dinner, add the avocado, tomato, lettuce, eggs, and cheese to the salad bowl. Pour over the vinaigrette and toss well.

Dinners Without Meat

Mushrooms

In addition to the common cultivated mushroom, certain wild species are highly prized at the dinner table during the damp spring and autumn months, like the ribbed, pale orange chanterelles and honey-comb-capped morels. Common in Europe, but more difficult to find here, except in its dried state, is the famous boletus edulis—called *porcini* in Italy, *cèpe* in France.

Two Asian mushroom varieties have become common in recent years—the meaty, brown shiitake and the astringent pale oyster, or pleurotte, mushroom. Both have been successfully cultivated, although shiitakes are still rather expensive. The most highly prized Asian mushroom is the matsutake. It has a perfumed taste and a meaty texture.

Traditional cooking has employed mushrooms for texture and flavor and to enhance other ingredients rather than as a food. This is a happy coincidence, since mushrooms are nutritionally poor. (They are very rich, though, in glutamic acid and are thus a natural source of MSG.) They add their own intense flavor to soups and sauces and can save bland vegetable dishes.

Mushrooms change composition after harvesting, and storing them tightly wrapped only hastens spoilage. Purchase only the whitest cultivated mushrooms, refrigerate them, loosely covered, and use as quickly as possible. When choosing chanterelles, look for ones with a solid texture, neither mushy nor wet. Shiitakes should have dark, plump caps with white undersides; remove the stringy stems. Oyster mushrooms should be white with unbroken caps; trim off the stems, which are bitter except on the smallest mushrooms.

OPEN-FACED MUSHROOM, ARUGULA, AND BRIE SANDWICHES

MAKES 4 SANDWICHES

7 hese sandwiches are a bit sloppy, so eat them with a fork and knife—it feels more like dinner that way, too. Try to use as many meaty mushrooms—shiitake and porcini, for example—as you can in the mélange.

Begin dinner with a white bean and vegetable soup, or something starchy like a pasta or risotto.

> *2 pounds assorted fresh or dried mushrooms, such as porcini, morel,*
> *   chanterelle, shiitake, oyster, and/or cultivated white*
> *2 tablespoons olive oil*
> *1 teaspoon minced garlic*
> *½ cup finely diced onion*
> *1 tablespoon red wine vinegar*
> *Salt and freshly ground black pepper to taste*
> *½ cup arugula*
> *4 slices country bread*
> *4 slices Brie*

1. Reconstitute any dried mushrooms by soaking in warm water to cover for 1 hour; drain. Cut morels and chanterelles in half or quarters, depending on size; remove and discard the stems from shiitake and oyster mushrooms; trim and slice cultivated mushrooms.

2. Heat the oil in a skillet over medium heat. Add the mushrooms, garlic, onion, vinegar, 1 tablespoon water (or strained soaking liquid), and salt and pepper, cover, and cook for 3 minutes. Uncover, increase the heat to high, and cook until the mushrooms are tender and most of the liquid is absorbed, about 5 minutes. Transfer the mushrooms to a bowl and let cool.

3. Toast or grill the bread. Preheat the broiler. Add the arugula to the mushrooms and toss to mix.

4. Place the bread on a baking sheet and pile on the mushrooms. Lay a slice of cheese over each sandwich and broil until the cheese is melted. Serve immediately.

VEGETABLE-STUFFED CABBAGE

SERVES 6

I'm fond of raisins and rice in a traditional stuffed cabbage filling, because they sweeten and lighten the meat. This vegetarian version is a culinary trompe l'oeil. I leave out the raisins because the filling is already sweet enough from the natural sugar in the carrots, parsnip, and onion. The eggplant lends a meaty texture. The whole dish is peasant in character— simple and rich without the heaviness of meat.

1 small eggplant (about ¾ pound), peeled
2 medium carrots (about ¼ pound), peeled
1 parsnip or turnip (about ½ pound), peeled
2 medium onions, quartered
1 large leek (about 1 pound), white part only
2 small yellow squash
½ cup cooked rice
1 tablespoon minced garlic
2 tablespoons rice wine vinegar or malt vinegar
3 tablespoons soy sauce
1 teaspoon tomato paste
½ teaspoon dried thyme
1 teaspoon ground white pepper
1 teaspoon dried sage
1 large head green cabbage
1 cup water, chicken stock, or canned low-sodium chicken broth
¾ cup sour cream
Vegetable oil, for brushing

1. Grind the eggplant, carrots, parsnip, onions, leek, and squash in a meat grinder fitted with the coarse disc; or roughly chop the vegetables and pulse in a food processor until coarsely ground. Put into a large pot and add the rice, garlic, vinegar, soy sauce, tomato paste, thyme, pepper, and sage. Mix well. Cover and cook over medium heat for 10 minutes. Uncover and cook, stirring occasionally, until the mixture is dry, about 15 minutes. Scrape into a bowl and set aside.

2. Bring a large pot of water to a boil. Core the cabbage and add it to the boiling water. As the outer leaves begin to soften, remove the cabbage from the water and carefully remove the large outer leaves one at a time. Return the cabbage to the water and repeat the procedure until you have about 15 leaves. (Save the remainder of the cabbage for another use.)

3. Lay a cabbage leaf out flat on a work surface. Place about ½ cup of the vegetable mixture in the center of the leaf, fold over the sides of the leaf, and roll up tightly like a jelly roll. Repeat with the remaining leaves and stuffing.

4. Place the cabbage rolls, seam side down, in a roasting pan or pot just large enough to hold them in a single layer. Add the water (or chicken stock), cover, and place in the oven. Turn the oven on to 350°F and bake for 30 minutes.

5. Pour off the liquid in the roasting pan into a bowl and whisk in the sour cream. Increase the oven temperature to 400°F. Brush the cabbage rolls with a little oil and bake for 10 minutes, or until the surface browns slightly. Arrange the cabbage rolls on a platter and pour the sour cream sauce over the top.

Tarte à l'Oignon

SERVES 4

This is a dinner of onion soup without the soup—the flavors that we love in the bistro favorite are here in pie form.

Prepare a composed salad of lightly cooked vegetables, some hard-cooked eggs, and crunchy lettuce. Serve it at the same time as the tarte.

8 tablespoons (1 stick) unsalted butter or margarine
2 cups all-purpose flour
1 egg yolk
2 tablespoons plus 2 teaspoons ice water
2 tablespoons olive oil or unsalted butter
8 medium onions, thinly sliced (about 12 cups)
2 tablespoons minced garlic
¼ teaspoon ground mace
1 teaspoon salt
½ teaspoon ground white pepper
2 tablespoons white wine vinegar
1 cup grated Gruyère cheese
1 egg, beaten

1. Prepare the pastry: Cut the butter into small cubes. Place the flour in a food processor, add the butter, and pulse lightly until the mixture reaches the

(continued)

138   consistency of coarse meal. Add the egg yolk and water and pulse just until the dough begins to form a ball. Divide the dough in half, shape it into 2 disks, wrap in plastic wrap, and let rest in the refrigerator for 30 minutes before using.

2. While the dough is resting, heat the olive oil over medium heat in a heavy-bottomed pot. Add the onions, garlic, mace, salt, pepper, and vinegar. Cook, stirring occasionally, until the onions caramelize and turn a dark golden brown, about 30 minutes. Transfer to a bowl, mix in the cheese, and let cool.

3. Remove the pastry from the refrigerator and roll out each disk to a 12-inch circle. Line a 10-inch tart pan with one and place it in the freezer for 15 minutes; place the second circle in the refrigerator.

4. Preheat the oven to 375°F.

5. Remove the tart pan from the freezer and fill with the onion mixture. Remove the second pastry round from the refrigerator and lay it over the filling. Trim off the excess dough from around the edge and crimp the two edges together. Prick the surface of the tart in several places with a fork and brush lightly with the beaten egg. Bake for 30 minutes, or until golden brown.

6. Serve hot from the oven.

Politically Correct Dinners — Grains, Beans, and Pasta

Red Bean, Pasta, and Sausage Stew
Tomato, White Bean, and Blue Cheese Chili
Vegetable Chili
Duck and White Bean Chili
Seafood Chili
Garbanzo, Lamb, and Olive Stew
Cassoulet

IN OTHER CHAPTERS

*A*s Reay Tannahill has observed, early man and woman nomaded around, the men hunting, the women gathering roots and vegetables. Herds moved from winter haven to summer pasture, and while grains, obviously, stayed where they were, you had to be in the right place at the right time to catch them exploding off the stalk.

Slowly, people began to settle in camps next to fields of grain rather than carry the harvest long distances back to the cave. Eventually, they learned how to cultivate grains, then how to hull them, to separate wheat from chaff, so they could make bread and pasta. In Asia, it was the soy bean and, later, rice that were to transform the land and socialize the population. In the Americas, it was corn and beans.

At the end of the nineteenth century, a trend toward "manufactured" food and perfect unblemished fruits and vegetables began to take hold in America. White became Mom's preferred color when it came to food. It symbolized refinement and purity—the miracle of American agribusiness. It celebrated sameness—the power of American democracy. Throughout the first half of the twentieth century, our food was smooth and bland.

The 1960s ushered in a counterculture—the age of tie-dye and macrobiotic cooking. The college generation abandoned the eating habits of its childhood—eggs and bacon in the morning, greasy school lunches of mystery meat or bagged sandwiches on enriched white bread, meat and potatoes for supper—for a diet richer in unrefined grains, more vegetarian and benign.

Food became beige. Hippies opened macrobiotic restaurants. Ying gave way to yang. Granola replaced ham and eggs, soy beans and tofu replaced meat, brown rice replaced the converted variety. Chocolate cake became carrot cake. All food, especially bread, was made crunchy with the addition of seeds and grains. This new diet was sane and nutritious in its balance of food groups, but did not make for particularly delicious—or refined—meals.

Politically Correct Dinners—Grains, Beans, and Pasta

We tend to believe, unfortunately, that moving up the socioeconomic scale means forsaking less expensive grains and carbohydrates for a diet weighted toward the "good stuff," the more expensive meat, fish, and poultry. Most people, as they mainstream into American culture, forsake their ethnic eating habits and try to follow what they think to be a true-blue American dietary model—lots of rich gravies, lots of animal protein. Group after immigrant group has been encouraged to give up its core food in favor of a more American model. (It's not surprising, then, that much of what people consider comforting in food is starchy and smooth. It's what filled us up before we were "privileged" enough to grace our table with a steak.)

But as we give up our potatoes, beans, and rice for hot dogs, hamburgers, and fried chicken, our health suffers. A diet heavy on grains and vegetables with a mere supplement of animal protein is still the ideal. Legumes and grains are a terrific source of protein, without the dreaded fat that we're told to avoid. Now football players in training are encouraged to eat lots of pasta, rice, and other grains rather than two or three meals of roast beef a day. Grain, beans, and pastas give more energy.

Most of the dinners in this chapter are vegetarian, although that wasn't my original intent. Meat just didn't seem a necessary ingredient in many of these dishes. There are, though, two recipes using chicken livers—paired with pasta shells and added to an artichoke risotto—one with ham, and another with sausages. There are three variations on a classic chili recipe—blue cheese, vegetable, and duck—as well as a quite traditional meaty cassoulet.

Some of my favorite meals are found in this chapter, as well as the inspirations for many future dinners. Buckwheat noodles, for example, are a flavor revelation, and when you get around to making these noodles yourself, you'll be addicted. They've already become a great jumping-off point for many of my new creations.

The idea of mixing two starches together in the same recipe is not a new one, but it's still a good one. I'm always pleased with the results when I cook Riso and Risotto or Buckwheat Noodles with Potatoes.

Chick-pea flour is an ingredient that had been languishing in my imagination (and getting stale in my cupboard). Try using it instead of cornmeal in a polenta (see page 168) or instead of buckwheat for blini (see page 169). And couscous, another often overlooked staple, makes wonderful pancakes (see page 150).

So don't be afraid to serve a dinner built around grains, beans, and pasta. It's politically and nutritionally correct—high in fiber and high in protein, low in animal fat—and more delicious than you would believe. Chic is now risotto, not ris de veau.

BUCKWHEAT NOODLES

MAKES ABOUT ½ POUND NOODLES, ENOUGH FOR 4 SERVINGS

*L*ose the image of Grandmother toiling in the kitchen rolling out hand-made noodles. Egg noodles are softer than pasta and easy to roll out. And the reason to make your own is to make them out of the many flours available, such as buckwheat, rye, chick-pea, masa harina (hominy flour), or even just whole wheat. What's needed in a noodle is gluten, a protein found in wheat flour that gives elasticity to a dough. Buckwheat, which has little gluten, is combined with high-gluten bread flour to make this dough. Toast the buckwheat first to bring out its flavor. These noodles have a more prominent flavor than Japanese soba; soba can, nevertheless, be substituted for your homemade noodles.

½ cup buckwheat flour
½ cup bread flour
2 eggs
1 teaspoon olive oil or walnut oil
1 teaspoon salt
¼ teaspoon ground white pepper

1. Preheat the oven to 350°F.

2. Spread the buckwheat flour in a baking pan and toast in the oven for 20 minutes, stirring occasionally.

3. Combine the buckwheat flour and bread flour in a bowl and mix well. Place one quarter of the flour mixture in the bowl of an electric mixer fitted with a dough hook or into a food processor. Add the eggs, oil, salt, and pepper and beat or process until smooth. Slowly add the remainder of the flour and beat until a stiff dough is formed. Turn the dough out onto a floured work surface and knead for 5 minutes. Cover the dough and let rest for 1 hour before rolling out the noodles.

4. Roll the dough out to a nearly paper-thin sheet. Roll up loosely jelly-roll fashion and cut into ¾-inch-wide noodles. (The noodles will keep for several days in the refrigerator.)

Politically Correct Dinners—Grains, Beans, and Pasta

BUCKWHEAT NOODLES WITH POTATOES AND SMOKED SALMON

SERVES 4

*W*e sometimes forget that food should "chew" well. Combinations of starches always feel good in your mouth, like this pairing of noodles and potatoes. It's a winning combination, but you need a flavor oomph, like some good smoked salmon.

½ pound potatoes, cut into ½-inch dice
3 tablespoons olive oil
3 tablespoons unsalted butter
2 medium onions, finely diced
¾ cup half-and-half
8 ounces smoked salmon
2 teaspoons chopped fresh dill
½ teaspoon salt, or to taste
½ teaspoon ground white pepper
1 recipe Buckwheat Noodles (page 143) or ½ pound Japanese soba noodles

1. Place the potatoes in a pot, cover with cold water, and bring to a boil. Immediately drain.

2. Heat the oil and butter in a skillet over medium heat. Add the potatoes and cook, without stirring, until browned on the bottom, about 10 minutes. Add the onions and cook, stirring occasionally, for 5 minutes. Add the half-and-half, increase the heat to high, and boil until lightly thickened. Remove from the heat and add the salmon, dill, and salt and pepper.

3. Meanwhile, cook the noodles in boiling salted water until just tender, 4 to 5 minutes; drain.

4. Arrange the noodles in four soup bowls and spoon the potatoes, salmon, and sauce over the top.

BUCKWHEAT NOODLES WITH THREE BRAISED LETTUCES

SERVES 4

*M*ost Americans are unaware of the delight of cooked lettuces. They make a wonderful, flavorful cooked vegetable. The bitter lettuces—endive, escarole, chicory—are tastier cooked than the rather dull butter and lime-stone varieties.

1 head escarole lettuce

2 heads Belgian endive

1 head Boston lettuce

1 recipe Buckwheat Noodles (page 143) or ½ pound Japanese soba
noodles

5 tablespoons olive oil

1 cup chicken stock or canned low-sodium chicken broth

1 teaspoon salt

½ teaspoon freshly ground black pepper

2 tablespoons minced garlic

1 teaspoon ground coriander

½ teaspoon dried thyme

½ teaspoon dried rosemary

2 tablespoons white wine vinegar

½ cup heavy cream

½ pound Fontina cheese, grated

2 tablespoons chopped fresh parsley

1. Remove and discard the tough outer leaves from the escarole, leaving the lighter green center. Cut in half lengthwise. Remove and discard any discolored outer leaves from the endive and halve them lengthwise. Remove and discard any damaged outer leaves from the Boston lettuce and cut in half lengthwise.

2. Bring a pot of salted water to the boil and cook the noodles for 4 minutes. Drain, toss with 1 tablespoon of the olive oil, and set aside.

3. Preheat the oven to 350°F.

4. Heat the remaining ¼ cup olive oil in a large skillet over medium-high heat. Add the lettuces and cook until golden. If necessary, brown the lettuce in batches. Replace all the lettuce in the skillet, add the stock and salt and pepper, and cook for 4 minutes. Remove the escarole and Boston lettuce and

(continued)

Politically Correct Dinners—Grains, Beans, and Pasta

cook the endive 4 minutes longer. Squeeze the excess liquid from the lettuces back into the skillet, and set the lettuces aside.

5. Add the garlic, coriander, thyme, rosemary, vinegar, and cream to the braising liquid, and cook over medium heat until thickened and reduced to the consistency of a sauce. Remove from the heat.

6. Toss the noodles with sauce and mound in the center of a baking dish. Arrange the lettuces around the noodles. Sprinkle with the Fontina cheese and place in the oven until bubbling hot, about 10 minutes. Sprinkle with the parsley and serve immediately.

BUCKWHEAT WAFFLES WITH CHIPPED HAM

SERVES 4

*T*his may seem like breakfast fare, but it's really a substantial dinner dish. The waffles have a toasty flavor that complements the ham.

Begin the meal with a vegetable soup, and serve an aged Cheddar.

½ cup buckwheat flour
1 cup bread flour
2 teaspoons baking powder
2 eggs, separated
1½ cups half-and-half
3 tablespoons melted unsalted butter
3 tablespoons unsalted butter
1 medium onion, finely diced (about ¾ cup)
4 medium carrots, peeled and thinly sliced (about 1 cup)
1 cup finely chopped ham (5 to 6 ounces)
3 tablespoons all-purpose flour
½ cup milk
Pinch of ground mace
Salt and ground white pepper to taste

1. Preheat the oven to 350°F.

2. Spread the buckwheat flour in a baking pan and toast in the oven for 20 minutes, stirring occasionally.

3. Combine the buckwheat flour, bread flour, and baking powder. Using an electric mixer set at medium speed, gradually beat in the egg yolks, half-and-half, and melted butter. Beat the egg whites until stiff, and fold them into the batter. The batter will measure about 2 ½ cups.

4. Heat waffle iron and cook the waffles according to manufacturer's directions. Keep waffles warm in a low oven as you make the remainder.

5. While the waffles are cooking, melt the 3 tablespoons butter in a skillet over medium heat. Add the onion and carrots and cook for 5 minutes. Add the ham and cook for 1 minute. Stir in the all-purpose flour, then the milk, and season with the mace and salt and pepper.

6. Place a waffle on each plate and spoon some of the ham mixture over the top. Serve immediately.

Couscous with Sausage

SERVES 4

*C*ouscous is the name of a North African dish based on a crushed semolina pasta, as well as the name of the pasta itself. The French have adopted it, and versions of it seem to be everywhere. Len Deighton, the writer of spy thrillers, lives in France and claims that couscous "is one of those ethnic dishes that gets better as it loses authenticity." This recipe, then, should be really good, Len. Let your guests make their couscous as spicy as they like by offering them Harissa, a red pepper condiment, on the side.

You can find quick-cooking couscous in most markets in larger cities. If you can't, though, substitute a tiny pasta shape such as pastina.

Serve dinner on the floor and lounge on pillows. Get out your old Oum Khalsoum records and play them as background music. Serve a plain mixed green salad, a platter of cheese, and some fresh and dried fruits for dessert, or maybe some halvah.

1 cup dried chick-peas
3 tablespoons olive oil
4 chicken thighs
1 pound lamb stew meat
2 onions, roughly chopped
2 tablespoons minced garlic
2 cups peeled and seeded tomatoes
4 cups chicken stock or canned low-sodium chicken broth
1 teaspoon ground cumin
1 teaspoon dried oregano
1 teaspoon salt, or to taste
½ teaspoon freshly ground black pepper
2 medium carrots, peeled and cut into large chunks
2 turnips, peeled and cut into large chunks
4 merguez sausages or hot Italian sausages
2 cups quick-cooking couscous
Harissa (recipe follows)

1. Place the chick-peas in cold water to cover, and soak overnight. Drain.

2. Heat the olive oil in a large pot over medium heat. Add the chicken and lamb and cook, stirring occasionally, for 15 minutes. Add the onions and garlic and cook, stirring, for 10 minutes. Remove the chicken and set aside.

3. Add the tomatoes, stock, 6 cups water, the chick-peas, cumin, oregano, salt, and pepper. Cover, reduce the heat to low, and cook for 30 minutes. Add the carrots, turnips, and chicken and cook for 30 minutes.

4. Meanwhile, prick the sausages and place in a pot of boiling water for 1 minute. Drain and cut into 1-inch pieces. Add them to the pot for the last 10 minutes of cooking.

5. Cook the couscous according to the package directions; keep warm.

6. To serve dinner, strain the broth and arrange the meat and vegetables on a platter. Pour the broth into a soup tureen. Place the couscous in a covered serving dish. Or mound the couscous in individual soup bowls, arrange the meat and vegetables on top, and ladle the broth over. Accompany with Harissa.

HARISSA

¼ cup red pepper flakes
2 tablespoons minced garlic
1 teaspoon ground cumin
¼ cup water
¼ cup olive oil
Salt to taste

1. Combine all the ingredients in a small pot and cook over medium heat until most of the water has evaporated. Let cool, and serve as a condiment for couscous.

Couscous Pancakes with Red Pepper Sauce

SERVES 4

*T*his is a light dinner, but worthy of main-course status because you can't resist these pancakes. Make a lot of ratatouille in August and September when tomatoes are at their peak and can or freeze some. Ratatouille is best when each vegetable is sautéed separately, then combined for a final cooking, so the different flavors can marry but the ratatouille doesn't become an undistinguished stew.

1 cup plus 2 tablespoons cooked couscous or ½ cup uncooked couscous

6 tablespoons all-purpose flour

1½ teaspoons ground coriander

¾ teaspoon baking powder

1 teaspoon salt, or to taste

1 teaspoon ground white pepper, or to taste

3 eggs, lightly beaten

1 cup milk

1½ tablespoons melted unsalted butter, plus additional for cooking the pancakes

About 2 tablespoons olive oil

1 medium onion, finely diced (about ¾ cup)

1 large zucchini, sliced (about 2 cups)

1 medium eggplant (about 1 pound), peeled and diced

6 plum tomatoes, peeled, quartered, and seeded

2 tablespoons finely minced garlic

1 medium red bell pepper

½ cup heavy cream

½ cup plain yogurt

2 tablespoons finely chopped fresh parsley

1. Combine the couscous, flour, coriander, baking powder, and ¼ teaspoon each of the salt, and pepper in a bowl. Add the eggs and milk and mix well. Stir in the butter, cover, and set aside to rest for 20 minutes.

2. Meanwhile, preheat the oven to 350°F.

3. Heat 2 teaspoons of the oil in a 12-inch skillet over high heat. Add the onion and cook, stirring, until softened, about 5 minutes. Remove with a

slotted spoon and set aside. Cook the zucchini, then the eggplant, until softened, adding more oil as necessary, and set aside. Cook the tomatoes with the garlic, and season with the remaining ¾ teaspoon each salt and pepper. Transfer to a baking dish and stir in the onion, zucchini, and eggplant. Bake, uncovered, for 20 minutes. Remove from the oven and keep warm.

4. Meanwhile, cut the pepper in half, remove and discard the seeds and stem, and roughly chop the pepper. Place in a small saucepan and add the cream. Cover and cook over medium heat for 10 minutes. Transfer to a blender or food processor, add the yogurt, and process to a puree. Strain through a fine strainer back into the saucepan, and add salt and pepper as desired. Keep the sauce warm in a larger pan of hot water or on the side of the stove; do not reheat, or the yogurt will curdle.

5. Cook the pancakes: heat an 8-inch skillet over medium heat and brush with a little melted butter. Stir the batter and spoon 3 tablespoons of batter per pancake into the skillet, making 3 pancakes at a time. Cook until bubbles rise to the surface of the pancakes and break, about 1 to 2 minutes. Using a spatula, flip the pancakes and cook for 2 minutes. Remove the pancakes from the skillet, cover, and keep warm. Repeat with the remaining batter, using as little butter as possible without allowing the pancakes to stick to the bottom of the pan.

6. To serve dinner, stir the parsley into the hot ratatouille. Rewarm the pancakes in the hot oven if necessary. Arrange the pancakes on individual plates, and mound the ratatouille next to them. Spoon some sauce around, and serve.

GRAIN AND VEGETABLE PILAF

SERVES 6

*T*his is the kind of dinner we would have laughed at twenty years ago. But, what's the joke? Times have changed, and this is delicious.

One of the reasons many people prefer meat to vegetables is the texture. Meat is more substantial and requires cutting and chewing. But these grains all have a chewy texture, and each has a distinct flavor. And there's lots of garlic for flavor and texture too. Even if you're a big meat eater, you'll like this meal. Be sure to use a matured goat cheese to melt over the pilaf. Leave it long enough under the broiler and you'll have a gratinéed topping.

¼ *cup bulgur*
¼ *cup quick-cooking couscous*
¼ *cup wild rice*
¼ *cup barley*
¼ *cup olive oil*
24 garlic cloves, peeled
2 medium onions, finely diced (about 1½ cups)
1 cup cauliflower florets
1 red bell pepper, diced
1 yellow squash, sliced into ¼-inch-thick rounds
1 zucchini, sliced into ¼-inch-thick rounds
2 tablespoons poppy seeds
2 teaspoons dried sage
1 6-ounce jar marinated artichoke hearts, drained and cut into
  ½-inch dice
2 tablespoons chopped fresh parsley
2½ cups chopped, peeled fresh or canned tomatoes
1 teaspoon salt
12 ounces matured goat cheese, such as bucheron, sliced

1. Cook each type of grain separately in lightly salted water until soft (or cook according to package directions). Drain and set aside at room temperature.

2. Combine 3 tablespoons of the oil and the garlic in a Dutch oven or heavy casserole, cover, and place in the oven. Turn on the oven to 375°F and cook for 10 minutes. Add the onions and cauliflower, cover, and cook for 15 minutes. Add the pepper, yellow squash, zucchini, poppy seeds, and sage and

cook for 20 minutes. Remove from the oven, stir in the grains, artichokes, and parsley, and mix well. Keep warm.

3. Meanwhile, heat the remaining 1 tablespoon oil in a saucepan over medium heat. Add the tomatoes and salt, cover, and cook for 25 minutes. (The pilaf and sauce can be made ahead to this point, set aside at room temperature for an hour or so, and reheated when ready to serve.)

4. When it's time to put dinner on the table, preheat the broiler.

5. Reheat the pilaf in the oven, if necessary, and reheat the sauce, if necessary, over medium heat. Place the cheese on a broiling pan or heatproof platter and broil until bubbling and brown. To serve, mound the pilaf in wide soup bowls and scrape the melted cheese over the top. Spoon the tomato sauce around the pilaf and serve immediately.

RISOTTO WITH GRILLED VEGETABLES AND SMOKED CHEESE

SERVES 4

*R*isotto is a creamy base for other more flavorful ingredients—in this dish, grilled vegetables. Melted cheese serves as a sauce here, gathering up and uniting other ingredients with flavor. Serve a plate of sardines with fresh lemon and chopped onions to complement the risotto.

2 tablespoons chopped fresh basil
2 teaspoons chopped fresh thyme
1 teaspoon chopped fresh rosemary
3 tablespoons balsamic or red wine vinegar
5 tablespoons olive oil
1 teaspoon salt, or to taste
½ teaspoon freshly ground black pepper, or to taste
2 red bell peppers, halved lengthwise, cored, and seeded
1 medium zucchini, sliced diagonally into ½-inch rounds
1 eggplant, cup into ½-inch rounds
1 onion, cut into ½-inch slices
½ pound white mushrooms
4 tomatoes, peeled, seeded, and diced
2 tablespoons minced garlic
1 cup Arborio or short-grain rice
3 to 3½ cups boiling chicken stock, canned low-sodium chicken broth, or water
½ pound smoked Gouda, Swiss, Cheddar, or mozzarella cheese, grated

1. Preheat a grill or broiler.

2. Combine the basil, thyme, rosemary, vinegar, ¼ cup of the oil, the salt, and pepper in a bowl and set aside.

3. Grill or broil the peppers, zucchini, eggplant, onion, and then the mushrooms (without using any oil) until just tender. Roughly dice all of the vegetables into ½-inch pieces, add them to the herbs and oil, and toss. Add the tomatoes and toss.

4. Heat the remaining 1 tablespoon oil in a heavy pot over medium heat. Add the garlic and cook, stirring for 1 minute. Add the rice and stir to coat with the oil. Add ½ cup of the boiling stock and cook, stirring, until the liquid has

been absorbed. Continue cooking and adding the broth ½ cup at a time, stirring constantly, until the rice is barely tender.

5. Add the vegetables to the risotto and continue to cook, stirring in a little more stock as needed, until the rice is tender. Remove from the heat and stir in the cheese. Mound the risotto in wide soup or pasta bowls and serve immediately.

RISO AND RISOTTO WITH
TOMATO AND HAM

SERVES 4

7his dinner has all the charm and comfort of your favorite spaghetti in red sauce, but with a new twist and taste. The riso pasta is toasted to give it a nutty flavor and distinguish it from the rice. Begin dinner with a salad of crisp lettuce and raw vegetables. Make plenty of garlic bread, and serve a cheese course before dessert.

> 8 ripe plum tomatoes or 1 14½-ounce can whole plum tomatoes
> ¼ cup olive oil
> 1 cup riso or orzo pasta
> 1 medium onion, finely diced (about ¾ cup)
> 2 tablespoons minced garlic
> 3 tablespoons capers, drained
> 1 tablespoon chopped fresh oregano or 1 teaspoon dried
> ½ pound prosciutto or ham, diced
> 1 cup Arborio or short-grain rice

1. Bring a large pot of salted water to the boil. If using fresh tomatoes, blanch them in the boiling water for 1 minute, or until the skin cracks. Plunge the tomatoes into a bowl of ice water; drain and peel them. (Keep the water boiling.) Roughly chop the fresh or canned tomatoes and set aside.

2. Heat 1 tablespoon of the oil in a skillet over medium heat and cook the riso, stirring, until the grains begin to brown around the edges, about 1½ minutes. Add to the boiling water and cook for 3 minutes, or until barely tender. Drain, and set aside at room temperature.   *(continued)*

3. Heat 2 tablespoons of the oil in a skillet. Add the onion and garlic and cook for 1 minute, stirring. Add the tomatoes, capers, oregano, and prosciutto, cover, and cook for 10 minutes. Remove from the heat and set aside; keep warm.

4. Meanwhile, bring 3 cups lightly salted water to a boil.

5. Heat the remaining 1 tablespoon oil in a saucepan over medium heat, add the rice, and stir to coat with oil. Add ¼ cup of the boiling water and cook, stirring, until the liquid has been absorbed. Continue cooking and adding the boiling water ¼ cup at a time, stirring constantly, until the rice is tender and creamy, but not mushy. (You may not need all the water.) Remove from the heat and stir in the cooked riso.

6. Mound the risotto in soup bowls. Make an indentation in each mound and ladle some tomato sauce into it. Serve piping hot.

CHICKEN LIVER AND ARTICHOKE RISOTTO

SERVES 4

I love to combine chicken livers and risotto because their soft textures go together so nicely. This is an altogether comforting dish. Even folks who are not fans of liver will enjoy its flavor here, accented with the saltiness of the capers, bacon, and mustard.

8 baby artichokes or canned marinated artichoke hearts, drained
1 lemon, cut in half (if using fresh artichokes)
1 pound chicken livers
¼ cup dry white wine
2 tablespoons olive oil
1 medium onion, finely chopped (about ¾ cup)
1 cup Arborio or short-grain rice
4 slices bacon, cut into 1-inch pieces
2 tomatoes, peeled, seeded, and chopped
2 tablespoons capers, drained
1 tablespoon Dijon mustard
2 tablespoons unsalted butter

1. If using fresh baby artichokes, bring a large pot of water to a boil and add the lemon. Meanwhile, remove one or two layers of the tough, darker green outer leaves from each artichoke and trim about ½ inch off the bottom.

2. Add the baby artichokes to the boiling water and cook for 10 to 12 minutes, until tender; drain. Cut them in half lengthwise and set aside. If using canned artichoke hearts, drain and halve.

3. Trim the livers of any connective tissue and dark spots, place in a bowl, and add the white wine. Let stand at room temperature while making the risotto or refrigerate for up to 8 hours.

4. Bring 3 cups lightly salted water to a boil.

5. Heat 1 tablespoon of the oil in a saucepan over medium heat. Add half the chopped onion and cook for 2 minutes. Reduce the heat to low, add the rice, and stir to coat with the oil. Add about ¼ cup of the boiling water and cook, stirring constantly, until the liquid is absorbed. Continue cooking and adding water ¼ cup at a time, stirring constantly, until the rice is soft but still al dente. (You may not need all the water.) Remove from the heat, cover, and keep warm.

6. Place the bacon and remaining 1 tablespoon oil in a skillet over medium heat and cook for 3 minutes, stirring. Add the remaining onions and cook for 3 minutes, stirring occasionally. Add the liver and wine, tomatoes, capers, and mustard. Increase the heat to high and cook for 6 to 7 minutes, stirring frequently. Add the artichokes and heat through. Remove from the heat and whisk in the butter.

7. Scoop the risotto onto a platter and make a well in the center. Spoon the liver, artichokes, and sauce into the well and serve immediately.

Fresh Herbs or Dried?

Tarragon, dill, cilantro, thyme, rosemary, basil, oregano, and marjoram are summer flavors, and the fresh versions of these herbs always do their job better when we throw them into a dish and cook them only briefly. Happily, summer recipes depend on quick-cooking techniques.

Add dried herbs to those dishes that cook for a long time—wintery roasts, stews, and dishes using legumes such as split peas, lentils, and chick peas, and grains such as rice, barley, and bulgur. The sweet flavor of root vegetables makes a nice foundation for the mellow flavors of dried herbs and spices. In general, fresh herbs release their flavor quickly and become dead after too long in the heat. Dried seeds and stems, however, benefit from long cooking that enables their flavors to develop.

Because dried herbs have a more mellow flavor than fresh, they can easily be combined with other ingredients because they won't dominate a dish, but use them with discretion. For example, rosemary is a very strong herb when its leaves are freshly cut. When fresh, its flavor predominates and it fights with sage, basil, or thyme and most other fresh herbs. I use garlic, onion, or lemon as background to support fresh rosemary's flavor. Dried, it is a great background for other flavors; it combines well with garlic, onion, parsley, clove, lemon, dill, caraway, celery seed, and thyme.

Dried tarragon is the winter version of my favorite summer herb, and when I combine it with dried seeds it becomes nearly as delightful as the fresh version. It usually needs a hint of celery and fennel seeds to make it taste "more like" tarragon, and more than tarragon.

In this way, many dried herbs depend on other flavors to make them more interesting. Using only one dried herb or spice usually results in a lackluster dish, where each mouthful tastes the same. I rarely add fresh oregano, thyme, and marjoram to the same dish, because they are too much alike and they become a muddle. But I always use them in combination when dried because the mix makes the resulting flavor fuller, rounder, and more like the fresh version of any one of them.

The general rule for using dried herbs is to substitute ½ to 1 teaspoon dried for each tablespoon of fresh. But this rule has many exceptions, so please taste carefully and decide for yourself. Remember, it's you who are the boss, not the recipe you're following.

SAVORY RICE AND SHRIMP PUDDING

SERVES 6

*T*his savory version of the beloved dessert has the same texture as a rice dressing. It holds its form when it's baked in a mold—a fancy presentation for a simple dish. It is, after all, the centerpiece of a divine shrimp dinner.

4 tablespoons unsalted butter or margarine

1½ cups chicken stock or canned low-sodium chicken broth

1 medium onion, finely diced (about 1 cup)

2 celery stalks, finely sliced (about 1 cup)

1 cup long-grain rice

1 teaspoon salt

¼ cup fresh bread crumbs

4 eggs

2 cups milk

1 tablespoon chopped fresh thyme

1 teaspoon dried summer savory

1 teaspoon ground mace

½ teaspoon freshly ground black pepper

1½ pounds large shrimp

¾ pound sugar snap peas

1 tablespoon tomato paste

¼ cup dry sherry

½ cup heavy cream

1. Preheat the oven to 375°F. Butter a 2-quart fluted ring mold or baking dish with 1 tablespoon of the butter.

2. Bring the stock to a boil. Meanwhile, melt 2 tablespoons of the butter in a 1-quart pot with a heat-resistant handle over medium heat. Add the onion and celery and cook, without coloring, for 5 minutes. Add the rice and stir to coat all grains with butter; do not let the rice brown.

3. Pour the boiling stock over the rice and stir in the salt. Cover and bake until the rice has absorbed all the liquid and is tender, about 15 minutes.

4. Transfer the rice to a bowl. Add the bread crumbs and mix well. Add the eggs, milk, thyme, savory, mace, and pepper, mix well, and scrape into the buttered mold or baking dish. Bake until set, about 35 minutes. (The rice pudding can be baked an hour or so ahead and set aside at room temperature.)

5. Meanwhile, peel the shrimp, but leave the last tail section of shell and

(continued)

the swimmer tail intact. Butterfly each shrimp by cutting down the back to the tail section, remove and discard the vein, and refrigerate until dinnertime.

6. When you are ready for dinner, reheat the pudding in a 350°F oven if necessary. Heat the remaining 1 tablespoon butter in a skillet over medium-high heat. Add the shrimp and sugar snaps and cook for 1 minute, tossing. Add the tomato paste, sherry, and cream and cook until slightly thickened, about 2 to 3 minutes. Remove from the heat. Run a knife around the edge of the pudding and unmold onto a serving platter. Spoon the shrimp and sugar snaps, with the sauce, into the center of the mold or around the pudding. Serve immediately.

MUSHROOM AND BARLEY RISOTTO

SERVES 4

*Y*ou may think that rice is rice, but it's just not so. Basmati rice has a decidedly toasty aromatic flavor, and you should take the trouble to seek it out for this recipe. Converted long-grain rice, which most of us buy automatically, is flavorless by comparison and would be overshadowed by the barley taste. Serve a salad and bread to complete the meal.

> 2 ounces dried mushrooms, such as porcini, morels, chanterelles, or
>   black Chinese or Polish mushrooms
> 2 tablespoons olive oil
> 2 medium onions, finely diced
> ¾ cup pearl barley
> 2½ cups chicken stock, canned low-sodium chicken broth, or water
> ½ teaspoon salt
> ½ teaspoon ground white pepper
> 3 bay leaves
> ¾ cup basmati rice
> 1 tablespoon minced garlic
> 2 pounds mixed fresh mushrooms, such as button, shiitake, and
>   oyster, trimmed
> ½ cup heavy cream
> 2 tablespoons chopped fresh parsley

1. Soak the dried mushrooms in 1½ cups warm water for 2 hours. When they are soft, strain the water through cheesecloth and reserve. Squeeze out excess water from the mushrooms.

2. Heat 1 tablespoon of the oil in a medium ovenproof pot, over medium heat. Add the onions and cook, stirring occasionally, for about 10 minutes, or until softened. Add the barley, 1 cup of the reserved mushroom liquid, 1½ cups of the broth, the salt, pepper, and bay leaves, cover, reduce the heat to low, and simmer for 1 hour.

3. Meanwhile, bring the remaining 1 cup broth to a boil.

4. Preheat the oven to 350°F.

5. When the barley has simmered for 1 hour, add the rice and stir in the boiling broth. Cover, place in the oven, and cook for 20 minutes.

6. Meanwhile, heat the remaining 1 tablespoon oil in a 1-quart pot over medium heat. Add the dried mushrooms and garlic and cook, stirring, for

(continued)

Politically Correct Dinners—Grains, Beans, and Pasta

about 2 minutes. Add the fresh mushrooms and cook for 5 minutes. Add the cream, increase the heat to high, and cook until the liquid has reduced to the consistency of a sauce. Stir in the parsley.

7. Mound the risotto in pasta or soup bowls and spoon the mushrooms over the top.

ONION AND ORZO PILAF

SERVES 4

*T*he orzo, mushrooms, artichokes, and tomatoes all can be prepared up to a day in advance and refrigerated. Bring to room temperature before assembling and serving. Begin with chilled corn soup and serve garlic bread.

> 6 tablespoons olive oil
> 3 medium onions, finely diced
> ¾ cup orzo pasta
> Salt and freshly ground black pepper to taste
> ¼ cup chopped fresh basil
> 1 pound white mushrooms
> 1 teaspoon ground coriander
> ¼ cup dry white wine
> 2 tablespoons balsamic vinegar
> 2 tablespoons minced garlic
> 1 lemon, cut in half
> 4 large artichokes
> 12 small plum tomatoes or 1 28-ounce can whole plum tomatoes, drained

1. Heat 2 tablespoons of the oil in a large skillet over high heat. Add the onions and cook, stirring, for about 7 minutes, or until the onions soften and begin to turn a light golden color. Transfer to a bowl.

2. Bring 1 quart salted water to a boil. Heat 1 tablespoon of the oil in a 3-quart pot over medium heat and add the orzo. Cook, stirring, until the edges of the orzo begin to turn golden, about 3 minutes. Pour in the boiling water, cover, and cook for 5 minutes. Drain. Add the orzo to the onions and mix well. Season with salt and pepper, stir in the basil, cover, and set aside.

3. Place the mushrooms in a large skillet and add the coriander, wine, vinegar, 2 tablespoons of the oil, the garlic, and salt and pepper to taste. Cover and cook over low heat for 15 minutes, or until the mushrooms have released their liquid and softened. Transfer to a bowl, cover, and set aside.

4. Prepare the artichokes: Fill a 2-quart pot with water and add the juice of the lemon. Keep the lemon halves for rubbing the cut surfaces of the artichokes as you work. Cut the stems off each artichoke, and cut off the top, leaving a base about 1 inch high and exposing the center choke. With a sharp knife, trim all around the sides and bottom to remove the dark green exterior. Add each artichoke to the water as it is ready. Cover the pot and bring the water to a boil over high heat. Cook for 20 minutes, or until the artichokes are tender. Remove the artichokes from the water. When cool enough to handle, scoop out and discard the center chokes.

5. While the artichokes are cooling, if using fresh tomatoes, drop them into the boiling artichoke water and cook for a minute, or until the skins crack. Remove and plunge into a bowl of ice water, drain, and peel.

6. Meanwhile, preheat the oven to 375°F.

7. Place the fresh or canned tomatoes in a baking dish, sprinkle with salt and pepper, and drizzle with the remaining 1 tablespoon olive oil. Cover, and bake for 20 minutes. Remove from the oven and let cool.

8. When it's time to serve dinner, mound the orzo on a large, deep platter. Arrange the artichokes and tomatoes around the orzo and spoon the mushrooms and their liquid into the artichoke bottoms.

LINGUINE WITH WHITE SHELLFISH SAUCE

SERVES 4

7 his dinner is soupy, so serve it in wide-rimmed soup or pasta bowls. If you live in an area where there is an abundance of fresh seafood, add whatever you like to the list of ingredients; calamari is especially good. You're not supposed to serve grated cheese with seafood dishes, but I think it's fine to do so here.

¼ cup olive oil
2 tablespoons minced garlic
1 medium onion, finely minced (about ¾ cup)
12 small Manila or littleneck clams, scrubbed and rinsed
12 mussels, scrubbed and debearded
12 jumbo shrimp, peeled and deveined
½ teaspoon ground white pepper
¼ cup dry white wine
2 tablespoons fresh lemon juice
½ cup bottled clam juice or canned low-sodium chicken broth
¾ pound linguine
Salt to taste
3 tablespoons finely chopped fresh parsley

1. Heat the oil in a large pot over medium heat. Add the garlic and onion and cook, stirring, for about 5 minutes. Add the clams, mussels, shrimp, pepper, wine, lemon juice, and clam juice or broth, cover, and cook for 5 to 6 minutes. Remove the shellfish and discard any unopened clams or mussels.

2. Meanwhile, cook the pasta in boiling salted water according to the package directions; drain.

3. Taste the seafood cooking liquid for salt and add as needed. Stir in the parsley.

4. Place the pasta in four soup or pasta bowls. Arrange the shellfish on top, and pour the cooking liquid over.

CREAMY CHICKEN LIVERS AND PASTA

*C*hicken livers steeped in Madeira should feel and taste like fine liver mousse. Keep the livers creamy by cooking them over medium heat. And if you think they might be starting to overcook, immediately retrieve them from the sauce and set them aside on a plate. As they cool, they continue to cook.

1½ pounds chicken livers
¾ cup Marsala wine
8 ounces large shell macaroni
3 tablespoons olive oil
1 28-ounce can whole plum tomatoes, drained
1 medium onion, finely minced (about ¾ cup)
½ cup heavy cream
1 teaspoon salt
½ teaspoon freshly ground black pepper
3 tablespoons chopped fresh basil
3 tablespoons chopped fresh parsley

1. Combine the livers and Marsala in a small bowl and refrigerate for 1 hour.

2. Bring a large pot of salted water to a boil and cook the macaroni until tender, about 7 to 10 minutes. Drain, toss with 1 tablespoon of the oil, and set aside.

3. Heat the remaining 2 tablespoons oil in a skillet, add the liver and marsala, and cook for 2 minutes over medium heat. Turn the livers, add the tomatoes and onion, and cook for 2 minutes. Add the cream, salt, and pepper and cook until the livers are just done and the juices have thickened to the consistency of a sauce, about 6 minutes. Pour the contents of the skillet over the pasta and toss gently. Cover and let cool to room temperature.

4. When it's time for dinner, add the chopped basil and parsley to the pasta and transfer to a serving bowl.

SERVES 4

Politically Correct Dinners—Grains, Beans, and Pasta

Corn, an American Favorite

It's difficult to imagine that corn was unknown except in the Americas before the sixteenth century. It was introduced relatively late to Asia, but eventually earned a secure place there, especially in Chinese and Thai cuisines. In sixteenth-century Italy and the Balkans, corn quickly replaced chestnuts as the staple of the poor man's diet.

There are five varieties of corn. Popcorn, the oldest cultivated variety, is particularly high in protein. Its hard hull doesn't allow moisture to escape, so when popcorn is heated, the moisture inside vaporizes and expands and bursts the hull.

Flint corn, long the favored variety of the Native North Americans, is still the favorite in Africa. It is a high-protein corn with a hard husk. Dent corn, used mainly as animal feed, is both starchy and sweet. Flour corn, low in protein and soft, is rarely seen outside of Central and South America, where it is prized for its grindability.

Sweet corn is the variety that most of us know; there are both winter and summer crops. Summer corn is lighter in color and less starchy than winter corn. Freshly picked and cooked—the hard-core corn eaters claim that more than 7 minutes from field to kitchen means the corn is ruined—the kernels pop when you bite them, exploding little bursts of sweet, syrupy flavor.

Although corn on the cob is most often boiled, it's much sweeter if the unhusked ears are soaked in water for 30 minutes and then grilled or broiled for about 15 minutes. Put the corn directly in the hot coals of a fire, or place about 6 inches from a broiler. The kernels steam and take on flavor from the husks.

Sweet corn is picked when still young and immature, when it stores more sugar than starch. During the summer, use the young corn in salads, soups, and as a vegetable. When you can find it, always buy white corn, which is less starchy and much sweeter than the yellow variety.

Use the older, more starchy corn for hearty recipes, where a stick-to-the-ribs satisfaction is what you're looking for. When using frozen corn or canned corn in a recipe, make certain to drain the kernels well before using. Often the frozen corn available is sweeter than fresh winter corn, so use it during the winter months when you want sweet corn as a vegetable.

SUCCOTASH SOUP

SERVES 4

*S*uccotash is a native American Indian dish. In summer, it was made with summer squashes, fresh beans, fresh young summer corn, and a variety of native peppers, both sweet and hot. Winter versions were probably restricted to dried beans, dried peppers, winter squashes, and gourds and dried corn—probably more like the succotash we can buy today in a can.

Serve warm tortillas instead of bread with this dinner soup.

½ cup dried lima beans
1 tablespoon flavorless vegetable oil
1 medium onion, diced (about 1 cup)
4 cups chicken stock or canned low-sodium chicken broth
2 branches fresh thyme or 1 teaspoon dried
1 small branch rosemary or ½ teaspoon dried
3 bay leaves
1 teaspoon salt, or to taste
½ teaspoon ground white pepper
2 small zucchini, cut into ½-inch rounds (about 1 cup)
1 red bell pepper, finely diced
2 ears corn, kernels removed (about 1 cup)
2 pounds large shrimp, peeled, split in half lengthwise down the
    back, and deveined
1 cup plain yogurt

1. Soak the lima beans overnight in water to cover. Drain.

2. Heat the oil in a large pot. Add the onion and cook, stirring occasionally, for 5 minutes. Add the stock, limas, thyme, rosemary, bay leaves, salt, and pepper and simmer over low heat, partially covered, for 1¼ hours.

3. Add the zucchini, pepper, and corn and cook for 5 minutes. Add the shrimp and cook for 2 minutes.

4. Remove from the heat and remove the bay leaves and branches of fresh herbs. Whisk the yogurt into the soup, and serve immediately.

Politically Correct Dinners—Grains, Beans, and Pasta

CHICK-PEA POLENTA WITH TOMATO SAUCE

SERVES 4

*P*olenta is a type of cornmeal mush that is popular in northern Italy and the Balkans. It's served warm from the pot, as a soft, creamy starch, or cooled, cut into cakes, and then grilled, sautéed, or fried. But polenta can be made with other flours, too. Before the arrival of corn in Europe it was made with chick-pea flour, as I have done here, or chestnut flour.

For this dinner okra and mushrooms are added to a classic garnish the French call "Portugaise," along with baked eggs.

8 ripe plum tomatoes or canned whole plum tomatoes
16 okra
1½ cups chick-pea flour
Salt and ground white pepper
¼ cup olive oil
16 white mushrooms, caps only
½ cup dry white wine
4 eggs
Grated Parmesan or Romano cheese, for serving

1. If using fresh tomatoes, plunge them into boiling water for 1 minute, or until skins begin to crack slightly. Immediately plunge into ice water to cool; drain. Peel the tomatoes, cut them in half, and squeeze out and discard the seeds. Chop the tomatoes and set aside. If using canned tomatoes, drain, chop, and set aside. Beginning just below the cap, slit each piece of okra lengthwise into quarters, leaving it still connected at the cap. Set aside.

2. Combine the flour, 1 teaspoon salt, and ½ teaspoon pepper in a heavy pot and add 2 cups cold water, stirring constantly. Cook over medium heat until the mixture comes to a boil, bubbles, and thickens, about 5 minutes. Remove from the heat and stir in 2 tablespoons of the oil. Pour into a lightly greased 9- by 5-inch loaf pan, smooth the top, and let cool.

3. When the polenta is cool, cut into 1-inch squares, remove from the pan, and toss with 1 tablespoon of the oil. Set aside.

4. Heat the remaining 3 tablespoons oil in an ovenproof skillet over medium heat, and add the okra and mushrooms. Cook for 3 to 4 minutes, stirring occasionally. Add the tomatoes and wine and cook for 5 minutes. Season to taste with salt and pepper. (The polenta and sauce can be prepared up to an hour in advance to this point and set aside at room temperature.)

5. When it's time to put dinner on the table, preheat the oven to 375°F.

6. Place the squares of polenta in a baking dish in a single layer and place in the oven. Make four small wells in the tomato mixture and carefully break an egg into each one. Cover the pan, place in the oven, and cook until the eggs are set, about 10 minutes. Remove vegetables and polenta from oven.

7. Arrange the polenta on plates and carefully spoon some of the vegetable mixture, including an egg, over each serving. Serve immediately, and pass some grated Parmesan or Romano on the side.

CHICK-PEA BLINI WITH YOGURT CHICKEN

SERVES 4 TO 5

*B*lini, the Russian buckwheat pancakes that are risen with yeast, are the traditional base for dollops of caviar. Here chick-pea flour and a hint of cumin give them an altogether different flavor that makes your mouth pucker.

Make your first course a beet or mixed vegetable soup.

1 cup buttermilk
½ cup warm beer
1 package active dry yeast
1 teaspoon sugar
¼ teaspoon ground cumin
2 teaspoons salt
1 cup all-purpose flour
½ cup chick-pea flour (available in health food stores and
  Middle Eastern markets)
3 tablespoons olive oil
2 pounds boneless, skinless chicken breast, cut into 1-inch cubes
¾ cup chicken stock or canned low-sodium chicken broth
¼ teaspoon ground white pepper
3 medium zucchini, thinly sliced (about 2 cups)
About 2 tablespoons melted butter
1 tablespoon chopped fresh dill or 2 teaspoons dried
¾ cup plain yogurt
1 tablespoon chopped fresh mint

1. Combine the buttermilk, beer, yeast, sugar, cumin, 1 teaspoon of the salt, and both the flours in a bowl and mix until smooth. Let rest, covered with a cloth, for 30 minutes.   *(continued)*

2. Heat the olive oil in a medium skillet. Add the chicken, cover, and cook for 2 minutes. Add the stock and pepper. If using dried dill, add it now. Increase the heat to high and cook, uncovered, until the broth has reduced by about two thirds. Add the zucchini and cook for 2 minutes, stirring. Remove from the heat, cover, and keep warm in a 200°F oven while making the blini.

3. Heat a 4-inch blini pan or a large nonstick skillet over medium heat, and brush lightly with melted butter. Add 2 tablespoons batter per blini and cook until the top surface of the blini begins to dry, about 2 minutes. Flip the blini and cook 1 to 2 minutes. Transfer to a plate, cover, and keep warm while you finish making the blini.

4. Arrange the blini on a serving platter. Stir the yogurt into the chicken and add the mint and, if using it, fresh dill. Spoon the chicken and zucchini over the blini.

Sweet and Split Pea "Porridge" with Sausages

SERVES 4

Pease porridge hot, pease porridge cold,
Pease porridge in the pot nine days old.

The pea originated in the Middle East, was domesticated around 6000 B.C., and quickly became a staple in the Mediterranean and India and China. It was an important alternative protein source in Europe in the Middle Ages. Today two varieties are cultivated—one for drying, and the other, picked while the peas are still immature, for eating fresh. Most people buy the latter frozen; they make good soup.

Split pea soup with hot dog slices floated in it is classic Americana and good eats. My dinner version follows, a soup—really a porridge—garnished with sausages, fresh peas, and pumpernickel croutons. Sour hints of fresh sorrel and lemon garnish the smoky flavor in the sausage. Offer sour cream for dolloping into the soup. Serve a salad of roasted red peppers and tomatoes.

1 tablespoon unsalted butter or margarine

2 medium onions, diced

1 small carrot, diced (about ½ cup)

2 celery stalks, diced

1 tablespoon minced garlic

6 cups chicken stock, canned low-sodium chicken broth, or water

¾ cup split peas

3 sprigs fresh thyme or ½ teaspoon dried

1 teaspoon salt, or to taste

½ teaspoon freshly ground black pepper

2 slices pumpernickel bread

2 tablespoons flavorless vegetable oil

8 sausages, such as kielbasa or sweet or hot Italian

1 cup fresh or frozen peas

¼ cup chopped fresh sorrel

2 tablespoons fresh lemon juice

Sour cream, for serving

1. Melt the butter in a large pot over medium heat. Add the onions, carrot, celery, and garlic and cook for 5 minutes to soften. Add the stock, split peas, thyme, salt, and pepper. Cover, reduce the heat to low, and simmer for 45 minutes, or until the split peas are soft.

2. Meanwhile, preheat the oven to 375°F.

3. Remove the crust from the bread and cut into ½-inch cubes. Put the oil in a small bowl, add the bread, and toss well. Spread on a baking sheet and toast in the oven, stirring occasionally, for 10 minutes. Let cool.

4. Heat a skillet over medium heat. Add the sausages and cook, turning occasionally, for about 7 minutes, to rid them of some fat. Remove from the pan and drain on paper towels, then cut into 1-inch pieces and set aside.

5. When the split peas are soft, add the fresh peas and sausages and simmer for about 7 minutes, or until the fresh peas are tender.

6. Stir the sorrel and lemon juice into the soup. Transfer the soup to a tureen, and serve sour cream and the pumpernickle, croutons on the side.

Politically Correct Dinners—Grains, Beans, and Pasta

RED BEAN, PASTA, AND SAUSAGE STEW

SERVES 3 TO 4

*U*se red beans rather than kidney beans for this dish—they're larger, exude more starch, and are less grainy. They thicken the broth, making it the tiniest bit opaque and adding texture.

¾ cup dried red beans

12 ripe plum tomatoes or 1 28-ounce can whole plum tomatoes

4 ounces shells or elbow macaroni

2 large leaves red or green Swiss chard

1 tablespoon olive oil

6 hot Italian sausages, cut into 2 or 3 pieces each

1 tablespoon minced garlic

½ cup dry white wine

1 tablespoon fresh oregano or 1 teaspoon dried

½ teaspoon salt, or to taste

½ teaspoon freshly ground black pepper

Grated Parmesan cheese, for serving

1. Place the beans in a pot, add enough water to barely cover, cover the pot, and cook over low heat until the beans are just soft, about 2 hours. Add water as necessary to keep the beans barely covered. Drain and set aside.

2. Meanwhile, if using fresh tomatoes, core them and plunge into boiling water for about 1 minute, or just until the skins crack. Then plunge into a bowl of ice water; drain. Peel the tomatoes, cut them in half crosswise, and squeeze out the seeds; if using canned tomatoes, cut them in half and squeeze out the seeds. Cut each tomato half in quarters and set aside.

3. Preheat the oven to 350°F.

4. Cook the pasta until al dente according to the package directions. Drain, and add to the beans.

5. Cut out the center stems from the chard leaves. Roughly chop the leaves and thinly slice the stems. Set aside.

6. Combine the oil and sausages in a Dutch oven, and cook over medium heat for 3 minutes. Pour off the fat, add the garlic, and cook, stirring, for 1 minute. Add the tomatoes, beans and pasta, wine, oregano, chard stems, salt, and pepper. Cover and bake for 20 minutes. (The stew can be prepared a few hours ahead to this point and reheated at serving time.)

7. When it's time to get dinner on the table, stir the chopped chard into the stew; if the stew appears dry, add up to 1 cup water. Bake for 5 minutes. Serve piping hot from the oven and offer grated cheese on the side.

Stop the Chuck Wagon, I Want to Get Off

Old favorites do need to change with the times. One of the most successful culinary makeovers of recent years is a Texas favorite, chili. Photographs of unusual chilies with glistening beans and slivers of unlikely meats have glossed the pages of cooking monthlies. And couples living in the skyrise penthouses of Chicago and New York are serving versions of chuck wagon food to thin guests with hyphenated last names. The phenomenon is not restricted to the States. In Paris, there are restaurants in the 7th and 16th *arrondissements* that serve hybrid versions of cassoulet—their equivalent of chili—as if gorgeously cooked white beans were a new caviar.

In fact, chili is more than just a spicy bean stew, and that's why it allows for so much delicious improvisation. A successful chili must have a variety of peppers, both hot and mild, and a strong foundation of tomato, onion, garlic, and cumin. And do add cinnamon, the secret ingredient that merges the various flavors, but keep it subtle—you don't want to call attention to it. Chili should cook slowly, with all the essential ingredients changing texture and exchanging flavor.

Remembering these simple guidelines, invent a chile using any ingredients you like, including leftovers. Cook up a batch of the chili on page 175, and divide it into family portions for the freezer. Then as mealtime approaches, add any number of ingredients to the defrosted base to give the chili a name—chicken, turkey, duck, ham, ground meat, lamb, even lobster, crab, or shrimp. Let your pocketbook and your intuition be the guide.

Wear rubber gloves when handling raw chile peppers, or wash your hands well after preparing them. Be careful not to rub your eyes. The capsicum—that's what makes the peppers hot—is volatile and will irritate the skin and eyes.

TOMATO, WHITE BEAN,
AND BLUE CHEESE CHILI

SERVES 8

I've come to prefer white beans for chili, either small navy, Great Northern, or cannellini. For me they have the perfect texture—not too soft and not too mealy.

This chili contrasts sweet stewed tomatoes, spicy hot chilies, and salty, smelly Roquefort.

> 2 poblano chile peppers
> 2 Anaheim chile peppers
> 2 red bell peppers
> 2 tablespoons vegetable oil
> 2 medium onions, diced (about 2 cups)
> 2 jalapeño peppers, or more to taste, seeded and finely minced
> 3 tablespoons minced garlic
> 15 tomatoes, seeded and diced, or 2 28-ounce cans chopped
>   tomatoes, drained
> 2 dried ancho or pasilla chile peppers, stems removed and
>   seeds discarded
> 2 teaspoons ground cumin
> ¼ teaspoon ground cinnamon
> 2 cups dried white beans
> 3 cups chicken stock, canned low-sodium chicken broth, or water
> ¾ pound Roquefort cheese, crumbled
> Salt to taste

1. Soak the white beans overnight in water to cover. Drain.

2. Roast, peel, and seed the poblano, Anaheim, and bell peppers (see page 203), then dice them.

3. Preheat the oven to 325°F.

4. Heat the oil in a large casserole or Dutch oven over medium heat. Add the onions and jalapeño peppers and cook, until the onions are translucent, about 5 minutes. Add the garlic, tomatoes, roasted peppers, dried chilies, peppers, cumin, cinnamon, beans, and chicken stock. Cover and bake for 1 hour.

5. Season the chili with salt and bake for 30 minutes longer, or until the beans are tender.

6. Stir the crumbled blue cheese into the chili, transfer to a serving bowl, and serve piping hot.

VEGETABLE CHILI

Omit the blue cheese; and if serving strict vegetarians, use vegetable broth, or water, instead of chicken stock. Heat a little olive oil in a large pan and cook 1 cup diced eggplant, ¾ cup zucchini in 1-inch chunks (about 1 medium zucchini), 1 cup chopped broccoli rabe or broccoli, and 1 cup fresh or frozen peas until tender. Add these vegetables to the chili once the beans are tender and bake 15 minutes longer. If you'd like, offer some grated Monterey jack or Cheddar cheese on the side, along with sour cream.

DUCK AND WHITE BEAN CHILI

Roast 2 duck legs per person in a 425°F oven for 30 minutes. Add to the chili after it has cooked for 30 minutes and cook together until done. Omit the blue cheese.

SEAFOOD CHILI

Sauté 1 pound peeled shrimp and 1 pound scallops in 1 teaspoon olive oil. Add to the chili once the beans are tender and bake 15 minutes longer.

GARBANZO, LAMB, AND OLIVE STEW

SERVES 4

*T*his stew is a Spanish or Moroccan fantasy, and it's better if allowed to sit, refrigerated, for a day before serving.

The garbanzo bean, or chick-pea, is one of the most important legume crops in India, where it's ground into flour; the Middle East, where it's pureed into hummus; Spain, where it's cooked in stews and soups; and Morocco, where it's an ingredient in couscous.

Garbanzos can seem to take forever to cook if you don't soak them first. They're marvelous in stew, where they absorb lots of flavor, without mushing into the broth. This stew is even more flavorful if prepared ahead.

1 cup dried garbanzo beans (chick-peas)
1 tablespoon flavorless vegetable oil
1½ pounds lamb stew meat
1 medium onion, roughly chopped
2 tablespoons all-purpose flour
½ cup dry white wine
3 cups chicken stock or canned low-sodium chicken broth
2 tablespoons tomato paste
1 tablespoon fresh oregano or 1 teaspoon dried
½ teaspoon freshly ground black pepper
⅓ cup pitted Kalamata olives
4 plum tomatoes, peeled and seeded
2 tablespoons chopped fresh parsley

1. Cover the garbanzos with cold water and soak overnight. Drain.

2. Heat the oil in a Dutch oven or ovenproof casserole over high heat. Add the meat, in batches if necessary, and brown well on all sides. Remove from the pot and set aside.

3. Lower the heat to medium and add the onion to the pot. Cook, stirring, until softened, about 5 minutes. Add the flour and cook, stirring, for 1 minute. Stir in the wine, stock, tomato paste, oregano, pepper, and garbanzos. Cover, place in the oven, turn the oven on to 350°F, and cook for 1 hour.

4. Return the meat to the pot and bake for 45 minutes longer, or until the meat is tender. Add the olives and tomatoes and cook for 15 minutes more.

5. When it's time to get dinner on the table, stir the parsley into the stew and ladle into serving bowls.

CASSOULET

SERVES 4 TO 5

*C*assoulet is a bean stew from the southwest corner of France. It's a peasant dish, with many variations, and in spite of what you may have read in cookbooks, there is no authentic version, only an authentic spirit. This is a dish primarily of beans and pork, and whatever else your larder holds—traditionally, sausage, lamb, and goose confit. In France, it is laden with goose fat, and a layer of bread crumbs is sprinkled over the top to soak up the fat and form a golden crust. It's unlikely that most American cooks will want to prepare the dish that way, so the recipe here is considerably defatted.

Serve with a simple green salad and a hearty red wine.

1 pound dried white navy beans
12 black peppercorns
2 branches fresh thyme
4 bay leaves
1 small branch fresh rosemary
1 small duck (about 4 pounds), cut into 8 serving pieces
½ pound pork stew meat
½ pound lamb stew meat
2 medium onions, diced (about 1½ cups)
¼ pound slab bacon, cut into ¾-inch cubes
2 tablespoons minced garlic
½ pound spicy pork sausages
Salt to taste

1. Soak the beans overnight in cold water to cover. Drain.

2. Preheat the oven to 300°F. Tie the peppercorns, thyme, bay leaves, and rosemary up in a small square of cheesecloth.

3. Heat a heavy ovenproof casserole or pot over medium heat and cook the duck pieces, turning once, to render some of the fat, about 15 minutes. Remove the duck and set aside. Increase the heat to high and add the pork. Brown well on all sides, remove from the pot, and set aside. Brown the lamb, remove from the pot, and set aside.

4. Pour off all but 3 tablespoons of the fat from the pot. Lower the heat to medium and add the onions. Cook, stirring, until softened, about 7 minutes. Add the beans, bacon, garlic, and the packet of herbs and return the duck, pork, and lamb to the pan. Add 4 cups water, cover, and bake for 2 hours.

(continued)

Politically Correct Dinners—Grains, Beans, and Pasta

5. Add the sausages and salt to taste, and bake for 1 hour longer.

6. Remove the bag of herbs, and serve the cassoulet directly from the casserole.

Dinner in the French Manner

*B*y the time of the French Revolution, the cuisine of France was already a developed one. But it was a cuisine held captive by aristocrats. The propertied class had adopted a style of cooking and eating that meant their food and dining habits were noticeably different from those of the bourgeoisie. And classical French cuisine would have remained an elitist, snobbish cuisine had the restaurant not come into being.

After the Revolution, the trade guilds were abolished, so anyone could be a chef; and the provincials who flooded into Paris, without family, were an endless source of patronage for the new restaurants. Most of the first restaurateurs were the former chefs of the late aristocracy.

These new restaurant chefs saw to the further development of French cuisine by continually trying to outdo each other. In the process, they demanded great ingredients for their stockpots. They stuffed, rolled, ground, pureed, creamed, buttered, and flamed their way to glory and the people wanted more. They sent legions of well-trained chefs and cooks throughout the world to set and maintain the standard of French excellence by which all other cooking is judged. French cuisine is one of rules and techniques. We wouldn't cook our own American food as well as we do if we hadn't been greatly influenced by France and its cooks.

French food is more than a list of ingredients—foie gras, white asparagus, triple cream cheeses, frog's legs, brains and sweetbreads, crème fraîche and butter. It's more than the sum of its regional specialties—pot au feu, cassoulet, homard à l'armoricaine, sauce Béarnaise. It's a state of mind, a mentality of eating.

Plan your menu carefully. The French look at the whole dinner as if it were a single recipe, with each course being an ingredient that has been chosen for what it adds to the meal.

Although the French may be known for their sauces, there are never two on the same plate. And they don't serve every course in sauce or follow one cream sauce with another. The model, even in France today, is lightness, both in the choice of ingredients and in the choice of dishes.

In the French manner, whether dinner is a long formal one or a more casual one, the cook exercises control over how the meal progresses. Things are served in separate courses. Each dish, although perhaps not *soigné* or fancy, gains importance by its unique presentation.

I've not strayed from this classic format here, but, because I find that traditional French cooking deemphasizes vegetables, some recipes are *plats composés*, dishes where a vegetable or starch is included as part of the main idea of the dish. These vegetables or starches are not meant to take the place of a side dish, though, and you may still want to serve a separate starch or a vegetable course. Then again, salad and cheese after the main course or a soup or some pâté to start may be enough. Consider the choices carefully so that your meal progresses nicely.

Although I've included a recipe for Braised Sweetbreads and another for a rich Chicken and Grapes with Crème de Foie, this chapter is not a compilation of fancy recipes that you'll want to cook only rarely. Included are the brasserie favorites I sought out when I was a student in Paris—blanquette de veau, leg of lamb, steak au poivre, and dover sole—given a *coup de moderne* through a reduction of the amount of cream and butter used.

The recipes for salmon—stuffed with herbs or buried in potatoes—are seemingly complicated, but in fact they are devised to be foolproof. A pork tenderloin dish incorporates my favorite dried legume, flageolet beans. This is tasty eating and may become your favorite pork recipe.

Two famous regional stews of France—cassoulet and potée—are found in other chapters (pages 177 and 56). The Provençal Grand Aïoli (page 20) is a meatless dinner, and the kind of food we don't always immediately associate with the French.

The French dishes in the chapter called Guess Who's Coming to Dinner—Turbans of Flounder and Crab (page 296) and—are fancy only in their flavors, not in the techniques involved.

Remember that in France, dinner always begins with a first course, perhaps a pâté or some marinated fish such as herring or mackerel. Then comes the main dish, sometimes accompanied by a starch or vegetable; often, however, the vegetable or starch is a separate course. Next is a green salad, then a cheese course, and finally, dessert. The portions in this chapter are American size, but if you're planning to serve a succession of dishes in the French manner, you may want to do a bit of trimming when it comes to the amounts of meat, poultry, or fish listed.

BAKED SALMON BURIED IN POTATOES

SERVES 4

*T*he thick potato crust guards the moisture of the salmon as it cooks. The dish is prettier if you shred the potato into the thinnest, longest filaments possible. The best device for accomplishing this is a daikon shredder of the sort used by sushi chefs, but the finest shredding blade on a food processor or a small Mouli hand grater will do just fine. If all you have is an old-fashioned box grater, yours will be a more rustic-looking dish.

Begin the meal with a plate of sautéed asparagus and mushrooms.

Kosher salt
Freshly ground black pepper
2 pounds russet potatoes (about 2 large potatoes), peeled
1 tablespoon fresh lemon juice
6 large scallions, thinly sliced
4 7-ounce skinless salmon fillets
½ cup finely minced shallots
½ cup dry white wine
½ cup white wine vinegar
8 tablespoons unsalted butter, cut into pieces
Ground white pepper to taste

1. Preheat the oven to 450°F. Cut four 9- by 12-inch sheets of aluminum foil. Heavily butter the foil and sprinkle with kosher salt and black pepper.

2. Shred the potatoes and toss with the lemon juice and scallions. Using half of the potatoes, make a nest on each piece of aluminum foil. Place a salmon fillet in each potato nest, sprinkle with salt and pepper, cover with the remaining potatoes. Press down on the potatoes and enclose tightly in the foil. Bake for 20 minutes.

3. Meanwhile, combine the shallots, wine, and vinegar in a saucepan and simmer over medium heat until most of the liquid has evaporated. Remove from the heat and whisk in the butter. Add salt and white pepper to taste and set aside in a warm place.

4. Preheat the broiler.

5. Remove the salmon from the foil packets and place on a broiler pan. Broil, 2 to 3 inches from the heat source, until well browned, about 2 minutes per side. Arrange the salmon on a platter and serve the sauce separately.

ROASTED SALMON WITH FINES HERBES STUFFING

SERVES 5 TO 6

*7*he cold weather prompts us to prepare the kind of recipes that produce "comfort" meals: long-cooked braises, stews, and roasts. But this cooking need not be restricted to the usual rich red meats and fatty birds. Unlikely ingredients, such as salmon, can be used to achieve a hearty dish that is at once rib-stickingly satisfying and lighter for the constitution.

1 cup minced onions

½ cup dry white wine

2 teaspoons salt

1 teaspoon ground white pepper

5 tablespoons unsalted butter

2 cups fresh bread crumbs

1 cup chopped fresh parsley

3 tablespoons chopped fresh tarragon

2 teaspoons chopped fresh thyme

1 whole side of salmon, skin and bones removed (about 2 pounds)

1 tablespoon vegetable oil

½ cup dry sherry

1. Combine the onions, wine, salt, pepper, and 2 tablespoons of the butter in a large pot and cook over medium heat for 5 minutes. Add the bread crumbs and cook, stirring constantly, for 3 minutes. Add the parsley, tarragon, and thyme. Transfer to a bowl and let cool.

2. Preheat the oven to 350°F.

3. Lay the salmon on a work surface and carefully slice it in half horizontally to give you 2 thin fillets. Cut out a piece of parchment paper larger than the 2 fillets side by side, and brush it with the oil. Lay the 2 pieces of salmon skinned side up on the parchment, head to tail, overlapping the edges slightly, to form a large rectangular shape.

4. Spread the cool stuffing evenly over the salmon. Roll up the salmon jelly-roll style, using the paper underneath to help roll it into a tight cylinder. Then wrap the paper around the salmon and transfer the salmon roll to a baking pan. Roast for 35 minutes.

5. Meanwhile, bring the sherry to a simmer in a small saucepan, over medium-high heat and cook until reduced by half. Remove from the heat and whisk in the remaining 3 tablespoons butter; set aside in a warm place.

6. Unwrap the salmon and place on a platter. Pour the sauce over and serve immediately.

Salmon

Salmon is found in both the Atlantic and Pacific oceans. They spawn in rivers, go down to the sea to live, then travel back to the spot where they were hatched to reproduce and complete their life cycle. While at sea they eat post-larval herring and other fish. It's this diet that gives the flesh its famous pink color. Once they enter the rivers on the return pilgrimage to their spawning grounds, they take no food.

A large industry has grown up in Scandinavia producing farm-raised Norwegian salmon. All salmon are considered fatty fish, but farmed salmon, which eat better than their wild cousins, have a lighter pink flesh, a less fishy flavor, and a finer texture.

Wild salmon has a fat content of about 17 percent. Farm-raised salmon is fattier. (Remember, those of you who restrict fat consumption, that this is healthful fat.) This fat protects the fish not only from the cold of the northern waters, but also from the inexactitude of the cook. Salmon can be cooked for a longer time than other fish without deteriorating. Even overcooking doesn't damage it as much as it might another, less unctuous, fish. I find farm-raised salmon the best for cooking.

Salmon's flavor—nutty, woodsy, almost gamey—allows it to be treated like meat, and, unlike many more delicately textured fish (which are usually best quickly sautéed, steamed, or broiled), salmon shines when roasted or braised.

RED SNAPPER ROASTED ON A BED OF FENNEL AND ONIONS

SERVES 4

*F*ish, like meat, roasts better on the bone. It cooks through more slowly and the flesh next to the bones benefits from the proteins that melt into it. Cook a whole fish rather than fillets for this dinner and you'll see what I mean. The sauce is made by enriching the pan juices with a nut of butter. Serve boiled potatoes with the platter of fish, fennel, and onions.

4 whole Florida or New Zealand red snapper (about 1 pound each)
  or 8 4-ounce snapper fillets
1 medium fennel bulb
1 medium onion
½ cup dry white wine
½ teaspoon celery seed
Salt and freshly ground black pepper to taste
2 teaspoons unsalted butter

1. Preheat the oven to 350°F.

2. If using whole fish, rinse and pat dry. Set aside.

3. Halve the fennel lengthwise, lay cut side down on a work surface, and slice lengthwise as thin as possible. Peel the onion, halve lengthwise, and slice lengthwise as thin as possible.

4. If using whole fish, arrange them in a baking dish and pour in the wine. Sprinkle with the celery seed and salt and pepper and arrange the fennel and onion over the top. Bake for 30 minutes. If using fillets, arrange the onion and fennel in the bottom of the baking dish, and add the wine. Bake for 15 minutes. Arrange the fillets on the onion and fennel, sprinkle with the celery seed and salt and pepper, and bake for 15 minutes.

5. Arrange a bed of the fennel and onions on a serving platter, and arrange the fish on top. Swirl the butter into the cooking liquid remaining in the pan and pour into a sauceboat. Serve immediately.

BAKED DOVER SOLE WITH
CREAMY CELERY AND POTATOES

SERVES 4

I use the most fabulous fish of them all for this recipe, but you can substitute any flat fish—flounder and sand dabs are the most commonly available. I've lightened this dish a bit by using half-and-half instead of heavy cream; you can lighten it further by substituting yogurt. Whisk it into the hot sauce immediately before serving. Just remember that you can't heat the dish again or the sauce will break.

12 tender, light green celery stalks
1½ pounds large waxy potatoes (about 3 potatoes)
¾ teaspoon salt, or to taste
Ground white pepper to taste
¼ cup dry white wine
1 tablespoon fresh tarragon or 1 teaspoon dried
¾ cup half-and-half
4 12-ounce Dover sole, skinned, or 1½ pounds sole, flounder, or
  other flat fish fillets
2 teaspoons melted unsalted butter
Lemon wedges, for garnish
1 tablespoon finely chopped fresh parsley

1. Preheat the oven to 375°F.

2. Lay each celery stalk on a work surface and, holding your knife nearly parallel to the work surface, sliver the celery diagonally into thin slices. Set aside.

3. Peel the potatoes and slice them into very thin rounds. Place in a 9- by 12-inch baking dish, sprinkle with ½ teaspoon of the salt and pepper to taste, and pour in the wine. Cover the baking dish with foil and bake for 15 minutes.

4. Add the celery, tarragon, and half-and-half to the potatoes and mix well. Cover and bake for 25 minutes longer. (The dish can be prepared ahead to this point and set aside at room temperature for up to 4 hours. When you're ready to serve dinner, reheat the oven to 375°F.)

5. When you're ready to get dinner on the table, arrange the fish on the celery and potatoes, sprinkle with pepper and the remaining ¼ teaspoon salt,

(continued)

and drizzle with the melted butter. If using whole fish, bake uncovered, for 25 minutes; if using fillets, bake for 15 minutes.

6. Using a large spatula, transfer the fish to a serving platter, overlapping it slightly. Mound the celery/potato mixture next to the fish. Garnish the fish with lemon wedges and sprinkle the potatoes and celery with the chopped parsley. Serve immediately.

CHÈVRE CHICKEN BREASTS
WITH SUMMER SQUASHES

SERVES 4

*S*outhern in spirit, the south of France that is, this dish is simple but astonishingly delicious. The vegetable juices that escape during cooking mix with the olive oil and make a natural sauce. Use an aged goat cheese that will ooze when melted, like a bucheron; the little fresh cheeses are not nearly so good for this dish. Serve a salad of mixed lettuces after the chicken, preferably with some arugula in it.

2 large boneless chicken breasts, with skin, split (about 1½ pounds)
Salt and freshly ground black pepper to taste
1 tablespoon olive oil
1 medium onion, finely diced
4 small zucchini, cut into 1-inch chunks
4 small yellow squash, cut into 1-inch chunks
1 tablespoon unsalted butter
4 slices aged goat cheese (about 6 ounces total)
2 tablespoons chopped fresh parsley

1. Preheat the oven to 375°F.

2. Pat the chicken dry and sprinkle with salt and pepper.

3. Heat the oil in a large skillet over medium heat. Add the chicken and cook until golden on both sides, about 5 minutes. Transfer to a plate and set aside to cool.

4. Meanwhile, add the onion to the skillet and cook, stirring, until soft, about 5 minutes. Transfer to a covered baking dish. Add the zucchini, yellow squash, and butter to the skillet and cook, stirring, for about 15 minutes, until soft. Scrape into the baking dish, add salt and pepper to taste, and mix well.

5. Place a slice of the goat cheese under the skin of each chicken breast half. Arrange the chicken on the squash, cover, and bake for 15 minutes.

6. Arrange the chicken breasts on a serving platter. Stir the parsley into the squash and mound next to the chicken. Serve immediately.

CHICKEN AND GRAPES
WITH CRÈME DE FOIE

SERVES 4 TO 6

*T*his is a very fancy dish that tastes much richer than it is. Pureeing a little chicken liver in the sauce gives the impression that the chicken is glazed with foie gras. Resist any temptation to peel the grapes before tossing them into the sauce—the skin is where all their tannin lies, and its nearly unidentifiable puckering taste makes the dish even better.

4 chicken drumsticks
4 chicken thighs
2 chicken breasts, split
Salt and freshly ground black pepper to taste
Flour for dusting
2 tablespoons flavorless vegetable oil
¾ cup Madeira or dry sherry
¼ cup heavy cream
3 bay leaves
1 branch fresh thyme or 1 teaspoon dried
2 chicken livers
1½ cups green seedless grapes

1. Preheat the oven to 375°F.

2. Rinse the chicken pieces and pat dry. Sprinkle with salt and pepper and dust with flour, shaking off the excess.   *(continued)*

Dinner in the French Manner

3. Heat the oil in a large skillet over medium heat. Add the chicken pieces without crowding the skillet, and cook until golden brown on all sides. Brown the chicken in batches if necessary. Transfer the thighs and drumsticks to a large casserole or Dutch oven, and set the breasts aside.

4. Add the Madeira, cream, bay leaves, and thyme to the thighs and drumsticks, cover, and bake for 10 minutes. Add the livers and chicken breasts and bake for 25 minutes.

5. Transfer the chicken pieces to a heatproof serving platter, cover, and keep warm in the oven while you finish the sauce. Remove the bay leaves and thyme sprig from the sauce, transfer the sauce and livers to a blender or food processor, and process until smooth. Taste for salt and add as needed. Strain the sauce into a saucepan, place over medium heat, and add the grapes. Simmer for 2 minutes, to heat the grapes. Spoon the sauce and grapes over the chicken and serve immediately.

BLANQUETTE OF VEAL AND CAULIFLOWER

SERVES 6

*B*lanquettes "talk" to me, and over the years I've improvised many different ones. But one thing remains constant: They're always white dishes made with white meat (usually veal but sometimes pork, rabbit, or chicken). Mine always have a hint of nutmeg and half a lemon cooked in the sauce. They're always delicious. And they're always served over rice.

> *3 pounds boneless veal stew meat*
> *6 cups chicken stock or canned low-sodium chicken broth*
> *1 medium onion, cut in half*
> *2 celery stalks, cut in half*
> *1 medium carrot, cut in half*
> *½ teaspoon salt, or to taste*
> *½ teaspoon black peppercorns*
> *¼ teaspoon ground nutmeg*
> *½ lemon*
> *5 tablespoons unsalted butter*
> *5 tablespoons all-purpose flour*
> *2½ cups cauliflower florets (from a 1-pound cauliflower)*
> *¾ cup sour cream*

1. Combine the veal and broth in a heavy 5-quart pot. Cover and bring to a boil over high heat, skimming off any scum that comes to the top of the pot. Add the onion, celery, carrot, salt, peppercorns, nutmeg, and lemon, reduce the heat to low, and simmer for 1¼ hours, or until the meat is just tender.

2. Meanwhile, melt the butter in a medium pot over low heat. Whisk in the flour and cook, stirring, for 2 minutes. Remove from the heat and set aside.

3. Remove the meat from the cooking liquid, using a slotted spoon, and set aside. Replace the butter/flour mixture over medium-low heat and strain the cooking liquid into it, whisking vigorously; discard the lemon and vegetables. Cook, stirring, until the sauce thickens, about 3 to 5 minutes. Add the cauliflower and cook for 15 minutes, skimming off any scum that rises to the surface.

4. To serve dinner, add the veal to the sauce and heat through. Place the sour cream in a bowl, whisk in ½ cup of the hot sauce, then stir this mixture into the stew. Do not reheat the stew after adding the sour cream, or the sauce will curdle. Pour the stew into a serving dish and accompany with rice pilaf.

BRAISED SWEETBREADS

SERVES 3 TO 4

*P*reparing sweetbreads in sherry is not uncommon, but I've added subtle nuances that make this dish especially tasty. Ground mace added to both the dusting flour and the sauce enhances and deepens the flavor of the sherry. Serving thinly sliced lemon cuts the richness of the cream sauce.

These sweetbreads are not blanched in boiling water before braising, a practice many cooks swear by, and so they keep their wonderful texture. But don't rush the cooking. They need a good long braising to soften and develop.

1½ pounds calf's sweetbreads
2 tablespoons all-purpose flour
⅛ teaspoon plus a pinch ground mace
½ teaspoon salt
¼ teaspoon freshly ground black pepper
3 tablespoons flavorless vegetable oil
2 tablespoons finely minced shallots
1 cup dry sherry
1 cup chicken stock or canned low-sodium chicken broth
½ cup heavy cream
2 tablespoons unsalted butter
Lemon slices, for garnish

1. Preheat the oven to 325°F.

2. Pat the sweetbreads dry. Peel off and discard just the most obvious membranes, without breaking the sweetbreads into small pieces. Combine the flour, ⅛ teaspoon mace, the salt, and pepper in a shallow bowl. Dust the sweetbreads with the seasoned flour, shaking off the excess.

3. Heat the oil in a heavy ovenproof frying pan over medium heat. Add the sweetbreads, in batches if necessary, and cook until they are dark golden on both sides, about 5 minutes per side. Do not crowd the pan or the sweetbreads will not brown.

4. Pour off any fat remaining in the pan, add the shallots, sherry, and broth, and bring to a boil. Cover, transfer to the oven, and cook for 45 minutes, turning the sweetbreads once.

5. Using a slotted spoon, transfer the sweetbreads to a platter. Add the cream and a pinch of mace to the cooking juices and boil over high heat until

the liquid has reduced to the consistency of a sauce, about 10 minutes. Remove from the heat and whisk in the butter.

6. Strain the sauce over the sweetbreads, and garnish with slices of lemon.

LAMB CHOPS WITH TARRAGON VINEGAR SAUCE

SERVES 4

I love any dish flavored with tarragon, but I especially like how its minty, peppery flavor goes with lamb. You'll like it for the same reasons you like mint jelly with lamb—you may even like it far better. Serve this with gratinéed potatoes.

12 thick-cut rib lamb chops (about 2 pounds)
Salt and freshly ground black pepper to taste
2 tablespoons finely minced onion or shallots
¼ cup red wine
¼ cup red wine vinegar
1 teaspoon brown sugar
1 tablespoon chopped fresh tarragon or 1 teaspoon dried
4 tablespoons unsalted butter

1. Heat a heavy skillet over high heat. Sprinkle the lamb chops with salt and pepper, place in the skillet, and cook for about 5 minutes on each side for rare. Transfer to a plate and keep warm in a 250°F oven while you finish the sauce.

2. Reduce the heat to medium and add the onion to the skillet. Cook, stirring, for 1 minute. Add the wine, vinegar, and sugar; if using dried tarragon, add it now. Cook until the liquid has reduced by half, about 3 minutes. Remove from the heat, and whisk in the butter and, if using it, the fresh tarragon.

3. Remove the chops from the oven and pour any juices that have collected on the plate, into the sauce. Pour the sauce over the lamb and serve immediately.

ROAST LAMB WITH RICE AND ONION PUREE

SERVES 6

*7*he onions that cook under this leg of lamb take on a great flavor. Puree them with cooked rice, and the result is a sweet, meat-flavored, stick-to-the-ribs mash.

1 bone-in leg of lamb (about 5 pounds)
5 garlic cloves, cut into ¼-inch slivers
2 tablespoons olive oil
1½ teaspoons salt, or to taste
Ground white pepper to taste
10 medium onions, finely sliced (about 7 cups)
½ tablespoon chopped fresh thyme or 1 teaspoon dried
2 cups cooked rice
½ cup heavy cream
¼ teaspoon ground nutmeg

1. Preheat the oven to 400°F.

2. Trim the excess fat from the leg of lamb, leaving only a thin layer. Using a small sharp knife, poke holes all over the meat and stuff in the slivers of garlic. Rub the surface of the lamb with the olive oil and sprinkle with the salt and pepper.

3. Combine the onions and thyme and mound in the middle of a roasting pan. Place the lamb fat side down on the onions. Place in the oven, reduce the temperature to 350°F, and roast for 1 hour.

4. Turn the lamb fat side up and roast 20 to 30 minutes longer for medium-rare, or until a meat thermometer registers 145°F.

5. Transfer the lamb to a cutting board and let rest for 15 minutes. Reheat the rice, if necessary.

6. Meanwhile, scrape the onions into a food processor, and add the rice, cream, nutmeg, and salt to taste. Pulse, scraping down the sides of the bowl, to a coarse puree. Transfer the puree to a vegetable dish.

7. Slice the lamb and arrange on a platter. Serve with the puree.

PORK TENDERLOINS WITH ROSEMARY AND FLAGEOLETS

SERVES 4

*P*ork tenderloins are very lean, and if you overcook them they will be dry. Cook them a little under medium for juicy results.

Flageolet beans are just the beans from a maturer French green bean. I don't know why they're so difficult to find in our markets, but they're worth searching out as they have a creamier texture than any other legume.

1 cup dried flageolets or baby lima beans
3 bay leaves
Salt and pepper to taste
3 tablespoons unsalted butter
1½ pounds pork tenderloin
1 tablespoon olive oil
1 onion, finely diced (about ¾ cup)
2 cups chicken stock or canned low-sodium chicken broth
¼ cup fresh lemon juice
1 tablespoon chopped fresh rosemary or 2 teaspoons dried

1. Place the beans and bay leaves in a pot and add water to barely cover the beans. Cover and bring to a boil, then reduce the heat to low and simmer the beans for 45 minutes. Add salt and pepper to taste and simmer until the beans are soft, about 30 minutes longer, adding only enough water as necessary so the beans don't dry out. Remove from the heat and stir in 1 tablespoon of the butter; cover and keep warm.

2. Meanwhile, preheat the oven to 375°F.

3. Sprinkle the pork with salt and pepper. Heat oil in an ovenproof skillet over high heat and brown pork on all sides, 6 to 7 minutes. Add the onion and cook, stirring, for 1 minute. Transfer to oven and cook for 12 minutes.

4. Transfer the pork to a plate, cover, and keep warm. Add the stock and lemon juice to the skillet; if using dried rosemary, add it now. Bring to a boil over high heat and boil until the liquid reduces by half and thickens, about 15 minutes. Remove from the heat and add any juices that have accumulated on the plate of pork. Whisk in the remaining 2 tablespoons butter; if using fresh rosemary, add it now. Taste for salt and pepper and add as needed.

5. Slice the pork on the bias into rounds about ½ inch thick. Arrange on a plate and spoon over some sauce. Serve the beans separately, and pass the remaining sauce.

Dinner in the French Manner

STEAK PAILLARDS AUX DEUX POIVRES

SERVES 4

*T*his brasserie favorite became expensive fare in the States because it was usually made with filet mignon steaks. But it's much better with an inexpensive but tastier cut of meat. This is a quick-to-cook dinner, excellent with mashed or baked potatoes. Serve a wilted spinach salad after the steaks.

4 7-ounce minute steaks (sometimes called breakfast steaks)
2 tablespoons coarsely cracked black pepper
Salt to taste
1 tablespoon vegetable oil
2 tablespoons minced onion or shallots
¼ cup brandy
1 tablespoon Dijon mustard
¼ cup heavy cream
1 tablespoon green peppercorns
1 tablespoon unsalted butter
Freshly ground black pepper to taste

1. Place the steaks between two layers of plastic wrap and flatten to ¼-inch thickness with a mallet or cleaver. Place on a plate, sprinkle both sides generously with the black pepper, and press the pepper into the steaks. Sprinkle with salt.

2. Heat the oil in a large heavy skillet over high heat until nearly smoking hot. Add the steaks and cook for 1½ minutes. Turn and cook about 1½ minutes longer for rare. Transfer the steaks to a platter and keep warm in a 250°F oven.

3. Pour off the fat from the skillet. Place the skillet over medium heat, add the onions, and cook for 1 minute, stirring. Add the brandy and shake the pan to ignite it (or use a match). Add the mustard, cream, and green peppercorns, and cook until the cream thickens slightly, about 1 minute. Remove from the heat, whisk in the butter, and taste for salt and pepper.

4. Remove the steaks from the oven and pour any juices that have collected on the plate into the sauce. Arrange the steaks on the plate and spoon the sauce over the top.

Dinner in the Italian Fashion

198   *Roast Lamb with Garlic, page 317*
           Veal Roast with Shallots and Lemon, page 313
           Cioppino, page 42
           Tomato and Pastina Aspic with Spiced Crab, page 15
           Individual Eggplant Parmesan, page 16

*I*talian cooking was the first in Europe to profit from the spice trade—in classical times, when Rome ruled the Western world and spices came from Asia, and then again at the end of the Middle Ages, when Venice, profiting most from the business of the Crusades, became a naval power and controller of the spice routes to India. By the sixteenth century, however, Portugal controlled the spice trade, and Italians had to pay the exorbitant price for spices to which the rest of Europe had become accustomed. But while the rest of Europe sent explorers to find a quicker route to India, Italy simply began to free its cuisine of the murky spice blends that characterized all European cooking at the time.

The *nuova cucina* that began to emerge in Italy in the sixteenth century relied upon native fresh herbs to flavor dishes. Italian cuisine is still known for its liberal use of basil, oregano, marjoram, thyme, parsley, sage, and rosemary, as well as capers, garlic, and onions. Italy was also the first European country to embrace the tomato, brought back from the New World. And, of course, olive oil had been used since Roman times. Italian cuisine became aromatic but lightly spiced.

Italian cuisine remains a varied, regional one that's based on the available local products. Cooking in Emilia-Romagna, the area around Bologna, is rich in dairy products and uses lots of cream; Piemontese cooking is characterized by mushrooms and truffles. Parma is famous for its hams and cheese; in Friuli one gets polenta of corn or chestnut flour; and Liguria is known for its seafood.

Many consider the cuisines of France and China the most sophisticated, and the proudest achievements of their chefs often depend on complicated culinary methods, the assistance of many cooks, and a plethora of ingredients. In Italy, the way people cook at home influences the *alta cucina* that's created by their chefs. Throughout Italy, the standard is for uncomplicated, robustly flavored dishes—the kind of simple yet elegant cooking that's done at home.

In this chapter you'll find recipes for more humble cuts of meat—for example, lamb or veal shanks, veal brisket, and breast of veal. Instead of veal scallopine, there are two recipes for pork scallopine. Vitello tonnato is a chilled braised Genovese dish that has become restaurant fare throughout Italy; it's a favorite of mine, but I've adapted the tuna sauce that accompanies it to work on pasta.

Italians are particular about their bread and buy it fresh daily. The

Tomatoes

The tomato, a native of the Andes, was domesticated in Mexico and was introduced to the Old World by Spanish explorers in 1523. By the end of the sixteenth century it was established in England, where it was known as the "love apple," but only as an ornamental plant. In fact, for over two hundred years, it was considered inedible, a poisonous plant, throughout most of Europe. Only in Spain and Italy was the tomato immediately incorporated into the diet. Large-scale consumption of tomatoes did not occur in the rest of Europe until the middle of the nineteenth century.

The tomato has undergone intense hybridization over past decades, with producers more interested in developing a tomato that ships well than one that tastes good. Most of today's tomatoes are shipped hard and unripe to reduce damage. They are then gassed with ethylene to promote ripening in local storehouses.

In late summer and early fall, look for tomatoes that are vine-ripened. At other times, look for those that are hothouse-grown. A hothouse can simulate nature's cycle of long, hot summer days. You'll recognize both these types of tomatoes by their intense red color, their strong tomato aroma, and, unfortunately, by their high price.

Tomatoes seem to be the plant of choice for most weekend gardeners. Not only are they extremely easy to grow, but of all the vegetables that one can produce in a small home garden patch, the difference in flavor between your garden variety and the storebought alternative is most astounding. Grow beefsteak tomatoes for salads, and Roma, or plum, tomatoes for sauces and canning. An organic ultimate in home cooking is probably the Tomato, Pastina, and Bread Stew included here, a scrumptious way of utilizing stale bread and overripe tomatoes. Two dishes using polenta—a soft polenta with flank steak, and little polenta cakes with seafood and chicken—are my own recipes for using this favorite corn mush. Baccalà-stuffed peppers are a discovery you will be happy to make if you're unfamiliar with salt cod.

Make "dinner in the Italian fashion" as elaborate as you like, serving an antipasto, pasta, fish, meat, vegetable, cheeses, and dessert. Or Americanize it by starting with a green salad and serving pasta alongside the main course. Whatever you do, you'll be serving a robust, unpretentious meal.

gardener shared some valuable advice with me: Give your plants plenty of water during the growing season, but stop watering them five to seven days before harvesting. Watering the ripening fruits will bloat them and destroy their flavor intensity.

I never serve tomatoes straight from the refrigerator—the cold temperature inhibits flavor. In fact, avoid refrigerating tomatoes at all if possible. The best way to prepare August tomatoes for eating is to drizzle slices with olive oil, sprinkle them with a little salt and freshly ground pepper, and allow them to marinate for 15 minutes and warm a bit. I slice tomatoes for salads from tip to stem, rather than across—the ratio of pulp to seed is more pleasing.

Before using tomatoes in most cooked preparations, you'll need to peel and seed them. Cut out and discard the stem. Bring a large pot of water to a rolling boil and add just a few tomatoes at a time; let them cook until the skins burst, about 1 minute. Remove them from the water and plunge immediately into ice water. The skins will peel off easily. Then halve the tomato crosswise and gently squeeze out the seeds. The tomatoes are now ready for cooking.

Many recipes for tomato sauce and soup include a little sugar to balance the acidity (tomatoes are a good source of citric acid). I prefer to leave my sauce or soup acidic—it allows the flavors of a good olive oil and fresh herbs to sparkle.

Whole peeled tomatoes in cans are better in any recipe than colorless, flavorless tomatoes out of season. But do taste them before adding them to a dish. Some are more "tomato-y" than others, some have sugar added, and some are very acidic.

Dinner in the Italian Fashion

TOMATO, PASTINA, AND BREAD STEW

SERVES 4

*I*talians do great things with old bread; my favorite is this stew. Make it thick and redolent of olive oil, and use overripe, bruised tomatoes and stale bread. Serve a plate of prosciutto, salami, melon, and fresh figs to complete dinner.

½ cup olive oil, plus additional, for serving
8 garlic cloves, crushed
2 medium onions, finely diced (about 1½ cups)
3 ounces stale Italian or French bread (about one quarter of
*   a medium loaf)*
6 cups peeled, seeded, and chopped ripe plum tomatoes or chopped
*   canned plum tomatoes (canned juices reserved)*
1 tablespoon fresh marjoram or 2 teaspoons dried
Salt and freshly ground black pepper to taste
½ cup dry white wine
2 cups water or juice from canned tomatoes, or more, if necessary
3 tablespoons pastina
Grated Parmesan and/or Romano cheese, for serving

1. Combine the olive oil, garlic, and onions in a large, deep skillet and cook over low heat, stirring occasionally, for 5 minutes, or until the onions are soft and translucent.

2. Roughly crumble the bread into ¼-inch pieces, add it to the skillet, and cook, stirring, for 1 minute.

3. Add the tomatoes, marjoram, salt and pepper, wine, and water or tomato juices, cover, and cook, stirring occasionally, for 20 minutes. Add the pastina and cook for 3 minutes. If the stew is too thick for your liking (sometimes fresh tomatoes don't have enough liquid), add a little extra water or juice from canned tomatoes.

4. Transfer the stew to a large soup tureen or serving dish, and offer grated cheese and additional olive oil on the side.

What's for Dinner?

*F*resh cod is a bland fish with a flaky texture, good for preparing fish sticks and patties and not much else. But a traditional method of salting, then air-drying the cod to a stiff cardboard appearance turns this lowly ocean denizen into an uncommonly delicious commodity. It's an important ingredient in Mediterranean cooking—called *baccalà* in Italy, *bacalao* in Spain, *bacalhau* in Portugal, and *morue* in France.

This is a recipe for a Mediterranean concoction of salt cod, mashed potatoes, garlic, and olive oil. It's usually served on toast, but I like it better stuffed into sweet red peppers.

Accompany the peppers with a simple pasta tossed with olive oil, garlic, and herbs and serve an arugula, tomato, and onion salad to complete the meal.

> *1 pound salt cod*
> *1 large potato, about ¾ pound, baked*
> *⅔ cup olive oil, plus additional for brushing the peppers*
> *2 tablespoons minced garlic*
> *4 red bell peppers*
> *¼ cup balsamic vinegar*
> *1 tablespoon unsalted butter*

1. Soak the cod in water to cover for 36 hours to 3 days, depending on the dryness of the fish, changing the water several times. The flesh should soften and become somewhat puffy and an opaque white throughout. Drain.

2. Place the cod in a pot, cover with cold water, and bring to a boil over high heat. Cook until flaky; depending on the salt cod this will take anywhere from 1 to 5 minutes. Drain and place in a bowl. Remove any skin and bones.

3. Scoop out the flesh of the potato, add to the bowl, and pound together with the cod. (A wooden mortar is good for the job.)

4. Combine the oil and garlic in a small saucepan and cook over high heat for 30 seconds. Slowly add the hot oil to the potato/cod mixture, pounding constantly until absorbed. Cover and set aside.

5. Roast the peppers: Place the peppers directly over a gas flame or under a preheated broiler. As the skin blackens, rotate the peppers until they are completely black on all sides. Place the peppers in a paper bag to steam for 2 minutes. Remove from the bag, hold under cold running water, and rub off

(continued)

the blackened skins. Core the peppers and remove the seeds, being careful not to split the peppers open.

6. Stuff the peppers with the cod mixture, arrange on a baking sheet, and brush with olive oil. Place in the oven, turn the oven on to 375°F, and bake for 25 minutes.

7. Meanwhile, heat the vinegar and 2 teaspoons water in a small sauce-pan. Whisk in the butter and remove from the heat.

8. Arrange the peppers on a serving platter, spoon the sauce over the top, and serve immediately.

ROASTED WHITEFISH WITH LEEK RISOTTO

SERVES 4

*I*n Italy, this dish would probably be made with *bronzino,* or striped bass, but whitefish is easier to locate here. Whichever one you choose to use, leave the skin on the fish and bake skin side up. Risotto, which we're used to stirring constantly on the stove top until cooked, is perfectly done in the oven with no trouble at all. Begin dinner with a platter of prosciutto or salami with melon or fresh figs.

1 cup Arborio rice
4 cups bottled clam juice, chicken stock, or canned low-sodium
  chicken broth
4 anchovies, finely chopped
½ teaspoon chopped fresh rosemary or ¼ teaspoon dried
½ teaspoon chopped fresh sage or ¼ teaspoon dried
6 large leeks, white part only, sliced into thin rounds (about 4 cups)
4 7-ounce whitefish or bass fillets
Freshly ground black pepper
3 tablespoons fresh lemon juice
1 tablespoon Dijon mustard
⅓ cup extra virgin olive oil

1. Preheat the oven to 350°F.

2. Combine the rice, 3 cups of the clam juice, the anchovies, rosemary, and sage in a 9- by 12-inch baking dish. Cover and bake for 30 minutes.

3. Scatter the leeks over the rice and arrange the fish on top, skin side up. Sprinkle with pepper, cover, and bake 15 minutes longer.

4. Meanwhile, combine the remaining 1 cup clam juice, the lemon juice, and mustard in a small saucepan. Bring to a boil over medium heat and cook until reduced by half. Remove from the heat and pour into a blender. Set the blender on medium speed and slowly drizzle in the oil, blending until well incorporated. Or use a food processor, adding the oil very slowly with the motor running.

5. To serve dinner, mound the risotto and leeks on a serving platter and arrange the fish around the rice. Spoon a little sauce over the fish and serve the remainder on the side.

Dinner in the Italian Fashion

CHICKEN AND SEAFOOD RAGOUT
WITH WARM POLENTA

SERVES 4

*C*hicken, garlic, and shallots all lend a sweet flavor to the briny seashore taste of the shrimp, clams, and mussels. Cooking these ingredients together fortifies the lightly creamed sauce that accompanies the dish. Polenta is the bread in this meal—use it to soak up all the delicious sauce on your plate.

You can make the polenta cakes well in advance. The remainder of the dish is quickly prepared. Begin dinner with a plate of olives, roasted peppers, and broccoli bathed in some garlicky olive oil.

3 tablespoons unsalted butter
½ cup yellow cornmeal
½ teaspoon salt, or more to taste
2 boneless, skinless chicken breast halves
4 large shrimp
2 tablespoons olive oil
4 large scallops
4 clams, scrubbed
4 mussels, scrubbed and debearded
1 teaspoon minced garlic
2 tablespoons finely minced shallots or onion
¼ cup dry white wine
½ cup chicken stock or canned low-sodium chicken broth
¼ teaspoon saffron threads or powder
½ teaspoon ground white pepper
¼ cup heavy cream

1. Generously butter an 8-inch square cake pan, using 1 tablespoon of the butter.

2. Combine 2¼ cups water, the cornmeal, salt, and 1 tablespoon of the butter in a 2-quart saucepan over high heat and bring to a boil. Reduce the heat and cook, stirring frequently, until the mixture begins to pull away from the sides of the pan, about 30 minutes. Pour into the prepared pan and spread the polenta into an even layer. Let cool completely.

3. Cut the polenta into 1-inch squares or circles, remove from the pan, and set aside. (The polenta can be prepared ahead and left at room temperature or refrigerated for several hours.)

4. Preheat the oven to 350°F.

5. Pull off the small tenderloins from the chicken breasts and set aside on a plate. Cut each breast lengthwise into 2 or 3 pieces, and add to the tenderloins. Peel the shrimp, leaving the tails intact, and devein them.

6. Toss the polenta cakes with 1 tablespoon of the oil, arrange on a baking sheet, and bake for 20 minutes, turning once.

7. Meanwhile, heat the remaining 1 tablespoon oil in a medium skillet over medium-high heat and add the chicken, shrimp, scallops, clams, mussels, garlic, and shallots. Stir well, then add the wine and cook for 1 minute. Add the stock, saffron, and pepper. As each ingredient is cooked, remove it from the skillet and set aside on a plate. The scallops will be cooked first; remove them as soon as they are opaque all the way through. Remove the clams and mussels as they open. Then remove the shrimp and chicken when cooked through. Add the cream to the skillet and cook until the liquid has reduced to the consistency of a sauce. Return all the ingredients to the skillet and swirl in the remaining 1 tablespoon butter; heat just until all the ingredients are warmed through. Taste and add salt as necessary.

8. To serve, heap the polenta cakes in the center of a serving platter. Arrange the chicken, shrimp, scallops, clams, and mussels around the polenta and spoon the sauce over the seafood and chicken.

STUFFED CHICKEN BREASTS

SERVES 4

*A*t first glance this dinner might seem like something dished up in the grand ballroom of your local hotel or at the country club—a combination of chicken and pasta meant to please the most and offend the fewest. In reality, this is a brave combination of flavors and textures, fussy enough to impress, yet honest enough to please even the most suspicious eater.

Serve a salad of mixed marinated mushrooms after the chicken. This dish is also a good one for the picnic hamper—just let the chicken cool, then slice it into rounds. Delicious. The vinaigrette-style sauce can be served warm or at room temperature.

¼ cup olive oil
1 small onion, coarsely diced (about ½ cup)
2 tablespoons minced garlic
2 anchovy fillets, chopped
¼ cup tightly packed fresh basil leaves
½ cup orzo or riso pasta
¾ cup chicken stock, canned low-sodium chicken broth, or water
Salt to taste
1 teaspoon freshly ground black pepper
1 egg white
1 tablespoon dry bread crumbs
2 large boneless chicken breasts, with skin, split
⅓ cup Marsala wine
¼ cup balsamic or red wine vinegar

1. Heat 1 tablespoon of the olive oil in a medium skillet over medium heat. Add the onion, garlic, and anchovies and cook, stirring occasionally, until the onion is softened, about 8 to 10 minutes. Scrape the mixture into a food processor, add the basil, and process until coarsely ground. Transfer to a bowl.

2. Meanwhile, combine the pasta and stock in a small pan, cover, and bring to a boil over medium-high heat. Cook for 5 minutes, or until the pasta is barely soft. Add the pasta and broth to the onion mixture. Season with salt and the pepper.

3. Add the egg white and bread crumbs to the onion mixture and mix well. Refrigerate until chilled.

4. Preheat the oven to 350°F.

5. Pull the small tenderloins off the chicken breasts and set aside. Remove the skin from each breast in one piece and set aside. Place the breasts between two sheets of plastic wrap or wax paper and flatten with a mallet or pounder to a ⅜-inch thickness; gently flatten the tenderloins.

6. Place the breasts skinned side down on a work surface and spread one quarter of the stuffing over each breast, leaving a 1-inch border. Gather up the edges around the stuffing, lay a tenderloin across the opening, and wrap the skin around each bundle. Place the bundles in a baking dish just large enough to hold them comfortably. Pour in the Marsala and vinegar, cover, and bake for 20 minutes.

7. To serve dinner, arrange the chicken on a platter and pour the cooking juices into a saucepan. Bring to a boil over high heat and boil until reduced by about half. Pour the sauce into a bowl and vigorously whisk in the remaining 3 tablespoons olive oil. Pour the sauce over the chicken and serve immediately.

TWO OSSO BUCCI

*T*he veal shank contains the meat closest to the hoof and most exposed to the harshness of the plains. Unlike the more "frou-frou" cuts of meat—the loin and tenderloin—this tough cut must be tamed through long cooking. Choose center-cut shanks no more than 2 inches thick. They need no additional trimming; the skin around them is necessary to hold the meat together during cooking. Braise them long enough so that they are tender but not completely falling apart. You should be able to eat them with just a fork.

BRAISED VEAL SHANKS WITH TOMATO-ORANGE SAUCE

SERVES 4

*C*ooking veal shanks with something tart always makes them taste even better. In this recipe, orange and lemon supply the tartness that helps cut the fattiness of the shanks.

Serve boiled potatoes in the same bowl as the shanks and their braising "soup," and encourage your guests to mash the potatoes with soup—it's the best way to eat this dish. An Italian Amarone, a thick red wine, is suggested with this rich veal.

8 center-cut veal shanks (about 14 to 16 ounces each)
¼ cup olive oil
1 medium onion, finely minced (about 1 cup)
1 celery stalk, finely diced (about ½ cup)
1 small carrot, peeled and finely diced (about ½ cup)
1½ cups fresh orange juice
¼ cup fresh lemon juice
4 sprigs fresh thyme or ½ teaspoon dried
Salt and freshly ground black pepper to taste
4 plum tomatoes
Grated zest of 1 orange
2 tablespoons finely chopped fresh parsley

1. Preheat the oven to 350°F.

2. Pat the shanks dry. Heat the oil over high heat in a roasting pan or Dutch oven large enough to hold the shanks in one layer. Add the shanks and brown well on both sides. Remove the shanks to a plate.

3. Reduce the heat to low and add the onion, celery, and carrot to the fat remaining in the pan. Gently cook the vegetables until soft, stirring to dissolve the residue on the bottom of the pan. Replace the meat in the pan and add the orange juice, lemon juice, thyme, and salt and pepper. Bring to a boil, cover, and transfer to the oven. Cook for 1½ hours, or until the meat is very tender but not falling apart, turning the shanks every 30 minutes. (The veal may be prepared a day in advance to this point. Let cool in the cooking liquid, and refrigerate. Reheat in the oven before proceeding with the recipe.)

4. Meanwhile, using a small paring knife, slice off the tops and bottoms of the tomatoes. Remove the seeds and core, leaving only the firm, outer pulp. Slice down one side of each tomato and open it out flat on a work surface. Cut the flesh into ¼-inch-wide julienne strips, then cut into ¼-inch dice. Set aside.

5. Transfer the veal shanks to a platter, turn off the oven, and keep the shanks warm in the oven while you finish the sauce. Pour the braising liquid into a large saucepan and discard the thyme sprigs. Bring to a boil over high heat and boil until the juices have reduced and look shiny. You should have about 2½ cups. Stir in the chopped tomatoes, orange zest, and parsley, and remove from the heat.

6. Pour the sauce over the veal shanks, and serve immediately.

VEAL SHANKS WITH VEGETABLE RICE

SERVES 4

7 his is the classic recipe for veal shanks—braised in stock with aromatic vegetables and lemon. I've added rice and zucchini, which cook in the rich *potage* making this a one-dish dinner. Serve with a raisiny Amarone wine.

8 center-cut veal shanks (about 14 to 16 ounces each)
Salt and freshly ground black pepper to taste
2 tablespoons flavorless vegetable oil
1 medium onion, finely diced (about 1 cup)
2 medium carrots, peeled and finely diced (about ¾ cup)
2 celery stalks, finely diced (about 1 cup)
3 cups chicken stock or canned low-sodium chicken broth
1 tablespoon finely minced garlic
2 bay leaves
2 sprigs fresh thyme or ¼ teaspoon dried
1 tablespoon tomato paste
1 lemon, cut in half
⅓ cup long-grain rice
1 small zucchini, finely diced (about ½ cup)
3 ripe plum tomatoes, peeled, or canned whole plum tomatoes

1. Preheat the oven to 375°F.

2. Pat the veal shanks dry and sprinkle with salt and pepper. Heat the oil over medium heat in a roasting pan, Dutch oven, or ovenproof skillet large enough to hold the shanks in a single layer. Add the shanks and brown well on both sides, about 5 minutes per side. Remove the shanks and set aside.

3. Pour off the fat from the pan. Return the pan to the heat and add the onion, carrots, and celery. Cook, stirring occasionally, until the vegetables soften, about 5 minutes.

4. Add the broth, garlic, bay leaves, thyme, tomato paste, and lemon. Replace the shanks in the pan. Raise the heat to high, bring to a boil, cover, and transfer to the oven. Cook for 1 hour, or until the meat is barely tender. Stir the rice into the cooking liquid and cook for 10 minutes. Add the zucchini and tomatoes and cook 10 minutes longer.

5. To serve, remove the shanks from the roasting pan. Remove and discard the bay leaves and lemon, taste the braising liquid for salt and pepper, and add as desired. Ladle the stewing liquid, with the rice and vegetables, into individual soup bowls, and place 2 shanks on top of each serving.

VITELLO TONNATO WITH PASTA

SERVES 6

*7*his chilled pot roast of veal flavored with tuna and anchovies is a native of Genoa, but it's a popular summer dish throughout Italy. The veal, which is fairly delicate (some would say bland), should soak up the personality of the braise, so prepare it early in the day, or up to several days in advance to let the flavor develop.

I prefer to buy cuts from free-range veal, which is usually organically raised. The flesh is not nearly as white as the formula-fed veal that we're familiar with, but it has much better flavor. It's not always as tender, but it's never dry. Serve a green salad with garden tomatoes or a dish of chilled broccoli rabe to complete dinner. Any leftovers will make very chic sandwiches.

1 onion, chopped

1 tablespoon minced garlic

½ cup plus 2 tablespoons olive oil

2 pounds veal roast (loin or leg)

1 6¾-ounce can tuna, drained and flaked

24 anchovy fillets

1 cup dry white wine

1 cup chicken stock, canned low-sodium chicken broth, or water

1 teaspoon dried thyme

2 bay leaves

1 teaspoon ground white pepper

½ pound pasta, such as penne or small shells

2 egg yolks

¼ cup capers

2 tablespoons finely chopped fresh parsely

1. Combine the onion, garlic, and 1 tablespoon of the oil in a 2-quart pot and cook over medium heat, stirring, for 5 minutes.

2. Add the veal, tuna, 6 of the anchovies, the wine, stock, thyme, bay leaves, and white pepper. Cover, reduce the heat to low, and cook for 45 to 50 minutes, or until a meat thermometer inserted into the veal measures 135°F. Remove from the heat and let the veal cool to room temperature in the broth.

3. Meanwhile, cook the pasta according to the package directions. Drain, toss with 1 tablespoon of the oil, and let cool. *(continued)*

4. Remove the veal from the cooking liquid and set aside. Boil the cooking liquid over high heat for 5 minutes, or until reduced by half. Transfer the contents of the pot to a bowl and let cool.

5. Remove the bay leaves from the cooking liquid and transfer the contents of the bowl to a food processor. Add the egg yolks and process until smooth. With the motor running, add the remaining ½ cup oil in a slow steady stream, and process until incorporated. Refrigerate the sauce and veal until ready to serve.

6. When it's time to serve dinner, toss the pasta with the capers, parsley, and half of the sauce, and arrange on a large platter. Slice the veal very thin and arrange the slices on the pasta. Spoon the remaining sauce in a ribbon over the veal and garnish with crisscrosses of the remaining anchovies.

VEAL BREAST STUFFED WITH LENTILS AND RICE

SERVES 6

*T*he texture of a well-braised or pot-roasted breast of veal is incomparable. Cook the meat with some moisture and baste frequently. The striated meat needs slow cooking so the fat and gristle melt into a wonderful texture. The result is an incredibly rich-tasting roast with a deliciously caramelized exterior.

When I tested this dinner, I went a bit overboard and ordered a whole breast from the butcher. It was enormous, weighing 14 pounds before boning, about 8½ when boned and trimmed. It was unwieldy to handle and took two of us to stuff and roll. And it barely fit in my largest roasting pan. I was glad, though, that I had cooked the whole thing and did not tire of it for the several days that it took to devour it. You'll most likely want to cook the more manageable quantity that this recipe calls for.

Begin this very rich dinner with a clear vegetable soup. Serve green vegetables or carrots with the breast and a salad after.

¼ pound pancetta, prosciutto, or bacon
3 tablespoons olive oil
1 onion, finely diced (about ¾ cup)
1 tablespoon minced garlic
¼ cup lentils
¼ cup Arborio rice
2 cups chicken stock or canned low-sodium chicken broth
2 tablespoons chopped fresh sage
Salt and freshly ground black pepper to taste
½ boneless veal breast (about 4 to 4½ pounds)
1 cup dry white wine
2 tablespoons fresh lemon juice

1. If using pancetta, unroll it and chop into ¼-inch pieces; or chop the prosciutto or bacon into ¼-inch dice.

2. Heat 1 tablespoon of the oil in a skillet over medium heat. If using pancetta or bacon, add it and cook for 2 minutes (do not add the prosciutto here). Add the onion and garlic and cook, stirring occasionally, 2 minutes. Add the lentils, rice, and stock. Reduce the heat to low, cover, and simmer until the broth is absorbed, about 30 minutes.

3. Scrape the rice mixture into a bowl. Add the sage and salt and pepper, and mix well. If using prosciutto, add it now. Let cool.

4. Lay the veal skin side down on a work surface and trim off any excess interior fat. Spread the stuffing over the veal, leaving a narrow border all around. Roll it up jelly-roll fashion and secure tightly with string.

5. Heat the remaining 2 tablespoons oil in a heavy casserole, just large enough to hold the veal, over medium heat. Add the veal, fat side down, and brown. Add the wine and lemon juice, reduce the heat to low, cover, and cook for 2 to 2½ hours or until the roast is very tender. Baste from time to time with the pan juices; move the roast each time you baste it so it doesn't stick to the bottom of the pan.

6. To serve dinner, untie the veal and slice it into pinwheel rounds. Arrange on a platter and spoon the cooking liquid over the meat.

VEAL BRISKET WITH PANCETTA AND PEAS

SERVES 4

*T*his brisket is inspired by the familiar carbonara, but I've eschewed the eggs and used sour cream or marscapone instead of heavy cream. Serve the veal with ziti or pasta shells. If possible, use pancetta, the cloved, aromatic Italian rolled bacon. You can splurge on these Italian ingredients because veal briskets are relatively inexpensive and a good bargain.

2 tablespoons flavorless vegetable oil
1 small veal brisket (about 2½ pounds)
1 medium onion, diced (about ¾ cup)
2 tablespoons all-purpose flour
1¾ cups chicken stock or canned low-sodium chicken broth
½ teaspoon salt, or to taste
½ teaspoon ground white pepper
3 bay leaves
½ teaspoon ground mace
½ teaspoon curry powder
¼ pound pancetta or thick-cut bacon
3 cups fresh peas or 1 package frozen peas
¼ cup sour cream or mascarpone cheese

1. Heat the oil in a Dutch oven over high heat. Add veal and brown lightly on both sides. Remove and set aside. Reduce heat to medium, add onion, and cook, stirring, until soft, about 3 minutes. Stir in flour and add broth. Cook, stirring, until liquid thickens slightly, about 3 minutes.

2. Replace the veal in the pot and add the salt, pepper, bay leaves, mace, and curry powder. Cover and transfer to the oven. Turn the oven on to 350°F and cook for 1¾ hours, or until the meat is very tender.

3. Meanwhile, if using pancetta, unroll it, cut into ½-inch-wide strips, and then cut the strips into ¼-inch-wide "lardons." If using bacon, cut it into ¼-inch-wide strips. Heat a skillet over medium heat. Add the pancetta or bacon and cook, stirring occasionally, for 4 minutes. Add the peas and cook for 3 minutes if using fresh peas, 5 minutes if using frozen. Remove from the heat, drain off the fat, and keep warm.

4. Remove the veal from the pot and keep warm on a plate. Strain the sauce from the veal into a saucepan or skillet and bring to a boil over medium heat. If using mascarpone, whisk it into the sauce until incorporated; remove from the heat. If using sour cream, place in a mixing bowl. Remove sauce from heat as soon as it boils and beat it into the sour cream. Do not reheat the sauce.

5. Slice the veal into thin slices. (Briskets are usually sold as a single piece with two easily separated sections of meat whose grains run in opposite directions. Cut through the fat that separates the two muscles. Trim well and slice the meat against the grain.) Arrange the veal on a platter. Spoon the pancetta and peas over and around the meat. Spoon the sauce over and serve.

PORK SCALLOPINE WITH LEMON AND CAPERS

SERVES 4

*7*his is a tart and salty preparation. The pork is served with a simple pan sauce made from olive oil and the meat juices. Accompany the pork with sautéed spinach and mashed potatoes.

1¾ pounds boneless pork loin
Salt and freshly ground black pepper to taste
Flour, for dusting
¼ cup olive oil
3 tablespoons fresh lemon juice
¼ cup chicken stock or canned low-sodium chicken broth
3 tablespoons capers, drained
1 tablespoon chopped fresh parsley
8 anchovy fillets

1. Cut the pork into 8 slices and pound each slice between sheets of plastic wrap to flatten it to a ⅜-inch thickness. Sprinkle with salt and pepper. Dust with flour, shaking off the excess.

2. Heat 1 tablespoon of the oil in a nonreactive skillet over medium heat. Add only as many slices of the pork as fit without crowding, and cook for 1½ to 2 minutes per side. Transfer the pork to a plate and keep warm in a 250°F oven while you cook the remaining pork, adding more oil as necessary.

3. Reduce the heat to medium and add any remaining olive oil, the lemon juice, stock, and capers to the skillet. Pour any juices that have accumulated on the plate of pork into the skillet, add salt and pepper as desired, and boil until the liquid has reduced to the consistency of a sauce, about 2 minutes. Immediately remove from the heat and add the chopped parsley.

4. Arrange the pork cutlets on a warm serving platter and spoon the sauce over them. Garnish with the anchovy fillets and serve immediately.

Dinner in the Italian Fashion

PORK SCALLOPINE WITH BROCCOLI RABE

SERVES 4

*I*talian broccoli, or broccoli rabe, is enjoyed as much for its stalks as for its flowering tops. Its flavor is much stronger than that of ordinary broccoli—more peppery and licorice-y. Serve mashed potatoes with this easy pork dish.

¾ *pound broccoli rabe, or broccoli florets from a medium head of broccoli*
1¾ *pounds boneless pork loin*
Salt and freshly ground black pepper to taste
4 to 6 tablespoons olive oil
2 heads Belgian endive, trimmed and cut diagonally into ¾-inch slices
2 tablespoons minced onion
2 tablespoons fresh lemon juice
2 tablespoons dry white wine
2 tablespoons unsalted butter

1. Bring a pot of salted water to the boil. Meanwhile, trim off the bottom ends of the broccoli rabe stems and cut the stalks into ¼-inch rounds. Cut the flowery tops into 1-inch pieces. Fill a bowl with ice water. Blanch the broccoli rabe or florets in the boiling water for 1 minute. Immediately drain and plunge into the ice water. Let cool, and drain on towels, then transfer to a plate and set aside.

2. Cut the pork into 8 slices and pound each slice between sheets of plastic wrap to flatten it to a ⅜-inch thickness. Sprinkle with salt and pepper.

3. Heat 1 tablespoon of the oil over medium heat in a large nonreactive skillet. Add the broccoli and endive and cook, stirring, for about 2 minutes. Add the onion and cook for 1 minute. Add salt to taste, then transfer the vegetables to a serving platter and keep warm in a 250°F oven.

4. Set the skillet over high heat and add another tablespoon of the oil. Add only as many slices of the pork as will fit without crowding and cook for 1½ minutes on each side, adding a scant amount of oil if necessary. Transfer the cutlets to a plate and keep warm in the oven while you cook the remaining pork, adding more oil as necessary.

5. Reduce the heat to medium, and add the lemon juice and wine to the skillet. Cook until the liquid has reduced slightly. Pour any juices that have

collected on the plate of pork into the skillet, remove the skillet from the heat,
and whisk in the butter.

6. Arrange the pork on top of the vegetables; spoon the sauce over.

BRAISED LAMB SHANKS

SERVES 4

*T*hese lamb shanks deserve a grain accompaniment—rice pilaf, couscous, bulgur, or buckwheat. Serve warm vegetables, such as braised endive,
roasted onions, or baked beets with a room-temperature vinaigrette as a
separate course.

2 tablespoons olive oil
4 lamb shanks (about 12 ounces each)
1 medium onion, finely diced (about 1 cup)
2 medium carrots, peeled and finely diced (about ¾ cup)
2 celery stalks, thinly sliced (about 1 cup)
1 tablespoon finely minced garlic
1½ cups dry red wine
1 lemon, cut in half
½ tablespoon salt
½ teaspoon freshly ground black pepper

1. Preheat the oven to 325°F.

2. Heat the olive oil over medium heat in a heavy roasting pan or Dutch
oven large enough to hold the shanks in one layer. Add the shanks and brown
on all sides, about 20 minutes.

3. Pour off all but 2 tablespoons fat from the pan. Add the onion, carrots,
and celery and cook for 5 minutes. Add the garlic, wine, 1½ cups water, the
lemon, salt, and pepper, cover, and transfer to the oven. Cook for 1½ hours,
or until the meat is tender, turning the lamb every 30 minutes and checking
to ensure that the liquid has not evaporated; if the pan seems dry, add
additional water as necessary.

4. To serve, transfer the shanks to a platter. Strain the sauce through a
fine sieve and discard the vegetables. Skim off and discard the fat from the
surface of the braising liquid, and serve with the shanks.

STUFFED FLANK STEAK
WITH CREAMY POLENTA

SERVES 4

*F*lank steak is a great cut for braising. In this dish, it's stuffed with a mushroom puree and braised in a broth accented by sun-dried tomatoes. The beef roulades are sliced and put back in the braising liquid to soak up even more flavor, then served with soft polenta.

¾ pound white mushrooms
1 medium onion, roughly diced
1 tablespoon salt, or to taste
½ teaspoon ground white pepper
1 1½- to 1¾-pound flank steak
1 cup chicken stock or canned low-sodium chicken broth
⅓ cup sun-dried tomatoes
2 tablespoons olive oil
1 cup fresh or frozen corn kernels
1¼ cups coarse yellow cornmeal

1. Combine the mushrooms and onion in a food processor and process to a puree. Add 1 teaspoon of the salt and ¼ teaspoon of the pepper and pulse to mix. Scrape into a skillet and cook over medium heat, stirring occasionally, until all the moisture has evaporated and the mixture is dry, about 15 minutes. Remove from the heat and let cool.

2. Lay the steak on a work surface and, using a sharp knife, slice the steak horizontally into 2 thin steaks. Place each one between two sheets of plastic wrap and flatten with a meat mallet.

3. Spread the mushroom mixture evenly over the steaks, leaving a narrow border all around. Starting at a long end, roll each steak up jelly-roll fashion. Secure with butcher's twine or string.

4. Place the beef roulades in a casserole or baking dish, cover, and place in the oven. Turn the oven on to 350°F and roast for 30 minutes. Add the stock and tomatoes and cook for 45 minutes, turning the beef once. Then remove the twine from the roulades and slice each one into 4 rolls. Place the beef rolls back in the braising liquid and keep warm.

5. Meanwhile, heat the oil in a pot over medium heat. Add the corn and cook for 5 minutes. Add the cornmeal, then slowly stir in 5 cups water. Stir

in the remaining 2 teaspoons salt and ¼ teaspoon pepper. Bring to a boil, reduce the heat to low, and cook for about 15 to 20 minutes, stirring frequently, until the polenta is smooth and creamy.

6. To serve dinner, mound the polenta onto a platter and make a well in the center. Arrange the steak rolls in the well, pour the braising liquid over, and serve immediately.

Asian Flavors

*A*sian cooking is as diverse in its various cuisines as is European cooking. We differentiate easily among Italian, German, and French food, for instance, because we are familiar with the various ingredients and the names of the dishes. We know that wiener schnitzel is Austrian; Italians serve the same piece of veal in a pool of tomato sauce, sprinkled with Parmesan cheese, making it Veal Parmigian; and Hungarian cooks flavor their veal with paprika and call it goulash.

Most of us are familiar enough with Asian cuisines to know the differences between Japanese, Chinese, Thai, and Indian dishes. But we are not so familiar with the subtleties of each of these cuisines.

For many, Asian cooking means a dish of cut-up meats and vegetables, flavored with soy, and served over crisp noodles. Well, I think we can do better than that, given the wealth of Asian products in American food markets and the sophistication of our palates. So, I've distilled a few basic ingredients to create a repertoire of Asian-flavored dishes. For instance, my "Szechuan formula" is a combination of garlic, dried hot chilies, soy, vinegar, and sherry; sometimes I finish the dish with a teaspoon of dark sesame oil. My Thai formula is chopped jalapeño chilies, curry, and coconut milk, always garnished with plenty of fresh cilantro. Fermented black beans, ginger, and coconut milk is another winning combination. For the Indian dishes, I prepare curry in a Western-style sauce or broth.

These dinners are Western culinary musings with an Asian flavor, variations on a theme meant to provide you with meals that don't depend on a trip to Chinatown, or a browse through a mail-order catalogue. I doubt that your local supermarket stocks thousand-year-old eggs, so there are no recipes that call for them. In my market, I'm lucky to be able to find 5-spice powder, various soy sauces, dark and light miso paste, fresh loquats, bok choy, and tamarind. But most of the time you can satisfactorily substitute for these exotic ingredients. If your spice cabinet is missing 5-spice powder, use a combination of fennel seed, clove, cinnamon, and pepper. You can air-dry fresh ducks yourself if you like, but it's unlikely that you will, so you can steam the duck before roasting for similar effect. You can stir-fry in a cast-iron skillet if you have the patience to do it in batches so that the skillet doesn't cool down too much. Understand that all ingredients are cut small so they cook quickly, evenly, and in the same amount of time.

CHINESE OMELETTES AND NOODLES IN BROTH

SERVES 4

*E*gg foo yung, a Milky Way of veggies and meat suspended in eggs, had already disappeared from hip Chinese restaurant menus when I rediscovered it. The Chinese kitchen staff of the restaurant where I worked often prepared it for themselves for dinner. A few eggs and a bowl of noodles with some broth made a soothing dinner. Here's my version of that much-envied meal.

Add cornstarch to the beaten eggs to help the omelettes puff when fried in oil. Drain them well on towels before serving. Almond cookies or fortune cookies are the perfect dessert.

>   ½ to ¾ cup peanut oil
>   ½ cup bean sprouts
>   2 celery stalks, thinly sliced
>   8 snow peas, cut into fine julienne strips
>   ¼ cup thinly sliced scallions
>   ½ pound ham, diced
>   5 tablespoons soy sauce
>   1 tablespoon cornstarch
>   9 eggs, beaten
>   ½ pound fresh Chinese noodles or fresh angel hair pasta

1 tablespoon dark sesame oil
1 tablespoon minced garlic
2 teaspoons minced fresh ginger
¼ teaspoon red pepper flakes
2 cups chicken stock or canned low-sodium chicken broth
1 cup bottled clam juice
2 tablespoons rice wine vinegar or white wine vinegar
¼ cup dry sherry
2 cups shredded iceberg lettuce
Cilantro (fresh coriander), for garnish

1. Heat 1 teaspoon of the oil in a wok or skillet over high heat. When the pan is nearly smoking hot, add the bean sprouts, celery, and snow peas. Cook, stirring constantly, for 1 minute. Immediately transfer the vegetables to a large bowl.

2. Add the scallions, ham, and 2 tablespoons of the soy sauce to the vegetables. Sprinkle in the cornstarch and mix well. Add the eggs and ¼ cup water and mix well.

3. Cook the noodles in boiling salted water for 5 minutes. Drain and keep warm.

4. Combine the sesame oil, garlic, and ginger in a large pot and heat over low heat for 1 minute. Add the pepper flakes, stock, clam juice, vinegar, sherry, and the remaining 2 tablespoons soy sauce. Cover, increase the heat to medium, and boil for 5 minutes. Remove from the heat and keep warm.

5. Heat about ⅜ inch of peanut oil in a large skillet over high heat. Add a generous ⅓ cup of the egg mixture and cook until the edges of the omelette puff, about 1 minute. Flip the omelette over and cook for about 30 seconds. Remove the omelette and place on towels to drain, cover and keep warm while you prepare the rest of the omelettes, adding more oil to the pan as necessary.

6. Divide the noodles and broth among four soup bowls. Make a bed of the shredded iceberg lettuce in each bowl and arrange the omelettes on top. Toss some cilantro on top and serve immediately.

GARLIC SHRIMP AND PASTA

SERVES 4

*W*oks were invented for utilizing heat most efficiently. They have a larger surface area than our European-style frying pans and so they will cook a greater quantity of ingredients at one time. However, all the ingredients must be cut in just the right size so that the heat penetrates them and cooks them quickly and evenly. Do all your peeling, paring, chopping, and slicing before you start cooking. Measure out all quantities and set everything out near the stove. Once you begin cooking, you'll have no time to stop for something you've forgotten.

Serve this quick stir-fry over pasta or rice.

1 small zucchini

1 teaspoon cornstarch

⅓ cup dry sherry

2 tablespoons soy sauce

2 tablespoons fresh lemon juice

½ pound pasta, such as spaghetti, linguine, or fettuccine

3 tablespoons peanut oil

2 red bell peppers, cored, seeded, and sliced into ⅜-inch-wide strips

1 pound large shrimp, peeled, deveined, and cut lengthwise into quarters

1 tablespoon finely minced garlic

½ pound white mushrooms, cut into ¼-inch slices

1. Trim off the ends of the zucchini and cut the zucchini into 1-inch lengths; then cut each piece lengthwise into ½-inch-thick sticks. Set aside.

2. Place the cornstarch in a small bowl. Slowly add the sherry, soy sauce, and lemon juice and stir until the cornstarch is dissolved. Set aside.

3. Cook the pasta in a large pot of boiling salted water according to the package directions. Drain.

4. While the pasta is cooking, heat the oil in a wok or large skillet over high heat. When the wok is very hot, add the peppers, shrimp, and garlic and cook, stirring, for 2 minutes, or until the garlic is golden. Add the mushrooms and zucchini and cook for 1 minute. Add the cornstarch mixture and cook until the sauce is thickened, about 30 seconds. Remove from the heat.

5. Arrange the pasta on a serving platter. Scrape the shrimp, vegetables, and sauce over the top, and serve immediately.

SCALLOPS AND GRAPEFRUIT FRIED RICE

SERVES 4

*F*ried rice is a dish of leftovers—rice and bits of vegetables or whatever. Improvise additions to this dinner with odds and ends from your refrigerator. A little ham or bacon would be good, as well as most vegetables. Day-old or leftover rice works best, or you can prepare rice early in the day and refrigerate it for a few hours before using in this recipe.

2 cups chilled cooked long-grain rice
¼ cup soy sauce
3 tablespoons peanut oil
1 small onion, finely diced
1 ear of corn, kernels removed, or ½ cup frozen corn, thawed
1 small red bell pepper, finely chopped
½ pound snow peas, finely chopped
1 tablespoon dark sesame oil (optional)
1½ pounds bay scallops
½ cup grapefruit juice
2 tablespoons unsalted butter

1. Toss the rice with the soy sauce and set aside.

2. Heat 2 tablespoons of the oil in a large skillet. Add the onion and cook for 1 minute. Add the corn and red pepper and cook, stirring, for 2 minutes. Add the snow peas and cook for 30 seconds. Add the rice and cook, stirring, for about 5 minutes. Remove from the heat and stir in the sesame oil, if desired. Shape the rice mixture into a ring on a serving platter. Keep warm in a 250°F oven while you cook the scallops.

3. Heat the remaining 1 tablespoon oil in a large nonreactive skillet over high heat until almost smoking hot. Add the scallops and cook for about 2 minutes, without stirring. Then, using a wooden spoon, stir to loosen the scallops from the bottom of the skillet. Add the grapefruit juice and cook for about 30 seconds. Using a slotted spoon, transfer the scallops to a plate. Reduce the heat to medium and boil the grapefruit juice until it has reduced by half and begun to thicken, about 5 minutes. Replace the scallops in the skillet, along with any juices that have collected on the plate. Cook for 30 seconds, remove from the heat, and whisk in the butter.

4. Spoon the scallops and sauce into the center of the rice ring, and serve immediately.

CURRIED HALIBUT WITH EGGPLANT CAVIAR

SERVES 4

*E*ggplant is native to India, but that's not why it's paired with curry sauce in this dinner. The mash of eggplant and olive oil that's called eggplant caviar (the many seeds in the puree look like so much fish roe) is deliciously acrid and contrasts with the sweetly aromatic curry.

Serve a sauté of peppers and tomatoes. Now dinner consists of three of the most commonly eaten members of the nightshade family. Potatoes are another, but you should resist the impulse and serve rice, a more appropriate accompaniment.

1 medium eggplant (about 1¼ pounds)
3 tablespoons olive oil
1 tablespoon minced garlic
2 tablespoons chopped fresh dill or 1 tablespoon dried
1 teaspoon salt, or to taste
½ teaspoon freshly ground black pepper, or to taste
½ cup dry white wine
1 small onion, sliced
1 celery stalk, roughly chopped
4 7-ounce halibut steaks or fillets
2 tablespoons curry powder
½ cup heavy cream
1 tablespoon unsalted butter

1. Prick the eggplant in a few places with a fork, place in a baking dish, and place in the oven. Turn the oven on to 425°F and bake, turning once, until the eggplant is shriveled and the skin looks burnt, about 35 minutes.

2. Transfer the eggplant to a work surface and let cool for about 10 minutes to make handling easier. Slit open the eggplant, scoop out all the seeds and flesh, and place in a bowl. Discard the skin.

3. Combine the olive oil and garlic in a small saucepan and cook over medium heat until the garlic turns light golden, about 3 minutes. Pour the garlic oil over the eggplant, and, using two forks, mash the eggplant until no large chunks of flesh remain. Add the dill, salt, and pepper and mix well. Scrape into an ovenproof bowl, cover, and place in a 250°F oven to keep warm while you poach the fish.

4. Combine the wine, ½ cup water, the onion, and celery in a large stainless steel pan and bring to a boil over high heat. Reduce the heat to low, add the halibut, cover, and simmer for 5 minutes, or until just cooked through. Transfer the halibut to a plate, cover, and place in the oven to keep warm.

5. Add the curry powder and cream to the fish poaching liquid, increase the heat to medium, and boil until the liquid reduces to the consistency of a sauce, about 10 minutes. Remove from the heat and whisk in the butter. Strain the sauce, discarding the onion and celery.

6. Mound the eggplant caviar on a warm serving platter and arrange the halibut fillets around it. Spoon the sauce over the fish.

Curry Powder

Originally a fairly simple combination of cardamom, ginger, pepper, mustard seed, and turmeric, curry powder has undergone changes that tell the history of a civilization looking east, north, and west. The spice trade from the East to Europe transformed curry powder into the concoction that we know today. Nutmeg, mace, and cloves were brought in from the Indonesian archipelago, coriander and cumin from the West. Fenugreek (the principal flavoring in imitation maple syrup), included in every recipe for curry that I've read, is native to southern Europe and Asia. The chile peppers that determine the heat of a curry were added only after their introduction from America at the end of the sixteenth century.

When adding it to a dish, cook curry powder first in a little of your oil or broth, allowing the flavors to blossom before you add the remainder of the liquid. Cooking it for a long time mellows the flavor without weakening it. I nearly always add fresh dill whenever I'm using commercial curry powder; it takes away an unpleasant stale quality.

PAN-FRIED MARINATED CATFISH

SERVES 4

*C*atfish are big business in the Southeast, where they are being farmed in manmade lakes. Since these fish don't have to scavenge on the muddy bottoms of rivers and lakes, their flavor is sweet, without any of the murky taste that traditionally makes catfish obvious candidates for breading in cornmeal and frying. And this new, improved version is firm-fleshed and will not fall apart when cooked.

Catfish is much used in Chinese cooking, where it's usually fried or cooked whole in a covered wok. Dredging in cornstarch gives the fish a dark golden coating and stops it from soaking up oil during frying.

3 tablespoons soy sauce
1½ cups fresh orange juice
3 tablespoons minced fresh ginger or 1 tablespoon ground
4 6- to 7-ounce catfish fillets
3 tablespoons unsalted butter
1 tablespoon grated orange zest
Cornstarch, for dredging
⅓ cup flavorless vegetable oil
1 tablespoon finely chopped fresh parsley

1. Combine the soy sauce, ½ cup of the orange juice, and the ginger in a nonreactive pan or shallow bowl. Add the catfish, cover, and refrigerate for at least 2 hours or up to 6, turning the fish occasionally in the marinade.

2. When it's time for dinner, place the remaining 1 cup orange juice in a saucepan and cook over medium heat until reduced by about half. Remove from the heat and whisk in the butter. Stir in the zest, cover, and keep warm.

3. Remove the fillets from the marinade and pat dry with a towel; discard the marinade. Dust the fillets with cornstarch, shaking off the excess.

4. Heat the oil in a 10-inch skillet over medium heat. When the oil is hot, add 2 of the catfish fillets. Fry until golden, about 3 minutes, then turn and fry until just cooked through, about 3 to 4 minutes depending on the thickness of the fillet. Drain on towels and keep warm in a low oven while you cook the remaining 2 fillets.

5. To serve, pour the sauce over the bottom of a warm platter. Arrange the catfish on top and garnish with the chopped parsley.

STEAK AND ONION STIR-FRY

SERVES 4

*7*his stir-fry is sure to please. The onions caramelize in the hot, dry wok and turn sweet, a delicious complement to the seared steak.

1½ cups long-grain rice

3 medium onions, peeled

1 teaspoon cornstarch

3 tablespoons soy sauce

¼ cup Madeira or dry sherry

¼ cup canned low-sodium chicken broth

2 tablespoons flavorless vegetable oil

1 pound beef tenderloin, cut into ½-inch-thick slices

1 teaspoon minced garlic

2 tomatoes, cut into 1-inch cubes

1. Bring 2¼ cups salted water to a boil in a medium pot. Stir in the rice, cover, and simmer for 15 to 20 minutes, or until the rice is tender and the liquid has been absorbed. Remove from the heat and keep warm.

2. Meanwhile, cut the onions in half lengthwise, lay each half cut side down, and cut into ¼-inch slivers. Combine the cornstarch, soy sauce, Madeira, and broth in a small bowl and stir to dissolve the cornstarch. Set aside.

3. Heat the oil in a wok or large skillet over high heat. When nearly smoking hot, add the onions and cook, stirring for 2 minutes. Remove from the wok and set aside. Add the steak and garlic and cook, stirring constantly, for 2 minutes. Add the tomatoes and the cornstarch mixture and cook until the sauce has thickened, about 1 minute. Return the onions to the wok and heat through. Remove from the heat.

4. To serve, arrange the rice in a ring on a serving platter. Spoon the steak and onions into the center. Serve immediately.

Asian Flavors

POACHED CHICKEN BREASTS
IN BLACK BEAN SAUCE

SERVES 4

*7*he white meat of chicken should always be poached in barely simmering liquid; when cooked at temperatures above 150°F, chicken gets chalky in texture and loses all juiciness.

The taste of fermented Chinese beans in this dish is pervasive, overpowering, and reduces the other flavors in the sauce to mere accents. If you cannot find these special black beans, don't make any substitution. The accent flavors—sherry, garlic, and ginger—will become the focus, and although the dish will be different, it will still be delicious.

> *¼ cup fermented Chinese black beans*
> *1 pound snow peas*
> *¼ cup dry sherry*
> *1 cup chicken stock or canned low-sodium chicken broth*
> *2 tablespoons finely minced garlic*
> *2 tablespoons finely minced fresh ginger or 1 tablespoon ground*
> *4 boneless skinless chicken breast halves*
> *3 tablespoons vegetable oil*
> *2 tablespoons dark sesame oil (optional)*
> *Cilantro (fresh coriander), for garnish*

1. Soak the black beans in water to cover for 15 minutes. Drain.

2. Meanwhile, fill a bowl with ice water. Cook the snow peas in boiling salted water for 30 seconds. Immediately drain and plunge into the ice water to chill, then drain and dry on a towel. Cut lengthwise into thin julienne strips and set aside.

3. Combine the black beans and sherry in a 2-quart saucepan and cook for 1 minute over high heat. Add the stock, garlic, and ginger and bring almost to a boil. Reduce the heat to low, add the chicken breasts, cover, and simmer for 3 minutes. Remove from the heat and let cool, covered, to room temperature.

4. Transfer the chicken breasts to a plate and return the pan to the stove. Bring to a simmer over medium heat and cook, uncovered, for 5 minutes, or until the liquid has reduced by one third. Transfer the black bean mixture to a blender. With the blender set at medium, slowly add the vegetable oil and then, if desired, the sesame oil. Serve warm or let cool to room temperature.

5. When it's time to put dinner on the table, pour the sauce onto a serving platter, and heap the snow peas in the center of the platter. Slice the chicken diagonally across the grain into thin strips, and fan the chicken breasts around the snow peas. Garnish with cilantro.

SAUTÉED CHICKEN BREASTS WITH GINGER AND MINT

SERVES 4

*W*hen boldly flavored dishes are cooked quickly, as is the case here, all the different flavors remain vital. Serve with some vegetables quickly stir-fried or sautéed just until crisp-tender and simple steamed rice.

1 tablespoon flavorless vegetable oil
4 boneless skinless chicken breast halves
1 tablespoon finely minced onion or shallots
½ cup dry white wine
1 cup chicken stock or canned low-sodium chicken broth
1 tablespoon finely minced fresh ginger or 2 teaspoons ground
4 tablespoons unsalted butter
2 tablespoons soy sauce
2 teaspoons chopped fresh mint

1. Heat the oil in a large skillet over high heat. Add the chicken breasts and cook for 2 minutes on each side. Add the onion, wine, stock, and ginger and cook until the liquid has reduced by half, about 4 minutes.

2. Remove the skillet from the heat and whisk in the butter. Stir in the soy sauce.

3. Transfer to a serving platter, sprinkle with the mint, and put dinner on the table.

Asian Flavors

ROAST SQUAB

SERVES 4

*O*f all the farm-raised game birds available in the market today—squab, quail, and pheasant are the most common—squab taste most like their wild counterpart.

Here the birds are garnished with crisp toasts spread with liver puree and accompanied with a red wine sauce. Serve with vegetables such as celery, zucchini, snow peas, and carrots, cut into julienne sticks and sautéed with bean sprouts.

1 teaspoon fennel seed
⅛ teaspoon ground cinnamon
⅛ teaspoon ground cloves
½ tablespoon salt, or more to taste
½ teaspoon cayenne pepper
4 14- to 16-ounce squab
8 garlic cloves, peeled
1 medium onion, peeled and cut into 8 wedges
8 bay leaves
8 small sprigs fresh thyme or ½ tablespoon dried
8 squab and/or chicken livers
¼ cup olive oil
1 cup dry red wine
8 slices French bread
2 tablespoons unsalted butter, at room temperature

1. Preheat the oven to 375°F.

2. Crush the fennel seed with a large knife or grind it in a spice grinder. Combine with the cinnamon, cloves, salt, and cayenne pepper.

3. Rinse the squab under cold running water and pat dry. Place 2 garlic cloves, 2 wedges of onion, 2 bay leaves, 2 thyme sprigs (or one quarter of the dried thyme), and 2 livers in the cavity of each bird. Rub the squab all over with the oil and then with the spice mixture. Tuck the wings under the birds, tie the legs together and arrange breast side down in a roasting pan. Roast, uncovered, for 15 minutes. Turn the birds over, pour the wine into the pan, and roast for another 15 minutes.

4. Meanwhile, arrange the bread on a baking sheet and place in the oven to dry out, about 10 minutes. Set aside.

5. Transfer the squab to a platter. Set aside the pan of cooking juices. When the squab are cool enough to handle, remove the onion, garlic, and livers from the cavities and cool to room temperature. Cover the squab and keep warm.

6. Place the onion, garlic, and livers in a blender or mini processor, add 2 tablespoons of the butter, and process until smooth. Taste for salt and add as desired. Spread the puree on the toasts and set aside.

7. Place the roasting pan over medium-high heat, bring the cooking liquid to a boil, and cook until it has reduced by about one third. Remove from the heat and whisk in the remaining 2 tablespoons butter. Transfer to a sauceboat.

8. To serve, arrange the squab on a serving platter, and arrange the toasts around them. Pass the sauce separately.

DUCK LEGS IN GINGER BROTH

SERVES 4

*T*his wonderful dish is somewhat time-consuming to make, but none of the techniques is beyond the realm of the average cook. The duck legs must be salted at least a day ahead.

Begin the dinner with fried rice or a pasta.

8 duck legs
3 tablespoons kosher salt
1 teaspoon black peppercorns
1 bulb garlic, cut in half crosswise
6 bay leaves
1 tablespoon chopped fresh thyme
4 cups chicken stock or canned low-sodium chicken broth
1 tablespoon peeled and finely slivered fresh ginger
1½ cups chopped sorrel leaves
3 tomatoes, seeded and chopped
1½ cups diced tofu (cut into ½-inch dice)
½ cup bean sprouts
Salt and freshly ground black pepper to taste

1. Sprinkle the duck legs with the kosher salt and refrigerate overnight or up to 2 days.

2. Rinse the duck legs, pat dry, and place skin side up in a deep baking dish just large enough to hold the legs tightly in one layer. Scatter the peppercorns, garlic, bay leaves, and thyme over the duck. Cover tightly, place in the oven, and turn on the oven to 300°F. Roast for 2½ hours.

3. Remove the duck legs from the fat. (The legs can be cooked several days in advance.) Strain the fat, discarding the solids, and reserve for another use (see Note).

4. Meanwhile, place the chicken stock in a large pot, bring to a boil over high heat, and boil until reduced to 3 cups. Set aside.

5. When it's time to put dinner on the table, preheat the boiler. Place the duck legs, skin side up, under the broiler to crisp the skin, about 2 minutes. Meanwhile, add the ginger, sorrel, tomatoes, tofu, sprouts, and salt and pepper to the hot broth and let steep for 1 minute. Arrange 2 duck legs in each soup bowl and ladle the soup out at the table.

NOTE: When your order duck legs from your poultry dealer, order a lot and salt and cook them all. They're good in many things other than this soup and any extras will keep, covered in duck fat, for up to one month in the refrigerator or up to four months in the freezer. Add the meat to chili, gumbo, or cassoulet and other bean casseroles. The legs are good in salads or just by themselves. Place any extra legs in a crock and pour the strained cooking fat over them.

ROAST DUCK WITH ORANGES

SERVES 2 TO 3

*I*f it were practical, we would air-dry ducks at home, forcing air between the flesh and the skin, and then hang them in a large oven by their necks so that the fat bathed the flesh as the bird roasted. Alas, it's not, so poach the duck before roasting to ensure a crisp, fatless bird.

> 1 4- to 5-pound duck
> 1 small head Napa cabbage
> 2 oranges
> 4 cloves
> 1 cinnamon stick or 1 teaspoon ground cinnamon
> 6 star anise or 1 tablespoon aniseed
> ½ cup soy sauce
> 1 head garlic, cut in half crosswise
> 1 onion (unpeeled), cut in half
> 2 tablespoons unsalted butter

1. Truss the duck.

2. Cut the cabbage in half lengthwise and cut out and discard the core. Grate the zest of 1 of the oranges and set aside. Section both oranges and set the sections aside. Finely shred the cabbage and set aside.

3. Combine the cloves, cinnamon, anise, soy sauce, garlic, onion, and 6 cups water in a large pot and bring to a boil over high heat. Add the duck, breast side down, reduce the heat to medium, cover, and simmer gently for 45 minutes, turning the duck once.

4. Meanwhile, preheat the oven to 350°F. *(continued)*

5. Remove the duck from the poaching liquid and place on a rack in a roasting pan. Roast for 1 hour. Pour off any fat that has collected in the roasting pan, scatter the cabbage around the duck, and roast for another 20 minutes, stirring the cabbage occasionally.

6. Meanwhile, skim all the fat from the surface of the duck poaching liquid. Strain the liquid into a pot and discard the solids. Bring to a simmer over medium heat and cook, uncovered, until the liquid has reduced to about ½ cup, about 1 hour; skim off the fat occasionally. Remove from the heat and set aside.

7. To serve, add the grated zest and the orange sections to the reduced sauce and reheat. Then remove from the heat and swirl in the butter.

8. Transfer the duck to a serving platter and surround it with the cabbage. Carve at the table and serve the sauce on the side.

Mexican Nights

The search for pepper brought the first Europeans to the New World. Instead, the Spaniards found, among the great civilizations of Central and South America, a cuisine based on corn and beans. They discovered, and brought back to the Old World, corn, tomatoes, potatoes, turkey, chocolate, vanilla, and chilies—but no pepper.

When most of us think of Mexican food today, we think of enchiladas and burritos—Mexican street food or snacks, basically tortillas filled with a little cheese or meat and moistened with some sauce. Authentic Mexican dinners are based on simple, fresh ingredients prepared in a straightforward way. Since most meats and poultry are tougher and stringier than their north-of-the border counterparts, braising is the cooking method of choice. A mostly peasant cuisine, Mexican cooking is richer in stews than in roasts. Grilling is also popular, especially for seafood.

And, despite our unfortunate familiarity with the greasy side, Mexican cooking is basically a healthful cuisine employing lots of corn, beans, and vegetables. Salsas mostly consist of chopped fresh tomatoes or tomatillos mixed with some chilies and onion. Other sauces are simply flavorful braising liquids thickened with tomato, tomatillo, or dried or fresh chile peppers.

But there is also subtlety and reason to Mexican cooking. The beans and corn that are the core of this cuisine are meant to foil the more spicy ingredients.

The omnipresent beans may be flavored with epazote (dried oregano is an acceptable substitute), perhaps a hint of cumin (please, not the deadly amount that most Mexican restaurants here use), and just a taste of chile— they're supposed to be mild.

Dairy products are little used in true Mexican cooking, often merely to accent the presentation of a dish—a dollop of sour cream, for example, smoothes the heat of certain fiery salsas. Mexican cheeses tend to be dry, salty, and mild. They're usually served in quesadillas or with eggs. Dairy products became part of the culinary picture only after livestock was introduced to the continent by the Europeans; traditional Mexican cooking uses corn oil or lard.

These are dinner improvisations with a Mexican style—there are writers more knowledgeable than I who can present a more accurate and complete guide to the fabulous cooking of this ancient country. Some, like the cheese-fried chicken breasts, are my own creations. Others are my interpretations of authentic dishes, like the fava and tripe stew. You needn't track down the most esoteric ingredients to make delicious Mexican dinners. Some purists will scream at me for not respecting to the letter a cuisine rich in tradition and based on regional products, but this is a peasant cuisine, and what's most respected in peasant cuisines is resourcefulness.

Two Salsas

S alsa is to a Mexican meal as ketchup is to hamburgers. Here are two recipes to start with.

GREEN SALSA

MAKES 1½ CUPS

10 tomatillos, husks removed
1 serrano or 2 jalapeño peppers, halved lengthwise and seeded
½ red onion, finely diced
2 tablespoons chopped cilantro (fresh coriander)
2 tablespoons fresh lemon juice
2 tablespoons olive oil
Salt to taste

1. Bring a large pot of salted water to a boil. Add the tomatillos and chile pepper(s), cover, and cook for 2 minutes. Drain.

2. Puree the tomatillos and chilies in a food processor. Strain into a bowl and discard solids. Add onion, cilantro, lemon juice, oil, and salt. Chill. Serve.

RED SALSA

MAKES 1½ CUPS

2 tablespoons flavorless vegetable oil
10 plum tomatoes, cut in half
1 red bell pepper, roughly diced
1 carrot, peeled and roughly diced
3 garlic cloves, peeled
2 serrano or 4 jalapeño peppers, halved lengthwise and seeded
½ red onion, finely minced
2 tablespoons fresh lemon juice
Salt to taste

1. Heat the oil in a large skillet over medium heat. Add the tomatoes, bell peppers, carrot, garlic, and chilies. Add ¼ cup water, cover, and cook for 20 minutes, or until the vegetables are very soft.

2. Transfer the contents of the pan to a food processor and puree. Strain into a bowl and discard the solids. (Or pass through a food mill.) Refrigerate.

3. When chilled, stir in the chopped onion, lemon juice, and salt. Serve.

Mexican Nights

CHILAQUILES

SERVES 4

*T*his is a dish of cut-up tortillas soaked in eggs, then all scrambled together. You can add shredded cooked beef, pork, or chicken, or leave it vegetarian. Meatless or not, this dinner wants a big vegetable salad to open—or perhaps a chilled gazpacho or corn soup.

6 eggs
4 corn tortillas, cut into 8 wedges each
2 avocados
2 tomatoes
¼ cup lime juice
¼ cup olive oil
Salt and freshly ground black pepper to taste
2 tablespoons unsalted butter or margarine
1 cup diced or shredded cooked beef, chicken, or pork (optional)
2 onions, finely diced (about 1½ cups)
1 teaspoon chili powder
½ teaspoon ground cumin
Cilantro (fresh coriander), for garnish

1. Break the eggs into a large bowl and beat them lightly. Add the tortillas and let sit for 15 minutes.

2. Meanwhile, cut the avocados in half lengthwise, and remove the pits. Using a paring knife, slice the flesh in each half lengthwise into ½-inch slices without cutting through the skin. Using a large spoon, scoop the flesh out of the skin in one piece. Lay one half, cut side down, on each plate and fan out the slices. Cut the tomatoes into thin slices and arrange next to the avocado on each plate. Drizzle with the lime juice and oil, and sprinkle with salt and pepper.

3. Heat the butter in a large skillet over medium heat. Add the meat, if desired, onions, chili powder, and cumin. Cook, stirring occasionally, for 5 minutes. Add the eggs and tortillas and cook, stirring, until the eggs are cooked to desired doneness.

4. Arrange a mound of eggs on each plate next to the avocado and tomatoes and garnish with cilantro. Serve immediately.

SEAFOOD POSOLE

SERVES 4

*T*his is a dark, tomato-y stew that's discreetly flavored with hints of cocoa, cumin, Pernod, and cinnamon. It's a combination that you'll find seductive.

Posole (called hominy in this country) is made by soaking corn in an alkaline mixture such as unslaked lime or wood ash and cooking it until it puffs up. Its soft texture enables it to soak up flavor when it cooks, so it tastes a little different in every dish. Uncooked dried posole is ground into flour called masa harina (hominy flour) and used to make tortillas and tamales.

1 tablespoon olive oil
1 small onion, diced
3 tablespoons finely minced garlic
Pinch of ground cloves
2 tablespoons cocoa powder
1 teaspoon ground cumin
2 jalapeño peppers, seeded and diced
2 cups fish stock, bottled clam juice, or chicken stock or canned
   low-sodium chicken broth
3 tablespoons Pernod
1 cinnamon stick or ¼ teaspoon ground cinnamon
Salt to taste
1 14½-ounce canned stewed tomatoes
1 15½-ounce can posole (hominy)
10 ounces skinless fish fillets (from a firm-fleshed white fish such as
   snapper, halibut, or sea bass), cut into chunks
8 jumbo shrimp
8 clams, scrubbed
8 mussels, scrubbed and debearded
1 cup fresh or frozen corn kernels
8 sprigs cilantro (fresh coriander), for garnish

1. Combine the olive oil, onion, and garlic in a large pot and cook for 2 minutes over medium heat. Add the cloves, cocoa powder, cumin, and jalapeños and cook for 1 minute. Add the fish stock, Pernod, cinnamon, and salt and bring to a boil. Reduce the heat and simmer, uncovered, for 25 minutes. *(continued)*

Mexican Nights

2. Strain the broth into a clean pot and discard the solids. Add the tomatoes and their liquid and the posole and its liquid to the broth and cook over medium heat for 10 minutes.

3. Add all the seafood and the corn, cover, and cook until the clams and mussels open, about 7 minutes. Discard any unopened shells.

4. Transfer the stew to a large tureen and garnish with the sprigs of cilantro.

SHELLFISH GAZPACHO

SERVES 4

*G*azpacho is such a favorite of mine that I sometimes think it alone will satisfy as a meal. Wrong. It just starts the juices flowing. When I order it in a restaurant I usually end up having a seafood dinner. And a second bowl of gazpacho to go with it. This seafood gazpacho combines them both.

3 to 4 tablespoons olive oil

8 large shrimp, peeled and deveined

8 large scallops

8 small clams (such as littlenecks or Manilas), scrubbed

8 mussels, scrubbed and debearded

1 cup dry white wine

2 tablespoons sherry vinegar

1 small onion, chopped (about ½ cup)

2 tablespoons plus 1 teaspoon minced garlic

1 medium cucumber, peeled and seeded

2 dashes Tabasco sauce, or more to taste

3 cups tomato juice

¼ cup mayonnaise

Salt and freshly ground black pepper to taste

2 large red bell peppers

8 slices French bread

1. Heat 2 tablespoons of the olive oil in a skillet over medium heat. Add the shrimp and scallops, cover, and cook until cooked through, about 4 minutes. Remove the shrimp and scallops and place in the refrigerator to chill. Add the clams, mussels, wine, vinegar, onion, and 2 tablespoons of the garlic to the pan, cover, increase the heat to high, and cook until the clams and mussels open, about 5 minutes. Remove from the heat. Remove the clams and mussels from the pan, discarding any unopened ones, and place in the refrigerator to chill. Transfer the contents of the pan to a food processor or blender.

2. Add the cucumber, remaining 1 teaspoon garlic, the Tabasco, and 1 cup of the tomato juice to the cooking liquid and process until smooth. Add the mayonnaise and process until well incorporated. Add salt and pepper to taste. Pour the gazpacho into a bowl, stir in the remaining 2 cups tomato juice, and refrigerate until well chilled.

3. Meanwhile, preheat the broiler. *(continued)*

Mexican Nights

4. Roast the peppers and remove the skin and seeds (see page 203). Cut each pepper in half lengthwise. Refrigerate. Brush the slices of bread with the remaining olive oil. Toast them under the broiler, turning once, until golden brown. Set aside to cool.

5. When it's time for dinner, place a pepper half in each soup bowl and arrange 2 shrimp and 2 scallops in each pepper half. Spoon the gazpacho around the peppers and add the clams and mussels. Place 2 croutons on top of the shrimp and scallops in each bowl, and serve immediately.

PAELLA

SERVES 6 TO 8

*P*aella, a Spanish creation that became a classic in Veracruz, was originally prepared over an open fire in the fields during harvest. So it's a one-dish meal and easy to put together.

You must use short-grain rice to create this remarkable dish. Vary the other ingredients—they don't really matter that much as long as they're cooked with the proper rice. After all, this is peasant food, and it's meant to feed a crowd of people easily. You probably don't own a *paella*, the skillet whose name lent itself to the dish, but you can use a large roasting pan with fine results.

¼ cup olive oil
3 pounds chicken pieces
1 large onion, diced
3 red bell peppers, diced
1 tablespoon minced garlic
1½ cups short-grain rice, such as Arborio
2 teaspoons salt
1 teaspoon ground white pepper
4 to 4½ cups chicken stock or canned low-sodium chicken broth
½ teaspoon saffron threads or powder
3 pounds plum tomatoes, peeled, seeded, and chopped
   (about 3 cups)
12 large shrimp
12 clams, scrubbed
12 mussels, scrubbed and debearded
Lemon wedges, for garnish

1. Preheat the oven to 350°F.

2. Heat the oil in a large skillet over medium heat. Add the chicken, in batches if necessary, and brown well on all sides. Transfer to a plate. Drain off the fat from the skillet and add the onion and peppers. Cook for 5 minutes, stirring occasionally. Remove from the heat, add the garlic, rice, salt, and pepper, and stir to coat the rice with the oil. Transfer the contents of the skillet to a roasting pan.

3. Meanwhile, bring 4 cups of the chicken stock to a boil.

4. Add the boiling stock, saffron, and tomatoes to the roasting pan and arrange the chicken on top. Cover and bake for 25 minutes. Add the shrimp and bake, uncovered, for 10 minutes longer. If the rice seems dry, add a little more stock or water. Add the clams and mussels and cook until they open, about 8 minutes. Discard any unopened shells.

5. Remove from the oven and serve immediately, garnished with lemon wedges.

CHEESE-STUFFED CHICKEN BREASTS
WITH CHILE SAUCE

SERVES 4

*I*f chicken Kiev were resurrected south of the border, this is what it would look and taste like. It's a more satisfying dish to prepare than the original, though, because it comes out right every time. You don't have to worry about the butter leaking out during cooking, or being absorbed by the chicken if it sits a minute too long before serving. This chicken always oozes cheese.

This is an easy dish for a party because after you fry the stuffed chicken breasts they can sit for up to an hour before finishing them in the oven. Fry up some ripe plantains and serve them as a first course, dolloped with sour cream. Serve a side of mixed rice and black beans and plenty of salsa.

½ cup flour plus additional, for dusting

½ cup dark beer or stout

2 egg whites

Salt and freshly ground black pepper

6 ripe plum tomatoes or canned plum tomatoes, drained

1 large onion, finely diced (about 1 cup)

½ cup plus 1 tablespoon vegetable oil

2 dried pasilla chile peppers, stems and seeds removed, or 1 tablespoon chili powder

1 teaspoon ground cumin

¼ cup heavy cream

4 slices sharp Monterey jack or Cheddar cheese

2 large boneless chicken breasts, with skin, split

1. Place the ½ cup flour in a bowl and slowly stir in the beer. Add the egg whites, ½ teaspoon salt, and ¼ teaspoon pepper and mix well. Set the batter aside to rest for 20 minutes.

2. If using fresh tomatoes, bring a large pot of water to the boil. Plunge in the tomatoes and cook for about 1 minute, or until the skins crack. Immediately plunge the tomatoes into a bowl of ice water; drain. Peel the tomatoes, cut them in half crosswise, and squeeze out the seeds. If using canned tomatoes, remove and discard the seeds.

3. Combine the onion and 1 tablespoon of the oil in a small Dutch oven or ovenproof casserole, place in the oven, and turn the oven on to 375°F. Cook for 10 minutes. Add the tomatoes, chile peppers or chili powder, cumin, cream, and salt to taste and cook for 30 minutes. Transfer to a blender or food processor and process until smooth. (The sauce can be prepared up to an hour ahead and set aside at room temperature.)

4. Meanwhile, insert a slice of cheese under the skin of each chicken breast, making sure the cheese is covered by the skin.

5. Heat the remaining ½ cup oil in a heavy skillet over medium heat until it is almost smoking hot. Dredge the chicken breasts in flour, shaking off the excess, then dip each breast in the beer batter and let the excess run off. Add the chicken skin side down to the hot oil and fry, turning once, until golden on both sides, about 1 minute per side. Drain on paper towels, and transfer to a baking dish. (The chicken can be prepared up to an hour ahead and set aside at room temperature.)

6. When it's time to get dinner on the table, place the chicken in the 375°F oven and heat for 15 minutes. Reheat the sauce over medium heat if necessary. Pour the sauce onto a serving platter and arrange the chicken breasts on top.

TAMALE PIE

SERVES 8

*W*hen they served shepherd's pie at school, all the kids made faces—no one trusted what it was made of. This pie is similar in its own "mystery meat" kind of way. After all, you can't really identify any of the ingredients. But trust the chef on this one; it's a winner.

Serve guacamole and chips and a big salad with crisp lettuce and fresh jicama. Drink plenty of margaritas if you don't have to drive home afterward.

1½ cups dried red beans
1½ pounds pork stew meat
1 teaspoon salt, or more to taste
1 tablespoon ground cumin
2 cups chicken stock or canned low-sodium chicken broth, plus additional, if necessary
12 dried corn husks, soaked in water until pliable and drained
Tamale Batter (recipe follows)
2 tablespoons vegetable oil
1 medium onion, roughly chopped
12 plum tomatoes, halved
1 jalapeño pepper, or more to taste, halved and seeded
1 teaspoon cocoa powder
3 cups grated Monterey jack cheese

1. Soak the beans overnight in water to cover. Drain.

2. Combine the pork, salt, 2 teaspoons of the cumin, and the broth in a heavy pot or Dutch oven. Cover, place in the oven, and turn the oven on to 350°F. Place the beans in another heavy pot, cover with water, and place in the oven. Cook both the meat and beans for 2 hours, checking every 30 minutes and adding a little water, if necessary. Remove from the oven, but leave the oven on.

3. Transfer the meat and any juices to a bowl. Using two forks, shred the pork. Set aside. Transfer the beans and any liquid to a food processor and blend until smooth. If the beans are too dry, add a little chicken broth or water.

4. Line two nine-inch pie pans with the corn husks. Spread the Tamale batter evenly over the corn husks. Divide the shredded pork between the pans. Spread the beans over the pork. Cover the pie pans with foil and bake at 350°F

for 30 minutes. Remove the foil, sprinkle the cheese over the pies, and bake for 10 minutes.

5. Meanwhile, heat the oil in a medium pot. Add the onion and cook over medium heat, stirring occasionally, for 5 minutes. Add the tomatoes, jalapeño, cocoa powder, the remaining 1 teaspoon cumin and salt to taste, cover, and cook for 15 minutes. Transfer to a blender and blend until smooth. Pass the sauce through a strainer into a small serving bowl.

6. Serve the pies piping hot from the oven and offer the tomato sauce on the side.

TAMALE BATTER

1¼ cups masa harina
¾ cup yellow cornmeal
1 tablespoon baking powder
1 teaspoon salt
½ teaspoon freshly ground black pepper
¾ cup solid vegetable shortening
1 medium red bell pepper, roughly diced
1 medium green bell pepper, roughly diced
1 medium onion, roughly diced
2 cups cooked corn

1. Combine the masa harina, cornmeal, baking powder, salt, and pepper in a bowl and mix well. Add 1¾ cups water and mix until incorporated. Set aside.

2. Heat the shortening in a large skillet over medium heat. Add the peppers, onion, and corn and cook, stirring, for 10 minutes. Transfer to a food processor and pulse to break up the corn kernels.

3. Transfer to a bowl. Add the masa harina mixture and mix well. The batter keeps, covered, for up to 3 days in the refrigerator, or it can be frozen for up to 3 months.

SAUSAGE POSOLE

SERVES 4

*P*osole, or hominy, has more texture than flavor, but this underused staple has a remarkable ability to absorb the essence of whatever it's cooked with.

Although fat is a great conductor of flavor, once you've cooked the sausages with the other ingredients, you may want to skim off any that accumulates on the top of the stew, although precooking the sausages rids them of much of their fat.

6 hot Italian sausages
2 medium onions, roughly diced
3 green (unripe) tomatoes
1 tablespoon tomato paste
1 15½-ounce can posole (hominy), drained (reserve 1½ cups of the liquid)
1 teaspoon dried oregano
½ teaspoon salt, or to taste
½ teaspoon freshly ground black pepper, or to taste
2 tablespoons chopped fresh parsley
Lime slices, for garnish

1. Cut each sausage into 4 pieces. Place in a 3-quart pot, and cook over medium heat, turning occasionally, for 5 minutes. Transfer the sausages to a plate and set aside. Drain off the fat from the pot.

2. Add the onions to the pot and cook, stirring occasionally, for 5 minutes, or until softened.

3. Meanwhile, halve the tomatoes crosswise. Lay each half cut side down and cut each half into 6 wedges.

4. Add the tomatoes and tomato paste to the onions and cook, stirring for 2 minutes. Add the posole, reserved 1½ cups posole liquid, oregano, salt, and pepper, cover, raise the heat to high, and bring to a boil. Lower the heat to medium and simmer for 20 minutes. (The posole can be prepared ahead to this point and reheated before serving.)

5. When it's time to get dinner on the table, add the sausages to the pot and cook for 7 minutes. Remove from the heat and stir in the parsley. Spoon the stew into four soup bowls and garnish with lime slices. Serve warm tortillas instead of bread.

PORK TENDERLOINS BAKED WITH CREAMED CORN

SERVES 6

*T*his pork dinner soaks up rich flavor from the cream and vegetables. Pork tenderloin is the easiest cut to ruin. It's tender, a bit lacking in flavor, and so terribly lean that it gets dry if cooked too long. Don't cook it past medium doneness. Poke the meat with your finger—it should spring back. As soon as you see beads of juice escaping, it's done.

1½ pounds pork tenderloin
Salt
1 tablespoon vegetable oil or margarine
3 tablespoons finely minced onion or shallots
4 cups fresh (about 5 large ears) or frozen corn
½ cup chicken stock or canned low-sodium chicken broth
¼ cup heavy cream
1 teaspoon ground cumin
3 red and/or green bell peppers
18 okra
1 tablespoon unsalted butter
⅓ cup crumbled queso cotillo (see Note) or grated Parmesan cheese
Freshly ground black pepper to taste
Sprigs of cilantro (fresh coriander), for garnish

1. Preheat the oven to 375°F.

2. Sprinkle the pork with salt. Heat the oil in a large skillet over high heat. Add the pork and brown it all over. Transfer the pork to a baking dish and set aside. Reduce the heat to medium, add the onion to the skillet, and cook until soft, about 2 minutes. Add the corn, stock, cream, and cumin, increase the heat to high, and bring to a boil.

3. Pour the corn mixture over the pork, transfer to the oven, and bake for 15 minutes.

4. Meanwhile, cut the peppers in half lengthwise. Remove and discard the stem and seeds, and cut the peppers lengthwise into strips. Leaving the caps in one piece, slice the okra lengthwise into quarters. Heat the butter over medium heat in a large skillet, add the peppers and okra, and cook, tossing the vegetables occasionally, for about 5 minutes. Add ½ teaspoon salt and pepper to taste. Remove from the heat, cover, and keep warm. *(continued)*

5. Transfer the pork to a plate, cover, and keep warm. Transfer the corn mixture to a blender or food processor. Add the cheese and pulse this to break up the corn kernels; the mixture should be chunky. Add salt and pepper to taste.

6. To serve dinner, mound the corn in the center of a serving platter. Thinly slice the pork diagonally across the grain and arrange around the corn. Arrange the okra and peppers on the corn, and garnish with cilantro. Serve immediately.

NOTE: Queso cotillo is a dry, crumbly, salty Mexican cheese. It somewhat resembles hoop cheese but has more flavor.

LAMB CARNITAS

SERVES 4

*C*arnitas are cubes of meat that are browned in oil, then cooked until almost falling apart. Pork is the usual choice, but they can be made with any kind of flavorful meat as long as it's a stewing cut. Milk is the secret ingredient here, helping the resulting juices develop their proper texture. The meat and gravy melt into each other until it's hard to tell them apart. But this is not a sloppy Joe preparation. The meat remains in chunks—but only until you put them in your mouth, and then they seem to melt. Eat them in warm tortillas, with a green salsa and sour cream as garnishes.

1 cup dried lima beans or 2 cups canned
Salt
1¾ pounds lamb stew meat
About ¼ cup olive oil
Freshly ground black pepper
3 bay leaves
1 teaspoon ground coriander
2 teaspoons dried summer savory
1 cup milk
2 medium onions
2 ripe tomatoes
Warm tortillas, for serving

1. If using dried lima beans, soak them overnight in water to cover. Drain.

2. Preheat the oven to 350°F.

3. Place the soaked limas in an ovenproof casserole, barely cover them with water, and bake for 1 hour. Add 1 teaspoon salt and bake 1 hour longer. Check from time to time and add water as necessary if the beans start to dry out. Remove from the oven and keep warm.

4. Meanwhile, heat 1 tablespoon of the oil in a large heavy skillet over high heat. Add only as much of the lamb as will fit without crowding the skillet and brown well on all sides. Transfer the lamb to a Dutch oven. Repeat in batches, adding oil as needed.

5. When all the lamb is browned, add 1 teaspoon each salt and pepper, the bay leaves, coriander, savory, and ½ cup of the milk. Cover and bake for 30 minutes. Add the remaining ½ cup milk and cook, uncovered, until the meat is falling-apart tender, about 45 minutes. Remove from the oven, cover, and keep warm.

6. While the meat and beans are cooking, halve the onions lengthwise. Lay cut side down on a work surface and cut each half lengthwise into slivers. Toss with 1 teaspoon oil and set aside in a bowl. Halve the tomatoes crosswise, sprinkle with salt and pepper, and drizzle with oil. Set aside on a plate.

7. When it's time to put dinner on the table, preheat the broiler. Spread the onions in a heat-resistant dish and broil until the top of the onions begin to color; toss the onions and broil until the top begins to color again. Repeat until the onions are tender, about 7 minutes in all. Place the tomato halves, cut sides up, on top of the onions and broil for 3 minutes. Meanwhile, if using canned lima beans, heat them. Transfer to a serving dish and keep warm.

8. Arrange the onions and tomatoes on a platter. Transfer the lamb to a casserole dish, and serve the lima beans directly from the baking dish. To eat, scoop some of the meat, beans, and onions onto a tortilla and roll up.

TRIPE AND FAVA BEAN STEW

SERVES 4

7ripe is a variety meat that is little seen today except in Latin neighborhoods. In San Francisco's Mission District people bring their kettles to the neighborhood cafés to fill up with menudo, a tripe stew, for the family meal.

Include fava beans in this stew only if you can find them fresh, when they have a minty green flavor. I like to blanch tripe with a little vinegar and aromatics to mellow its flavor and give it a tender, falling-apart texture, then stew it with other flavorful ingredients to finish the cooking.

1 pound honeycomb tripe
¼ cup white wine vinegar
4 cloves
6 bay leaves
1 teaspoon black peppercorns
1 teaspoon salt, or more to taste
2½ cups fresh fava beans (2 pounds fresh beans in the shell)
24 pearl onions
18 garlic cloves
2 tablespoons unsalted butter
1 tablespoon sugar
1 tablespoon all-purpose flour
2 cups chicken stock or canned low-sodium chicken broth
¾ teaspoon dried summer savory
Freshly ground black pepper to taste

1. Place the tripe in a large pot with the vinegar, cloves, bay leaves, peppercorns, and salt. Cover with cold water, cover the pot, and bring to a boil over high heat. Reduce the heat to low and simmer for 2 hours. Drain the tripe and cool under cold running water. When the tripe is cool enough to handle, pat dry with towels and cut into strips about 1½ inches long and ½ inch wide.

2. Meanwhile, bring a large pot of salted water to the boil. Add the fava beans and cook for 5 minutes; drain. When cool enough to handle, peel the beans and set aside.

3. Peel the onions and cut an X in the root end of each one. Peel the garlic. Place the onions and garlic in a pan just large enough to hold them in one layer, and add the butter, sugar, and water to just cover. Cook over high heat until all the liquid has evaporated, then cook, shaking the pan, until the onions are golden. Remove from the heat and set aside.

4. When it's time to get dinner on the table, place the tripe in a large pot. Sprinkle with the flour and mix well. Add the chicken broth and savory, cover, and bring to a boil over medium heat. Reduce the heat to low and simmer for 5 minutes. Add the fava beans and cook for 5 minutes. Add the onions and garlic and cook just until heated through. Taste for salt and pepper and add as desired. Transfer the stew to a serving bowl and serve piping hot.

Last-Minute Dinners

Turkey Carbonara

Lamb Chops with "Fried Corn"

Broiled Lamb Chops with Prunes

Dill and Caraway Pork Tenderloins

Veal Scallopine with Leeks

IN OTHER CHAPTERS

*W*elcome to the world of last-minute dinners: a fantastic place where you are promised easy, delicious meals without too much fuss or mess.

Planning a quick dinner means, first, you want dishes that don't require a tedious setting up. All recipes require some advance work before the actual cooking begins, but the ones in this chapter keep it to a minimum without sacrificing deliciousness—after all, it's pointless to demand forty-five minutes, chopping and slicing before grilling a piece of meat for five minutes. With some foresight and organization, you can prepare batches of the little ingredients that you use regularly in your own cooking in batches to be stored in the refrigerator or freezer; it will save you those five minutes when they're important. You can sauté a batch of minced onions, freeze them in ice cube trays, and pop one out when a recipe calls for a tablespoon or so. The same is true of garlic, tomato paste, and pureed mushrooms.

And, of course, to get dinner on the table quickly, you need to choose appropriate ingredients—ones that are fairly small in size and cook quickly—fillets or steaks of fish rather than whole fish, boneless breasts of chicken or paillards of turkey, tender cuts of meat from the loin or sirloin, or cutlets that have been pounded to tenderness.

Dishes that cook quickly require the bold fresh taste of fresh herbs. Flavors that need time to mellow, as they would in a long-cooked stew, for instance, do not blend well when they are cooked quickly. Confusion results from too many different flavors in a single dish.

Last-minute dinners are suitable when you have family or guests who like to eat in the kitchen, or hang out in the kitchen. I often serve cocktails there while I throw together a dinner. The smells of cooking food act as an apéritif and get the gastric juices flowing in anticipation of the meal to come.

CURRIED CLAMS AND MUSSELS

SERVES 3 TO 4

I like tiny Manila clams for their brine and tenderness, and mussels for their sweetness and creamy texture. A strong broth results from the steaming of the seafood.

Serve a salad and a plate of charcuterie to complete the meal.

> 4 dozen Manila clams, scrubbed
> 4 dozen mussels, scrubbed and debearded
> 2 cups broccoli florets
> ¼ cup dry white wine
> 1 tablespoon curry powder
> 1 tablespoon finely minced garlic
> 1 cup peeled, seeded, and chopped tomatoes
> 1½ teaspoons chopped fresh dill or ¼ teaspoon dried
> ½ cup heavy cream (optional)
> Salt to taste

1. Combine the clams, mussels, broccoli, wine, curry powder, garlic, and tomatoes in a 3-quart pot. Cover and bring to a boil over high heat. If using dried dill, add it now. Add the cream, if desired, and boil, uncovered, until the clams and mussels open, about 5 minutes. Discard any unopened clams or mussels. Stir in the fresh dill, if using it, and add salt to taste.

2. Arrange the shellfish in individual bowls and ladle over the broth.

SOFT-SHELL CRABS STUFFED
WITH SMOKED SALMON

SERVES 4

S oft-shell crabs are Atlantic blue crabs that are caught from the late spring through the summer when they have molted their hard shells and not yet formed new ones. Buy them very fresh and in season only. Use larger crabs, about 4½ inches across, for stuffing.

Prepare a platter of summer vegetables to complete this dinner.

½ pound white mushrooms

2 tablespoons diced onion

1 egg white

Pinch of ground nutmeg

½ pound smoked salmon, ground in a food processor or finely
    chopped

½ teaspoon salt

Freshly ground black pepper to taste

8 large soft-shell crabs

Flour, for dusting

2 tablespoons vegetable oil

3 tablespoons unsalted butter

2 tablespoons fresh lemon juice

2 tablespoons finely chopped fresh parsley

1. Place the mushrooms and onion in a food processor and process until smooth. Scrape into a small skillet and cook over medium heat until the mixture is completely dry, about 10 minutes. Transfer to a bowl. Add the egg white and nutmeg and mix well. Add the salmon, salt, and pepper and mix well. Cover and refrigerate.

2. Lift up the flap on the underside of each crab and remove the white, spongy gills. Remove the tail flap, or apron. Using kitchen shears, cut off the face. Rinse the crabs under cold running water and dry well with towels. Stuff the crabs with the salmon mixture, placing it in the cavity left by the gills. (The crabs can be stuffed up to 2 hours in advance and refrigerated until serving time.)

3. When it's time to get dinner on the table, preheat the oven to 200°F. Dust the crabs with flour, shaking off the excess.

4. Heat the oil in a large skillet over high heat until almost smoking hot. Add the crabs shell side down, without crowding the pan, and cook for 1 minute, then turn and cook for 2 minutes. Cook the crabs in batches if necessary. Remove from the skillet and keep warm in the oven.

5. Wipe the skillet clean with a paper towel and set over medium heat. Add the butter and heat until it foams. When the foam begins to subside, add the lemon juice, and cook until the butter turns a hazelnut color. Remove from the heat and add the parsley. Pour the butter over the crabs, give a few turns of the pepper mill, and serve immediately.

Soft-Shell Crab Tempura

*G*iving these crabs a new shell—tempura batter—crisps them and keeps them very juicy. Make sure your oil is the right temperature to avoid greasy crabs. When the oil is hot enough, a droplet of water will make a "pinging" sound, and immediately bubble and dance on the surface of the oil as it turns to steam. A frying thermometer will read 365°F.

If you can't find wasabi powder—dry Japanese horseradish powder— add 2 teaspoons dry mustard to the soy, vinegar, and sherry for dipping. In keeping with the Japanese theme, serve a quick stir-fry of bean sprouts and snow peas or a salad of field greens, seaweed, and crispy Asian noodles.

> *6 tablespoons all-purpose flour*
> *1 egg white*
> *½ cup beer*
> *¼ teaspoon salt*
> *3 tablespoons dry sherry*
> *⅓ cup soy sauce*
> *2 tablespoons rice wine vinegar*
> *2 tablespoons wasabi powder*
> *12 small soft-shell crabs*
> *Peanut oil, for frying*

1. Place 4 tablespoons of the flour in a bowl. Add the egg white and mix well. Stir in the beer and mix well. Stir in the salt. Set the batter aside.

2. Combine the sherry, vinegar, and soy sauce and pour into four small ramekins or bowls. Mix the wasabi powder with enough water, adding it a few drops at a time, to form a paste. Place 4 mounds of wasabi on 4 small plates, or on the serving plates.

3. Lift up the flap on the underside of each crab and remove the white, spongy gills. Remove the tail flap, or apron. With shears, cut off the face. Rinse the crabs under cold running water and dry well on towels. Refrigerate until ready to serve dinner.

4. When it's time to get dinner on the table, heat ¾ inch of oil to 365°F in a heavy skillet over medium heat. Meanwhile, place the remaining 2 table- spoons flour in a paper bag. Add the crabs, one at a time, and shake to lightly dust. When the oil is hot, dip each crab in the batter and let the excess run off.

Add the crabs to the hot oil, without crowding the skillet, and fry for about 2 minutes on each side. Fry the crabs in batches, if necessary. Drain on paper towels.

5. Arrange the hot crabs on a platter and serve immediately with the dipping sauce and wasabi. The wasabi should be dissolved a hint at a time in the dipping soy, according to each diner's taste.

SHRIMP SCAMPI

SERVES 4

*O*h, what a familiar and simple dish this is, and well deserving of its beloved status. It's the kind of cooking that invites guests into the kitchen, so you might want to prepare the rest of your meal earlier. I would start with asparagus vinaigrette and accompany the scampi with pasta tossed with some olive oil and herbs.

> 20 jumbo shrimp
> 3 tablespoons olive oil
> 1 to 2 tablespoons finely minced garlic (to taste)
> 3 tablespoons fresh lemon juice
> ¼ cup dry white wine
> ½ teaspoon salt, or more to taste
> ⅛ teaspoon cayenne pepper
> 2 tablespoons unsalted butter
> 2 tablespoons chopped fresh parsley
> Freshly ground black pepper to taste

1. Peel the shrimp, leaving the last tail section of shell and the swimmer intact. Make an incision down the back of each shrimp and pull out the dark vein.

2. Heat the oil in a large nonreactive skillet over medium heat. Add the shrimp and cook, tossing or stirring, for 1 minute. Add the garlic and cook 1 minute. Add the lemon juice, wine, salt, and cayenne pepper, increase the heat to high, and cook until the liquid has reduced by about half.

3. Remove from the heat and stir in the butter until incorporated. Add the parsley and salt and pepper to taste. Transfer to a platter and serve immediately.

Last-Minute Dinners

STUFFED PRAWNS

SERVES 4

*T*his is "cute" food but it's not fussy, so even if you're not in the habit of stuffing anything other than a chicken or a turkey, don't worry. No one will think you're obsessive about dinner. Start the meal with a crisp garlicky Caesar salad and serve broccoli rabe or broccoli as your vegetable.

14 giant prawns, or jumbo shrimp (in the shell)
3 tablespoons olive oil
2 tablespoons minced onion
1 tablespoon minced garlic
¼ cup fresh bread crumbs
3 tablespoons finely chopped fresh parsley
¼ pound smoked salmon
2 egg whites
⅓ cup dry white wine
3 tablespoons unsalted butter, at room temperature

1. Remove the shells from 2 of the prawns. Devein them and set aside. Lay the remaining prawns on a work surface and make a deep slit down the back of each one through the shell to butterfly it. Remove and discard the vein, open out the prawns, and flatten with the side of a knife. Refrigerate until ready to stuff.

2. Heat 1 tablespoon of the olive oil in a small skillet over medium heat. Add the onion and garlic and cook, stirring, for 2 minutes. Transfer to a food processor. Add the bread crumbs, 2 tablespoons of the parsley, the peeled prawns, smoked salmon, and egg whites and process until smooth. Scrape the mixture into a small bowl.

3. Preheat the broiler.

4. Lay the butterflied prawns flat on a work surface. Spoon some of the stuffing into each prawn and lightly press the sides together around the stuffing. Arrange the prawns in a small ovenproof dish and brush with the remaining 2 tablespoons olive oil. Pour in the wine and broil for 5 to 6 minutes, or until the prawns (and stuffing) are opaque all the way through.

5. Transfer the prawns to a serving plate. Whisk the butter into the liquid remaining in the dish and add the remaining 1 tablespoon parsley. Pour the sauce over the prawns and serve immediately.

The Scallop

Scallops—the part we eat, that is—range in size from very small, about the size of a penny, to very large, weighing as much as five ounces. The smallest are called bay scallops, the largest, sea scallops. There are also medium-sized scallops referred to as cape scallops. In the days when you could still buy scallops in the shell, it was possible to know in which bay the scallops were found (the way you should still know from what waters oysters in the shell were harvested). But today, most scallops are removed from the shell in dockside processing factories. Then they are sorted according to size and packed into buckets for sale to the trade.

When you buy fresh scallops, there are several qualities to look for. They should be a translucent whitish color; certain scallops are slightly orange, which is fine, but avoid buying any that are an opaque white. They should be moist, but the faint amount of liquid around them should not be milky, a sign that they have begun to ooze their liquid and are probably a day or two past their prime. They should be whole, not broken into pieces—an indication that they have been poorly handled or, possibly, frozen. (I do not recommend buying frozen scallops, although I have had great success freezing fresh ones myself: Rinse the scallops and pat dry. Lay the scallops on a cookie sheet in a single layer and place in the freezer. When they are frozen, pack into airtight freezer bags and freeze for up to three months.) Scallops should have the scent of the shore at high tide. If they smell a little gaseous—a seaweed or kelp odor—avoid them.

Scallops can be grilled or broiled, sautéed, or poached. When sautéing or grilling, you want them to quickly take on a dark golden color—the result of caramelization, not burning. Quick cooking—in a very hot, uncrowded, pan, on a hot grill, or under a hot broiler close to the heat—not only brings out their sweetness but also keeps them from becoming stringy and tough. Simple sauce accompaniments are easy to prepare because the liquid the scallops release makes a flavorful base for them.

You won't find me steaming or poaching scallops except in citrus juice—the flavor simply can't compare with that of sautéed or grilled ones. I grill larger sea scallops and sauté smaller cape or bay scallops. If you insist on poaching, remember that scallops are high in the protein albumin and get as tough as rubber bands if cooked too long. Place in a rapidly boiling liquid and remove while still undercooked.

SAUTÉED SCALLOPS AND CELERIAC

SERVES 4

*S*hredded celeriac, or celery root, has the texture of a spongy carrot and an intense celery flavor. It plays the role of both green vegetable and starch, but you'll need more for dinner than just this dish. Start with a plate of pâté or cold cuts, with good bread and strong mustard, and serve a green salad.

1½ pounds small bay scallops or sea scallops
3 tablespoons unsalted butter
2 cups shredded celeriac (celery root)
Salt
1 to 2 tablespoons vegetable oil
Freshly ground black pepper to taste
1 tablespoon finely minced shallots
½ cup dry white wine
1 tablespoon chopped fresh tarragon or 1 teaspoon dried

1. If using sea scallops, remove and discard the tough muscle on the side of the scallops, and slice the scallops in half crosswise. Set aside.

2. Melt 1 tablespoon of the butter in a small pot or saucepan over low heat. Add the celeriac and ½ teaspoon salt, or to taste, cover, and cook for about 10 minutes, until softened. Remove from the heat and keep warm.

3. Meanwhile, heat 1 tablespoon oil in a large skillet over high heat. Pat the scallops dry with a towel and sprinkle with salt and pepper. When the oil is almost smoking hot, add only as many scallops as will fit without crowding the pan, and cook for 30 seconds without stirring. Then vigorously shake the skillet and cook 1 minute longer. Using a slotted spoon, transfer the scallops to a plate. (They should be only partially cooked.) Repeat with the remaining scallops, adding more oil as necessary. Discard the fat from the skillet.

4. Return the skillet to high heat and add the shallots, wine, and any juices that have collected on the plate of scallops. If using dried tarragon, add it now. Cook until the liquid has reduced by half. Return the scallops to the pan, and whisk in the remaining 2 tablespoons butter and the fresh tarragon, if using it. Immediately remove from the heat.

5. To serve dinner, make a ring of the celeriac on a platter and mound the scallops in the center; drizzle any sauce remaining in the pan over the scallops.

SAUTÉED SCALLOPS WITH PANCETTA AND APPLES

SERVES 4

*S*callops and bacon of any sort combine terrifically well. Actually, I'm fond of bacon as an accent to many seafood dishes. When you add the apple sticks to the skillet, be certain to just heat them through. The crisp contrast to the creamy scallops and the refreshing flavor make this a special dinner. Serve the scallops with mashed potatoes.

1½ pounds bay scallops or sea scallops
1 to 2 tablespoons olive oil
Salt and freshly ground black pepper to taste
¼ pound pancetta or bacon, chopped into ¼-inch pieces
1 teaspoon finely minced shallots
½ cup dry white wine
3 tablespoons unsalted butter
1 green (pippin) apple (unpeeled), cut into julienne sticks

1. If using sea scallops, remove and discard the tough muscle on the side, and slice the scallops in half crosswise.

2. Heat 1 tablespoon oil in a large skillet over high heat. Pat the scallops dry with a towel and sprinkle with salt and pepper. When the oil is almost smoking hot, add only as many scallops as will fit without crowding the pan, and cook for 30 seconds without stirring. Then vigorously shake the skillet and cook 1 minute longer. Using a slotted spoon, transfer the scallops to a plate. (They should be only partially cooked.) Repeat with the remaining scallops, adding more oil as necessary. Drain off the fat from the pan.

3. Reduce the heat to medium and add the pancetta or bacon and shallots to the pan. Cook, stirring, for 1 minute. Add the wine and any juices that have collected on the plate of scallops. Cook until the liquid has reduced by half. Return the scallops to the pan and reduce the heat to low. Whisk in the butter and then add the apple. Season to taste with salt and pepper and remove from the heat.

4. Turn out onto a serving platter and serve immediately.

PAN-ROASTED PEPPERED SCALLOPS

SERVES 4

*7*he versatility of scallops makes them a popular dinner choice. Here, they're treated like a French steak *à la minute*. They're briny with clam juice and spicy with mustard and pepper. Please, do sear them over the highest heat and don't stand over the skillet—the oil in the pepper will make you cough, unless you're not cooking hot enough.

The potato crisps are made from potatoes sliced as thin as potato chips. A mandoline is perfect for this; be attentive if you use the thin slicing blade of a food processor, so that you end up with uniform slices. Once you get the knack of assembling these potato sheets, you'll find yourself using them as accompaniment to many dishes.

1½ pounds large sea scallops (about 2 ounces each)
Cracked black pepper to taste
2 tablespoons melted unsalted butter
1 large potato (about ¾ pound)
Salt and freshly ground black pepper to taste
1 tablespoon green peppercorns
2 tablespoons minced shallots
½ cup dry white wine
½ cup fish broth or bottled clam juice
1 tablespoon Dijon mustard
2 teaspoons chopped fresh tarragon or 1 teaspoon dried
½ cup heavy cream
1 teaspoon vegetable oil

1. Remove and discard the tough muscle on the side of the scallops. Dip the scallops in cracked pepper, pressing so it adheres; use as much or as little pepper as you like, according to your taste. Set the scallops aside in the refrigerator, covered, for up to 3 hours.

2. Preheat the oven to 375°F. Line a 12- by 17-inch baking sheet with parchment paper or foil and grease with 2 teaspoons of the melted butter.

3. Thinly slice the potato. Form 4 circles of overlapping slices on the baking sheet and fill in the center of each round with another slice. Sprinkle with salt and pepper and bake for 20 minutes. Flip the potato circles over, brush with the remaining melted butter, and bake for 10 minutes, or until golden. Remove from the oven and set aside in a warm place.

4. Meanwhile, combine the green peppercorns, shallots, wine, broth, and mustard in a saucepan. If using dried tarragon, add it now. Cook over medium heat for 5 minutes. Add the cream and cook until the liquid reduces and thickens to the consistency of a sauce, about 5 more minutes. Remove from the heat, stir in the fresh tarragon if using it, cover, and keep warm.

5. Rub the oil over the bottom of a heavy cast-iron skillet and place the skillet over high heat. When the skillet is hot, almost smoking, add the scallops and cook for about 2 minutes. Turn the scallops and transfer to the hot oven to finish cooking, about 5 minutes for medium. Reheat the potatoes in the oven, if necessary.

6. To serve, pour the warm sauce onto a platter and arrange the scallops on the sauce. Arrange the potato circles around the scallops.

SCALLOPS POACHED IN GRAPEFRUIT JUICE

SERVES 4

*T*his dish is totally simple to prepare. The grapefruit tastes at once sweet and tart and the effect is completely exotic. Serve this over rice. Begin dinner with something salty, such as a plate of prosciutto, and follow with cheese and salad.

1 cup fresh grapefruit juice
1½ pounds bay or cape scallops
Salt to taste
4 tablespoons unsalted butter, cut into 8 pieces

1. Bring the grapefruit juice to a boil in a covered saucepan over high heat. Add the scallops and salt, cover, and simmer for 2 minutes. Using a slotted spoon, transfer the scallops to a plate.

2. Reduce the heat to medium and cook the liquid, uncovered, until reduced by about half. Add any juices that have collected on the plate of scallops and cook until the liquid has thickened slightly. Remove from the heat, add the scallops to the pan, and whisk in the butter until incorporated. Serve immediately.

SAUTÉED SCALLOPS WITH ROOT VEGETABLES

SERVES 4

*T*his dish emphasizes the sweet taste of scallops. Root vegetables have lots of stored sugars, and when shredded, they cook quickly, releasing all their sweetness. Use a food processor to shred the vegetables, or grate them by hand.

> 1½ pounds bay scallops or sea scallops
> 1 tablespoon unsalted butter
> 1 small onion, halved lengthwise and finely sliced (about ½ cup)
> 1 medium carrot, peeled and shredded (about ¾ cup)
> 1 medium parsnip, peeled and shredded (about ¾ cup)
> 1 small turnip, peeled and shredded (about 1¼ cups)
> 1 small knob celeriac (celery root), peeled and shredded
>   (about 1¼ cups)
> 1 teaspoon salt, or to taste
> ½ teaspoon ground white pepper
> 1 tablespoon vegetable oil
> ½ cup dry sherry

1. If using sea scallops, remove the tough muscle from the side and slice the scallops in half crosswise. Set aside.

2. Heat the butter in a large skillet over medium heat. Add the onion, cover, and cook for 2 minutes. Add the carrot, parsnip, turnip, celeriac, salt, and pepper, cover, and cook for 5 minutes. Remove the lid and cook, stirring for about 2 more minutes. Remove from the heat and keep warm.

3. Meanwhile, heat the oil over high heat in a heavy nonreactive skillet until almost smoking hot. Add the scallops, shake the pan to distribute them evenly, and cook for about 2 minutes without stirring. Add the sherry and cook for 30 seconds; then, using a slotted spoon, transfer the scallops to a plate. Reduce the heat and boil the cooking liquid until it has reduced by half and started to thicken, about 5 minutes. Return the scallops to the pan, along with any juices that have collected on the plate, and cook for 30 seconds. Remove from the heat and whisk in the butter. Taste for salt and add as desired.

4. Arrange a ring of the vegetables on a serving platter and spoon the scallops and sauce into the center. Serve immediately.

BROILED SALMON WITH A BARBECUE GLAZE

SERVES 4

*D*on't be shy about treating this recipe as if it were one for ribs. Remember that a barbecue glaze should be spread on meat, poultry, or fish and allowed to soak in before cooking. Its flavor is absorbed by the flesh, adding a subtle accent. Then, after cooking, brush a little more glaze over the surface. Fish, especially, can be overpowered if you're not restrained in the use of your glaze.

Accompany this salmon with sautéed red cabbage or boiled sauerkraut and potato salad.

2 tablespoons Dijon mustard
2 tablespoons brown sugar
2 teaspoons Worcestershire sauce
2 tablespoons white wine vinegar
½ teaspoon freshly ground black pepper
1 cup bottled clam juice, chicken stock, or canned low-sodium
*   chicken broth*
4 7-ounce salmon steaks or fillets
Lemon wedges, for garnish

1. Combine the mustard, brown sugar, Worcestershire sauce, vinegar, pepper, and clam juice in a saucepan, and cook over medium heat until reduced by half and the consistency of honey. Pour the glaze into a bowl, place in a bowl of ice water, and chill.

2. Lay the salmon in one layer in a glass baking dish. Pour the chilled BBQ glaze over the fish and let sit for 15 minutes. Meanwhile, light a barbecue grill or preheat a broiler.

3. Place the salmon about 6 inches from the heat source and broil for about 2 minutes on each side for medium, basting once with the glaze.

4. Arrange the salmon on a platter, garnish with lemon wedges, and serve immediately.

THREE SHAD RECIPES

*S*had is a migratory fish, swimming up the rivers in spring to spawn in fresh water. Overfishing and the damming of many rivers has contributed to the rapid decline of shad, both in Europe and in the United States.

Shad has many tiny bones; the French claim that cooking it with fresh sorrel causes the bones to dissolve. Although a nice excuse to pair the two, I've never found that to be the case. So, buy whole fish—the flesh discolors rapidly after filleting—and ask the fishmonger to cut out the strip of hairlike bones when he fillets them for you.

The highly prized roe sacs are a pair of long lobes. To prepare them, carefully separate the two lobes. Prick the membrane with the tip of a sharp knife in several places to keep the sacs from exploding during cooking. Old recipes often direct the cook to blanch the roe before cooking, but I find this ruins the creamy texture. Broil or sauté the roe, but do not overcook it or it will become rubbery.

I always serve white things with shad—tiny boiled potatoes and a vegetable such as turnips, parsnips, parsley roots, salsify, or cabbage.

SHAD ROE WITH BACON AND PERNOD

SERVES 2

*T*hank you, Elizabeth Montgomery, for this recipe of your mother's. I just added the Pernod. Ms. Montgomery prefers her roe cooked about 2 minutes past well done; we always laugh about this.

> *1 pair shad roe*
> *Salt and ground white pepper to taste*
> *1 tablespoon all-purpose flour*
> *¼ pound sliced bacon, cut into ½-inch-wide strips*
> *1 teaspoon unsalted butter*
> *1 tablespoon Pernod or Ricard*
> *1 tablespoon fresh lemon juice*
> *1 tablespoon finely chopped fresh parsley*

1. Using a small knife, carefully separate the two lobes of roe. Then prick the membrane in several places with the tip of the knife. Sprinkle the roe with salt and pepper, lightly dust with the flour, and set aside on a plate.

What's for Dinner?

2. Combine the bacon and butter in a medium skillet and cook over medium heat, stirring, for about 3 minutes. Add the roe and cook for about 5 minutes on each side.

3. Add the Pernod, lemon juice, and parsley and cook for 30 seconds. Arrange the roe on plates, spoon over the contents of the skillet, and serve immediately.

SHAD WITH SORREL

SERVES 3

*7*his is the classic French way of preparing shad, but I've made it more "puckery" by using yogurt rather than cream to finish the sauce.

¼ cup fish broth or bottled clam juice
¼ cup dry white wine
1 tablespoon fresh lemon juice
½ cup chopped sorrel
1½ pounds boneless skinless shad fillet, cut into 3 serving pieces
Salt and ground white pepper to taste
1 tablespoon unsalted butter
1 tablespoon plain yogurt

1. Combine the broth, wine, and lemon juice in a large nonreactive skillet and add the sorrel. Add the shad and sprinkle with salt and pepper. Cover and simmer over medium heat for 8 minutes.

2. Transfer the shad to a plate and keep warm. Replace the skillet over medium heat and whisk in the butter until incorporated. Remove from the heat and whisk in the yogurt.

3. Pour the sauce over the fish and serve immediately.

SAUTÉED SHAD WITH CAPER SAUCE

SERVES 4

*T*his oily river fish is delicious with a contrasting acidic sauce of capers and lemon juice.

Serve potatoes boiled in their jackets with the shad. Steam or boil a mélange of vegetables, toss them with a vinaigrette, and serve as a warm first course.

1 tablespoon finely minced garlic
3 tablespoons drained capers
1 cup dry white wine
2 tablespoons fresh lemon juice
¼ cup heavy cream
3 tablespoons unsalted butter
4 7-ounce shad or whitefish fillets
Flour, for dusting
1 tablespoon vegetable oil

1. Combine the garlic, capers, wine, and lemon juice in a 1-quart saucepan and cook over high heat until reduced by one third. Add the cream, reduce the heat to medium, and cook until the liquid starts to thicken, about 3 minutes. Remove from the heat and whisk in 2 tablespoons of the butter. Set the sauce aside in a warm place.

2. Pat the fish dry with towels. Dust with the flour, shaking off the excess.

3. Heat the oil and remaining 1 tablespoon butter in a skillet over medium heat. Add the fish and sauté until golden, about 6 minutes per side.

4. Arrange the fish on a heated platter and nap with the warm sauce. Serve immediately.

SWORDFISH PAILLARDS WITH
MADEIRA ORANGES

SERVES 4

*T*hese thin slices of swordfish, called paillards, cook rapidly but don't dry out. Serve them with wild rice—its woodsy flavor makes a great contrast to the sweet citrus in the swordfish dish.

> *1½ pounds swordfish fillet (in one piece) or 4 7-ounce*
> *   swordfish steaks*
> *Salt and freshly ground black pepper to taste*
> *2 to 3 teaspoons flavorless vegetable oil*
> *½ cup Madeira or dry sherry*
> *½ cup fresh orange juice*
> *1 tablespoon cider vinegar*
> *2 teaspoons grated orange zest*
> *¼ cup walnut oil*

1. If using 1 large swordfish fillet, cut it into 8 thin slices. If using steaks, slice each steak crosswise into 2 thin pieces. Sprinkle with salt and pepper on both sides.

2. Cook the swordfish in batches so as not to crowd the skillet, or the fish will not cook quickly enough. Heat about 1 teaspoon of the oil in a heavy skillet over high heat. When the pan is nearly smoking hot, add the swordfish and cook about 1 minute on each side, or until just cooked through. Transfer the swordfish to a plate and keep warm in a low oven while you prepare the sauce.

3. Reduce the heat to medium, add the Madeira, orange juice, vinegar, and zest to the skillet, and cook until the liquid has reduced by about half, about 4 minutes. Remove from the heat and pour into a bowl. Vigorously whisk in the walnut oil. Taste for salt and add as desired.

4. Pour any juices that have collected on the swordfish plate into the sauce and arrange the swordfish on a serving platter. Spoon the sauce over the fish and call everyone to the table.

BAKED SWORDFISH AND CUCUMBERS

SERVES 4

*T*hick-cut swordfish should be baked to keep it moist. The more intense direct heat of a broiler or sauté pan would dry it out before it was done.

In this dish, the spicy, salty flavor of the mustard is offset by the cleansing cucumbers.

3 tablespoons white wine vinegar
3 tablespoons dry white wine
1 tablespoon Dijon mustard
1 tablespoon chopped fresh dill or 2 teaspoons dried
4 7-ounce thick-cut swordfish steaks
½ teaspoon salt, or to taste
¼ teaspoon ground white pepper
2 cucumbers
3 tablespoons unsalted butter

1. Preheat the oven to 375°F.

2. Mix together the vinegar, wine, and mustard and pour into a glass or other nonreactive dish that is just large enough to hold the swordfish. If using dried dill, add it now. Add the swordfish and sprinkle with the salt and pepper. Set aside.

3. Peel the cucumbers and halve lengthwise. Scoop out the seeds. Cut the cucumbers on the diagonal into ½-inch slices. Scatter the cucumber over the swordfish and bake for 20 minutes, turning the fish once.

4. Transfer the fish to a platter. Transfer the cucumbers and liquid to a pot, bring to a boil over high heat, and cook until the liquid has reduced by about one third. Remove from the heat and whisk in the butter. Add the fresh dill if using it. Spoon the sauce and cucumbers over the fish and serve immediately.

SEAFOOD BEIGNETS

SERVES 4

*B*eignets are batter-coated French fritters. Some are sweet, some are savory. These are made with diced seafood in a tempura batter, fried into crispy cakes.

The rice flour, available in Asian markets and health food stores, results in a lighter, less starchy fritter.

¼ cup rice flour
1 egg
1 egg white
¼ cup beer
Salt
¼ teaspoon ground white pepper
2 teaspoons curry powder
1 tablespoon chopped fresh dill or 1 teaspoon dried
½ pound (raw) shrimp, chopped
½ pound skinless salmon fillets, chopped
½ pound skinless whitefish fillet, chopped
1 cup finely sliced scallions
About ¼ cup flavorless vegetable oil
2 carrots, peeled and cut into julienne strips
1 small zucchini, cut into julienne strips
2 celery stalks, cut into julienne strips
½ cup bean sprouts
Freshly ground black pepper to taste

1. Place the flour in a bowl. Whisk in the egg and egg white, then slowly stir in the beer. Stir in ½ teaspoon salt, the white pepper, curry powder, and dill. Cover the batter and let rest for 15 minutes.

2. Add the shrimp, salmon, whitefish, and scallions to the batter and refrigerate for up to 30 minutes.

3. When it's time to cook dinner, heat 1 tablespoon oil in a skillet over medium heat. Add the carrots, cover, and cook for 2 minutes. Add the zucchini and celery and cook, tossing the vegetables, about 2 minutes more. Add the sprouts and cook for 1 minute. Remove from the heat and season with salt and black pepper. Make a bed of the vegetables on a serving platter, and keep warm in a 250°F oven while you make the beignets. *(continued)*

Last-Minute Dinners

4. Heat a large frying pan over medium heat and add 2 tablespoons oil. Spoon ⅓-cup portions of the seafood batter into the skillet, without crowding, and cook for 2½ to 3 minutes on each side. As each batch of beignets is done, transfer to the oven to keep warm while you fry the remainder, adding more oil to the pan as necessary.

5. Arrange the beignets on the vegetables and serve immediately.

Tarragon Chicken Breasts with Crabmeat Sauce

SERVES 4

Voilà! Veal Oscar returns as a light, tasty chicken dish. The Béarnaise sauce is replaced by a tarragon reduction, and chicken goes great with the crab. Serve with mashed or boiled potatoes and follow with a green salad garnished with hearts of palm.

1 pound asparagus
1 cup chicken stock or canned low-sodium chicken broth
1 tablespoon Pernod
2 tablespoons finely minced onion or shallots
1 teaspoon minced garlic
½ teaspoon celery seed
½ teaspoon aniseed
½ teaspoon salt, or to taste
½ teaspoon ground white pepper
4 boneless, skinless chicken breast halves
1 tablespoon chopped fresh tarragon or 1 teaspoon dried
¼ cup heavy cream
6 ounces crab leg meat, picked over for shells and cartilage
1 tablespoon unsalted butter

1. Trim off the bottom 1½ inches of the asparagus stalks. If the asparagus is thick, peel it.

2. Combine the stock, Pernod, onion, garlic, celery seed, aniseed, salt, and pepper in a large nonreactive skillet, cover, and bring to a boil over high heat. Add the asparagus and cook until tender, about 2 to 4 minutes, depending on the thickness. Transfer the asparagus to a platter, cover, and keep warm in a 250°F oven.

3. Reduce the heat to low and add the chicken breasts to the skillet. If using dried tarragon, add it now. Cover and simmer until the breasts are cooked through, about 7 minutes. Remove the breasts and keep warm in the oven.

4. Increase the heat to high, add the cream, and boil until the liquid is thick enough to coat the back of a spoon. Add the crabmeat and cook for 1 minute to heat through. Remove from the heat, whisk in the butter, and add the fresh tarragon if using it.

5. Arrange the asparagus on individual plates and place a chicken breast on top of each serving. Arrange the crabmeat on the chicken and spoon the sauce around. Serve immediately.

CHICKEN BREASTS XERES

SERVES 4

*T*his recipe was quite the vogue about fifteen years ago, when sherry vinegar was the vinegar of choice. These days it's balsamic vinegar that's all the rage. Both work equally well here. In fact, if you like vinegar as much as I do, any good-quality one will make a delicious sauce.

Serve the chicken over pasta or rice or accompanied by mashed potatoes. Start with a plate of mozzarella, tomatoes, and roasted peppers dressed with lemon juice and olive oil.

2 large boneless chicken breasts, with skin, split (about 1½ pounds)
Salt and freshly ground black pepper to taste
½ pound white mushrooms
6 tablespoons olive oil
⅔ cup sherry vinegar
2 tablespoons tomato paste
2 tablespoons chopped fresh parsley

1. Trim excess skin from the chicken breasts. Sprinkle with salt and pepper and set aside. Quarter the mushrooms if large, halve smaller ones, and set aside.

2. Heat 1 tablespoon of the oil in a nonreactive skillet over high heat. Add the chicken and brown on the skin side only. Transfer to a plate and pour off the fat from the pan. Reduce the heat to medium, add the vinegar, and stir in the tomato paste. Return the chicken to the skillet, skin side up, cover, and cook for 3 minutes. Remove the lid and cook until the chicken is cooked through, about 6 minutes more.

3. Meanwhile, heat 1 tablespoon of the oil in a large frying pan. Add the mushrooms and cook for 3 to 4 minutes. Remove from the heat and keep warm.

4. Transfer the chicken breasts to a platter. Whisk the remaining ¼ cup olive oil into the pan juices and stir in the parsley. Pour any juices that have collected on the chicken platter into the sauce. Spoon the mushrooms around the chicken, pour the sauce over the chicken and mushrooms, and serve dinner immediately.

Turkey Carbonara

SERVES 4

*E*ggs and cream thicken into a rich sauce when warmed. Even the heat from steaming hot pasta will do it, as in a traditional pasta carbonara. In this recipe it's the warm pan that heats the sauce for the turkey. Serve it over pasta or rice or with polenta, and begin with a Caesar salad.

1½ pounds turkey cutlets, cut into ¼-inch-wide julienne strips
Salt to taste
½ teaspoon ground white pepper
2 eggs
3 tablespoons grated Parmesan or Romano cheese
½ cup heavy cream
¼ cup milk
½ pound bacon, diced
1 tablespoon olive oil
2 tablespoons minced shallots or onion
1 teaspoon minced garlic
2 tablespoons all-purpose flour
1 cup fresh or frozen peas

1. Pat the turkey julienne dry, sprinkle with salt and the pepper, and set aside.

2. Beat the eggs, cheese, cream, and milk together in a bowl and set aside.

3. Place the bacon and oil in a large skillet and cook over medium heat, stirring for about 2 minutes. Add the shallots and garlic and cook for 1 minute.

4. Meanwhile, place the flour in a paper bag, add the turkey, and shake to coat. Remove from the bag, place in a strainer, and shake off the excess flour.

5. Add the turkey to the skillet and cook, tossing, for about 3 minutes. Add the peas and cook for 1 minute. Stir in the egg mixture and cook for 30 seconds. Remove from the heat and stir for a minute or so, until the sauce thickens.

6. Serve over pasta or rice or serve with polenta.

Don't Throw Out the Flavor

Good cooking consists of retaining the essence of an ingredient in a flavorful concentration. The basic methods of cooking allow us to achieve this—if we don't throw out the flavor that's left in the pan or in the pot. Yet we might not realize that it's there unless we either reduce a bland liquid or magnify an already concentrated residue.

When we prepare a stew or pot roast, we start with water or a thin-flavored broth, aptly called stock—and enrich the braising liquid with the distillation of the proteins and flavors of the stew ingredients. You'd never think of throwing it out. It's the best part of the dish and it usually doesn't require any further fortification.

When you blanch or boil vegetables, there are flavors drawn out into the cooking liquid that can be retrieved. Keep this liquid and use it again and again for blanching vegetables. After a dozen or so times, what you thought was an inert liquid reduces to a dark, sweet vegetable glaze that can be used to flavor both vegetarian and meat dishes. It can also be the base for a flavorful hot or cold vinaigrette.

Those sticky, dark bits that remain on the bottom of the pan after your roast comes out of the oven—they are flavor. Don't throw them out. Dissolve them into another liquid, then concentrate it over high heat to make a sauce.

When preparing a sauce, begin with a flavorful liquid—juice, wine or spirits, broth or braising liquid, or a combination. Concentrate the flavor by boiling off the greater volume of water. (Water, of course, is neutral with no flavor of its own—reduce it and what do you get? A burnt pot.) You now have a too flavorful concentration, but there's not much of it.

Think of your reduction as being thirsty because you've gotten rid of all its water. This thirsty syrupy reduction will drink up cream and butter. Add some cream and cook the liquid again—cream is partly water, too, and you need to boil it off. Enrich the sauce by replacing some of the water in the cream with butter—your sauce will shine. Or forget cream and swirl a good nut of butter directly into the concentrated liquid—your butter sauce will sing with flavor.

Recently, chefs have been preparing reduction sauces using flavored oils instead of butter or cream. The reductions for these sauces are not as concentrated or thirsty and an acidic component, such as vinegar or lemon juice, is needed to stabilize them so they can be served warm or cold. When making these new-style sauces, choose vinegars and oils carefully because their flavors will be prominent.

LAMB CHOPS WITH "FRIED CORN"

SERVES 4

*W*hen you blacken the corn kernels for this recipe, they jump around the hot skillet and it seems like they're frying. They take on a popcorn flavor that's nice with the orange-rosemary sauce.

Serve broiled tomatoes and sautéed green beans as vegetables and begin the meal with potato pancakes.

> 2 teaspoons flavorless vegetable oil
> 12 thick-cut lamb rib chops (about 1¾ pounds)
> ½ teaspoon salt, or to taste
> Freshly ground black pepper to taste
> 3 ears sweet corn, preferably white, kernels removed (about 3 cups)
> 2 tablespoons finely minced onion
> ½ cup orange juice
> 1 teaspoon fresh or dried rosemary
> 4 tablespoons unsalted butter

1. Heat the oil in a heavy skillet over high heat. Sprinkle the chops with the salt and pepper, add to the skillet, and cook for about 5 minutes on each side for rare. Transfer to a plate and keep warm in a 250°F oven.

2. Pour off any fat from the skillet and return it to high heat. When nearly smoking hot, add half the corn and cook for 1 minute without stirring. Stir and cook for 1 minute more. The corn should be dark brown or even black in spots. Scrape the corn onto a plate, return the skillet to the heat, and repeat with the remaining corn.

3. Add the onion to the skillet, reduce the heat to medium, and cook, stirring, for 30 seconds. Add the orange juice and cook until reduced by half, about 5 minutes. Return the corn to the pan and add the rosemary. Reduce the heat to low and stir in the butter.

4. Pour any juices that have collected around the lamb into the skillet. Spoon the corn onto a platter, arrange the chops on top, and serve immediately.

BROILED LAMB CHOPS WITH PRUNES

SERVES 4

*M*arinating the lamb for several hours in whiskey improves its flavor, but if you're in a rush to get dinner on the table, you can cut down the time and the lamb will still taste good.

12 thick-cut lamb rib chops (about 1¾ pounds)
1 tablespoon brown sugar
⅓ cup whiskey
Salt and freshly ground black pepper to taste
2 tablespoons finely minced onion or shallots
½ cup chicken stock or canned low-sodium chicken broth
12 pitted prunes
¼ cup heavy cream
2 tablespoons unsalted butter
1 tablespoon chopped fresh parsley or mint

1. At least 4 hours before dinner, place the lamb in a glass or other nonreactive dish. Dissolve the sugar in the whiskey and pour over the lamb. Sprinkle with salt and pepper, cover, and refrigerate for up to 8 hours, turning once.

2. When it's time to prepare dinner, preheat the broiler.

3. Place the onion in a large saucepan, and add the broth. Drain the marinade from the lamb chops and add it to the saucepan. Bring to a boil over medium heat and cook until reduced by half, about 8 to 10 minutes.

4. Add the prunes and the cream and cook until the liquid has reduced to the consistency of a sauce, about 3 minutes. Remove from the heat and whisk in the butter. Taste for salt and pepper and add to taste. Keep warm.

5. Meanwhile, place the lamb chops under the broiler and broil for about 2 to 3 minutes on each side for very rare, about 4 minutes per side for rare, or 6 minutes for medium.

6. To serve dinner, spoon the prunes and sauce onto a serving platter, arrange the chops on top, and sprinkle with the chopped parsley or mint.

DILL AND CARAWAY PORK TENDERLOINS

SERVES 6

*P*ork tenderloins don't have the flavor of a roast or chops, so prepare them with a flavorful accompaniment. Use a pungent, resinous herb like rosemary or sage or pair them with the strong flavor of seeds such as cumin, celery, or coriander. My favorite is caraway, the seed that flavors rye bread.

Serve boiled or mashed potatoes and sauerkraut with this dish.

2 tablespoons olive oil
4 pork tenderloins (about 3½ pounds total)
Salt and freshly ground black pepper to taste
½ cup chicken stock or canned low-sodium chicken broth
2 tablespoons Dijon mustard
¼ cup heavy cream
2 teaspoons caraway seeds
2 tablespoons chopped fresh dill

1. Heat the oil over high heat in a large skillet. Sprinkle the pork with salt and pepper, add to the pan, and brown on all sides until light golden, about 7 minutes.

2. Meanwhile, combine the stock and mustard and mix well.

3. Add the stock mixture to the browned pork, cover, and cook for 5 minutes. Turn the tenderloins, add the cream and caraway seeds, and cook, uncovered, for 10 minutes.

4. Transfer the tenderloins to a platter. If the sauce seems thin, cook until it coats the back of a spoon.

5. To serve, slice the meat and arrange on a serving platter. Stir the dill into the sauce and spoon over the meat. Serve immediately.

VEAL SCALLOPINE WITH LEEKS

SERVES 4

*U*se a green, herby olive oil for this dish—not a rough Greek or Spanish one, but a Tuscan variety.

Serve a risotto and some sautéed mushrooms with the veal and follow with a green salad.

> *1¼ pounds veal eye-of-round roast or veal scallopine*
> *Salt and freshly ground black pepper to taste*
> *Flour, for dusting*
> *2 tablespoons unsalted butter*
> *4 leeks, white part only, thinly sliced (about 2 cups)*
> *About 2 tablespoons extra virgin olive oil*
> *2 tablespoons dry white wine*
> *1 tablespoon fresh lemon juice*
> *2 teaspoons chopped fresh sage or 1 teaspoon dried*

1. If you've bought a roast, cut it into 8 or 12 slices. Place the slices between two sheets of plastic wrap and pound them to a thickness of ¼-inch or less. If using scallopine, pound to the same thickness if necessary. Pat the meat dry with towels and sprinkle with salt and pepper. Dust with flour, shaking off the excess, and set aside.

2. Heat 1 tablespoon of the butter in a skillet over low heat. Add the leeks and salt and pepper to taste, cover, and cook for 20 minutes, stirring occasionally. Remove from the heat and keep warm.

3. Place a large frying pan over medium-high heat. Add enough oil to coat the bottom of the pan, and heat the oil. Add 4 or 5 pieces of veal, without crowding the pan, and cook for 2 minutes on each side. Transfer to a plate and keep warm while you cook the remainder, adding more oil as necessary.

4. Pour the wine and lemon juice into the pan and add any juices that have collected on the plate of veal. Add the sage and cook for 1 minute. Remove the sauce from the heat and swirl in the remaining 1 tablespoon butter.

5. To serve, make a bed of the leeks on a platter and arrange the veal on top. Spoon the sauce over the top and bring dinner to the table.

Guess Who's Coming to Dinner

*C*ooking for people is my favorite thing to do. At my restaurant I instruct the cooks, teach them how I want things done, and then watch to make sure it's done correctly and with passion. Having guests for dinner at home is about the only chance I get now to really cook. I invariably attempt to do too much, forgetting how spoiled I am at work where I have staff. But I have come up with a certain repertoire of special dishes that are fun to prepare at home and nourish both appetite and conversation.

Some of the recipes here are for family holiday gatherings; there are two ham recipes as well as a goose with sauerkraut and a stuffed turkey breast. Two roast pork loin dishes are suitable for a large dinner party where you have to leave the kitchen to greet guests; they can both sit in the oven for a while before serving.

I like serving a fish main course when I have a guest whose eating habits I don't know. With so many people avoiding red meat for health reasons and white meat for whatever reasons they can think up, fish is a safe alternative. Here there's Roasted Salmon and Beets and Turbans of Flounder and Crab. Among the company fish recipes in other chapters are Shad with Sorrel (page 279) and Baked Swordfish and Cucumbers (page 282).

When I know my guests well, I prepare my favorite lamb recipes, a roast lamb with garlic and sage and a rack with bacon vinaigrette. Blanquette of Veal and Cauliflower in Dinner in the French Manner (page 191) and Cassoulet (page 177) are both stupendous stews that I am proud to serve to company. In fact, there are more entertaining recipes scattered throughout the other chapters than there are collected here. I guess the message is that we should treat ourselves better—as least as well as we treat our guests.

TURBANS OF FLOUNDER AND CRAB

SERVES 4

*W*hen you've spent some time assembling a dish rather than simply putting dinner on a plate, the food must taste as good as it looks. This dinner tastes fancy, with onion, celery, and thyme enhancing the crab and a subtle nutmeg and sherry flavor in the sauce.

9 tablespoons unsalted butter
½ small onion, finely diced (about ¼ cup)
1 celery stalk, finely diced (about ¼ cup)
2 tablespoons all-purpose flour
¼ cup milk
½ teaspoon fresh thyme or ¼ teaspoon dried
⅛ teaspoon nutmeg, preferably freshly grated
¼ teaspoon Tabasco sauce
¾ pound fresh crabmeat
½ teaspoon salt, or to taste
Ground white pepper to taste
4 6-ounce flounder or sole fillets
1 cup dry sherry

1. Melt 3 tablespoons of the butter in a medium skillet over medium heat. Add the onion and celery, cover, and cook until soft, about 3 minutes. Sprinkle with the flour and cook, stirring, for 1 minute. Add the milk, thyme, nutmeg, and Tabasco and cook, stirring, just until the mixture thickens, about 30 seconds. Transfer to a bowl, add the crabmeat, salt, and pepper, and mix well. Let cool.

2. Preheat the oven to 375°F.

3. Use a coffee cup or a measuring cup to form the turbans: Line the sides of the cup with a 2-inch-high strip of parchment paper. Making sure that the thinner part of the fillet is toward the bottom of the cup, place a fillet (skin side in) against the paper, overlapping the ends of the fillet if necessary. Then push down gently so that most of the bottom of the cup is covered. It doesn't matter if the fillet doesn't fit perfectly into the cup. Fill the center of the cup with a quarter of the crab mixture. Now carefully pull the turban out of the cup and stand it up in a baking dish that is just large enough to hold the 4 turbans. Repeat to make 3 more turbans and place in the baking dish.

4. Pour the sherry into the baking dish, cover, and bake for 20 to 25 minutes, or until the crabmeat filling puffs up slightly.

5. Transfer the turbans to a serving platter and keep warm. Pour the cooking liquid into a saucepan and simmer over medium heat until reduced by about half. Remove from the heat and whisk in the remaining 6 tablespoons butter. Taste for salt and pepper and adjust to taste. Pour any juices that have collected around the turbans into the sauce, then spoon the sauce over the turbans and serve immediately.

ROASTED SALMON AND BEETS

SERVES 4

*B*eets and salmon are an amazing couple because they both have a kind of peaty, earthy flavor. I can't really describe how much I like this dish, and how sincerely eccentric the combination is.

Keep the rest of dinner pretty tame. Serve a cucumber salad, boiled potatoes, and lots of bread for soaking up the sauce.

> *2 medium beets (about 1 pound)*
> *½ cup red wine*
> *¼ cup fish stock or bottled clam juice*
> *Salt and freshly ground black pepper to taste*
> *1½ pounds salmon fillet, in 4 pieces, or 4 salmon steaks*
> *1 tablespoon unsalted butter*
> *1 tablespoon sour cream*
> *2 tablespoons chopped fresh dill, for garnish*

1. Trim off the beet tops. Peel the beets and slice them as thin as you can, using the slicing blade on a food processor or a mandoline.

2. Place the beets in a 2-quart baking dish. Add the wine, stock or clam juice, and salt and pepper, cover, and place in the oven. Turn the oven on to 425°F and bake for 30 minutes.

3. Meanwhile, pat the salmon dry and sprinkle with salt and pepper.

4. Place the salmon fillets on top of the beets and bake 15 minutes longer.

5. Arrange the salmon on a serving platter, leaving the center of the platter empty, and keep warm. Whisk the butter and sour cream into the beets and place them in the center of the platter. Sprinkle the salmon and beets with the dill and serve immediately.

FLATTENED CHICKEN AND MUSHROOMS

SERVES 3 TO 4

*F*lattening the chicken makes the dark and white meat cook at the same rate. I like this dish because the meat comes falling off the bone, something that's desirable in a larger roasting chicken with tougher but more flavorful meat. A large chicken like this has enough fat to self-baste as it roasts. It crisps and delights.

Serve a first-course soup, or something unexpected like potato pancakes.

1 4- to 5-pound roasting chicken
Several branches fresh rosemary
2 tablespoons olive oil
Salt and ground white pepper to taste
3 tablespoons Dijon mustard
2 pounds small white mushrooms
½ cup chicken stock or canned low-sodium chicken broth
½ cup sour cream or plain yogurt

1. Preheat the oven to 350°F.

2. Using a large sharp knife cut down the sides of the backbone of the chicken and remove the backbone. Lay the chicken flat on a work surface, skin side up, lay a large roasting pan over it, and press down on the roasting pan to flatten the chicken. Carefully insert the rosemary branches under the chicken skin. Rub the entire chicken with the oil, then sprinkle with salt and pepper. Place skin side up in a roasting pan and roast for 1 hour.

3. Remove the chicken from the roasting pan and brush both sides of the bird with the mustard. Scatter the mushrooms over the bottom of the roasting pan and lay the chicken on top. Roast for 35 minutes longer.

4. Transfer the chicken to a serving platter. Place the roasting pan over high heat, add the chicken stock, and cook, stirring, for 5 minutes. Remove from the heat and whisk in the sour cream. Spoon the mushrooms and sauce around the chicken and serve immediately.

Poussins with Celeriac and Wild Rice Stuffing

Serves 4

*P*oussins are the smallest, youngest chickens. They have the lightest, most tender flesh, and weigh about 12 to 14 ounces. These small birds cook quickly and are always tender. You can use Cornish hens in this recipe as well, but you probably won't have to baste them with butter, because they are fattier than the poussin.

The stuffing for this dish soaks up poultry flavor while it roasts. The celeriac acts as the bread. Serve a lot of simply prepared vegetables. You can begin dinner with something rich because the poussin really isn't—it just tastes that way.

1¼ pounds celeriac (celery root)
1¼ pounds onions, roughly diced
½ cup cooked wild rice
½ cup pine nuts
1 teaspoon fresh thyme or ½ teaspoon dried
2 teaspoons salt
½ teaspoon freshly ground black pepper
4 poussins or small Cornish hens
1½ cups chicken stock or canned low-sodium chicken broth
2 tablespoons melted unsalted butter
2 tablespoons unsalted butter, at room temperature

1. Remove and discard the celeriac tops. Using a paring knife, peel off and discard the thick, tough outer layer. Cut the celeriac into pieces small enough to fit in the feed tube of a food processor. Using the shredding blade, shred the celeriac.

2. Combine the onions and celeriac in a heavy pot, cover, and cook over low heat for 20 minutes, stirring frequently. Transfer to a bowl, add the rice, pine nuts, thyme, salt, and pepper, and mix well. Refrigerate until completely cool.

3. Preheat the oven to 400°F.

4. Stuff the birds with the cooled stuffing and tie the legs together with string. Place in a roasting pan, place in the oven, and lower the temperature to 350°F. Roast for 1 to 1¼ hours, until the juices from the thigh run clear. Baste occasionally with the melted butter. *(continued)*

5. Transfer the hens to a serving platter. Place the roasting pan over medium heat, add the stock and bring to a simmer, stirring to scrape up any dark bits on the bottom of the pan. Remove from the heat and swirl in the room-temperature butter. Pour the *jus* over the birds and serve dinner immediately.

ROAST CAPON WITH POLENTA STUFFING

SERVES 5 TO 6

*C*apons, neutered roosters, are large, have a good amount of dark meat, and are always best when roasted. I always stuff them, partly because then it takes longer for them to cook and the result is wonderful, falling-off-the-bone meat. I lay a double layer of cheesecloth wrung out with oil over the bird to act as a sort of baster helper. This marvelous trick will also work wonders for your usual roast chicken or your holiday turkey. It ensures a perfectly golden crisp skin. Although seldom seen in markets today, capons are easy to special order, even from your local supermarket.

Cook a variety of vegetable side dishes to serve with this perfect feast-day bird.

2 tablespoons unsalted butter or margarine
2 pounds white mushrooms, sliced
2 medium onions, diced
Salt
½ cup yellow cornmeal
Freshly ground black pepper
¼ teaspoon ground coriander
½ teaspoon dried thyme
1 8- to 9-pound capon
¼ cup olive oil or chicken fat
¼ cup all-purpose flour
2 cups chicken stock or canned low-sodium chicken broth

1. Melt the butter in a large skillet. Add the mushrooms and half the onions and cook over medium heat, stirring occasionally, until the onions are soft and all the moisture from the mushrooms has evaporated, about 15 minutes. Scrape into a bowl and set aside.

2. Pour 2 cups water into a medium pot, add ½ teaspoon salt, and bring to a boil over high heat. Pour in the cornmeal in a slow, steady stream, stirring constantly, and cook for 1 minute. Then reduce the heat to low and cook, stirring constantly, for 15 minutes. Scrape the polenta into the bowl of mushrooms. Add ¼ teaspoon pepper, the coriander, and thyme and mix well. Let cool to room temperature.

3. Meanwhile, preheat the oven to 450°F. Remove the giblets from the cavity of the capon, rinse the bird, and pat dry. Moisten a large sheet of cheesecloth with the oil and set aside.

4. Turn the wings underneath the capon. Stuff the cavity as tightly as possible with the cool stuffing, and tie the legs together. Sprinkle the bird with salt and pepper, place in a roasting pan, and roast for 15 minutes. Reduce the heat to 350°F. Fold the cheesecloth in half and lay over the bird. Roast for about 2 to 2½ hours longer, about 15 minutes per pound, or until a thermometer inserted into the center of the stuffing reads 180°F. Every 30 minutes, lift the cheesecloth, baste the bird, and replace the cheesecloth.

5. Transfer the capon to a platter. Drain off the fat from the roasting pan, reserving ¼ cup. Return the reserved fat to the pan, place over low heat, and stir in the flour. Cook, stirring, for 1 minute. Add the stock and cook, scraping up any dark bits that have stuck to the bottom of the roasting pan, until reduced by about half. Remove from the heat. Taste and add salt and pepper as desired.

6. Remove the stuffing from the capon and place it in a serving bowl. Place the bird on a platter and pour the gravy into a sauceboat.

TURKEY CUTLETS WITH AN APPLE, POTATO, AND ONION MACÉDOINE

SERVES 4

*T*he macédoine of diced apples, onion, and potatoes is the only vegetable you need on this elegant plate. Begin dinner with a pre-set or chilled first course—a steamed artichoke, for example, or a salad of smoked trout; or serve a chilled or hot soup. Prepare the macédoine before the guests arrive and cook the cutlets at the last minute.

Turkey cutlets risk cooking to dry, tough slabs even if you are attentive. This flour and egg coating keeps them moist, but be certain to shake off all excess flour and let the egg run off. Too much of it will absorb oil and will remind you rather too much of a turkey omelette.

> 2 green apples, such as Granny Smiths
> 1 tablespoon fresh lemon juice
> 1 medium onion, roughly diced (about ¾ cup)
> ½ pound waxy potatoes (unpeeled)
> ½ teaspoon salt, or to taste
> ½ teaspoon ground white pepper
> 2 tablespoons melted unsalted butter
> ¼ cup dry white wine
> 2 tablespoons cider vinegar
> 2 eggs
> Flour, for dusting
> 1 to 2 tablespoons vegetable oil
> 8 slices turkey cutlet (about 1¾ pounds total)

1. Peel and core the apples, and cut into ¼-inch dice. Place in a bowl and toss with the lemon juice. Add the onion to the bowl and set aside.

2. Cut the potatoes into ¼-inch dice. Place in a pot and add cold water to barely cover. Bring to a boil over high heat and cook for 2 minutes. Drain.

3. Add the potatoes to the onion and apples and toss well. Scrape into a baking dish, add the salt, pepper, butter, wine, and vinegar, and mix well. Cover and place in the oven. Turn the oven on to 375°F and bake for 40 minutes. Remove and keep warm.

4. Meanwhile, break the eggs into a bowl. Add 1 tablespoon water and beat lightly. Spread the flour on a plate.

5. When it's time to get dinner on the table, heat 1 tablespoon of the oil in a skillet over medium heat. Dust 3 or 4 of the cutlets in flour and dip in the beaten egg, letting the excess run off. Add to the hot oil, without crowding the pan, and cook for 1 minute on each side, or until golden on both sides. Drain on paper towels and keep warm. Repeat with the remaining cutlets, adding more oil to the skillet as necessary.

6. Scrape the macédoine onto a serving platter and arrange the cutlets on top. Serve immediately.

ROAST STUFFED TURKEY BREAST

SERVES 5 TO 6

*W*hole turkey breasts are stuffed with a small dice of ingredients and then roasted. Some of the stuffing will undoubtedly run out of the turkey during roasting; just scrape it up and transfer it to your serving platter—it will be slightly overcooked and some of the cheese will have burned, which only adds a special flavor to the dish. Slice the breast to serve, and each slice will show a nice vein of colorful stuffing.

> *1 whole boneless turkey breast (about 3 pounds)*
> *Salt and freshly ground black pepper to taste*
> *4 tablespoons vegetable oil or unsalted butter, at room temperature*
> *1 medium onion, finely chopped (about ¾ cup)*
> *2 cups chopped fresh spinach or ¾ cup frozen spinach, thawed and*
> *   drained*
> *½ pound Black Forest ham, finely diced*
> *1 tablespoon chopped fresh sage or 1 teaspoon dried*
> *¼ teaspoon ground mace*
> *½ pound raclette or Gruyère cheese, grated*
> *1 cup Marsala wine*
> *½ cup heavy cream*

1. Cut the turkey breast in half. Remove the tenderloins from each breast and reserve for another use. Lay the breasts skin side down on a work surface and, using a thin sharp knife, cut a lengthwise slit in the side of each breast, forming a pocket. Sprinkle the pockets with salt and pepper and set the turkey aside in the refrigerator. *(continued)*

Guess Who's Coming to Dinner

2. Combine 2 tablespoons of the oil or butter and the onion in a large saucepan and cook over medium heat, stirring occasionally, until the onion softens, about 7 minutes. Add the spinach and ham and cook for 5 minutes, stirring occasionally. Transfer to a bowl, add the sage and mace, and allow to cool.

3. Preheat the oven to 350°F.

4. Add the cheese to the spinach and ham and mix well. Stuff this mixture into the turkey breasts, then sew the slits closed. Rub the turkey with the remaining 2 tablespoons oil or butter, then sprinkle all over with salt and

Roasting

No other method quite matches roasting for cooking large joints of meat or whole birds. Until the late nineteenth century, however, working people didn't have roasts; they ate foods cooked in a pot over the same hearth fire that provided heat for the home—potages, stews, braises, and pot roasts. Only the wealthy could afford both the animal and the fuel required for this inefficient method of cooking, where as much as half the heat produced escapes. Even today, roasts are "special" meals, reserved for major feast days.

Roasting always makes me think of those good bits stuck to the bottom of the heavy roasting pan. When I was growing up, I, like most youngsters, didn't want sauce (and my mother didn't make sauces or gravies anyway), but we got to scrape the bottom of the roasting pan. Now, of course, we're more sophisticated. We don't throw away the flavor, but use the delicious concentrate to make sauce or gravy.

Most roasting should happen slowly. Slow cooking results in tender flesh. But if your roast is a tender cut to begin with and not too large, say under five pounds and less than four inches thick—a fillet of beef for example—do not roast it slowly or it will dry out. You want the outside crisp while keeping the interior rare and still juicy. On the other hand, if you have a really large or a really tough piece of meat, you should roast it for a long amount of time at a low temperature.

Roasting is easy. First you want to form a crust on the surface. Contrary to popular culinary lore, this does not preserve the internal pepper. Place the breasts in a roasting pan, skin side down, and roast for 20 minutes. Turn the breasts and roast for 30 minutes longer.

5. Remove the turkey from the pan along with any stuffing that has fallen out, and keep warm. Pour the Marsala into the roasting pan, stir to scrape up any burnt bits stuck on the bottom of the pan, and pour into a medium saucepan. Add the cream, bring to a simmer over high heat, and cook until reduced to the consistency of a sauce, about 7 to 8 minutes. Pour into a sauceboat.

6. Slice the turkey against the grain into thin slices, arrange on a platter, and serve. Pass the sauce separately.

juices. What it does do, however, is caramelize the proteins, giving a wonderful taste to your roast. Place roasts weighing more than five pounds in a hot oven—400°F—and turn the heat down to 350°F after five minutes. To avoid overcooking smaller roasts, sear them on top of the stove over high heat, then transfer to a 350°F oven.

Whenever possible, buy a bone-in roast. The bone adds flavor and the meat nearer the bone cooks more slowly, enabling you to get that desirable crusty surface while maintaining a good rare-to-medium-rare meat temperature.

Poultry comes with its own "crust"—the skin, which also acts like a natural basting bag. As a bird roasts, the fat layer under the skin melts, basting the meat. As the fat dissolves, the skin crisps, forming the crust. Begin cooking chickens and other fowl in a 400°F oven, but immediately reduce the heat to 350°F. Because the fat underneath the skin is rendered as the skin crisps, even if you don't want to eat skin for health reasons, roast your birds with the skin on and remove it before serving.

The microwave oven will neither concentrate interior juices nor help in the formation of a crust. You can help a microwaved roast, meat or poultry, along with a preliminary cooking by first searing it well on all sides in a very hot pan with only a small amount of oil.

Let roasted meat and poultry rest for a few minutes after removing it from the oven to give the juices time to relax. This ensures that the meat will not give up all its juices once carved.

Since roasting happens by itself—all you need to do is baste from time to time—you can spend more energy on side dishes or another course such as a soup, salad, or dessert.

ROAST GOOSE WITH CUMIN APPLES

SERVES 6 TO 8

*M*ost people whine about goose—it's too fatty, they say; they're afraid it will be dry; there's not enough meat on it. So we rarely eat it these days—and what a shame that is. Goose is a magical bird to eat. Its flesh is dark and rich. It's gamey but it's not game. Yes, it's fatty, but with proper cooking it crisps up nicely. Cook it in two stages: The first cooking defats the bird and the second readies the bird for dinner. Many vegetable dishes can accompany this special bird. I serve glazed Brussels sprouts, pureed carrots or pureed celeriac, and gratinéed potatoes, among others.

1 8- to 10-pound goose
Salt and freshly ground black pepper to taste
3 cups drained sauerkraut (1 27-ounce can)
6 green apples, such as Granny Smiths
3 tablespoons fresh lemon juice
6 tablespoons unsalted butter
2 tablespoons cumin seed or 1 teaspoon ground

1. Rinse the goose and pat dry. Prick it all over with a large fork, and sprinkle with salt and pepper. Turn the wings underneath the bird and tie the legs together. Place on a rack in a deep roasting pan, cover tightly, and place in the oven. Turn the oven on to 450°F and cook for 20 minutes. Reduce the heat to 350°F, uncover, and roast for a total of 20 minutes per pound.

2. Transfer goose to cutting board. Strain fat and reserve for other use.

3. When the goose is cool enough to handle, untruss it and, using poultry shears, cut into 8 serving pieces. (The goose can be prepared to this point up to 6 hours in advance and refrigerated.)

4. Arrange a bed of sauerkraut in a large baking dish and arrange goose pieces, skin side up, on top. Cover and bake at 350°F for 30 minutes.

5. Meanwhile, peel and core the apples. Roughly dice into ½-inch pieces, place in a small bowl, and toss with the lemon juice.

6. Melt the butter in a medium skillet over medium heat. Add the apples and cumin and cook, tossing occasionally, for 5 minutes. Remove from the heat and keep warm.

7. To serve, arrange the sauerkraut and goose on a serving platter. Spoon the apples and their sauce over the goose and serve immediately.

What's for Dinner?

Ham with Sweet and Sour Root Vegetables

SERVES 10

*T*his is most definitely a winter meal, with all those glazed root vegetables accompanying the ham. It's a wonderful holiday dish, especially with baked yams or mashed potatoes. Simply cooked green vegetables such as spinach and Brussels sprouts are perfect accompaniments.

½ ham (about 5 to 6 pounds)
2 cups distilled white vinegar
3 tablespoons honey
5 tablespoons prepared mustard
½ pound carrots
½ pound parsnips
½ pound rutabagas
½ pound turnips
2 pints pearl onions (about 2 pounds)
2 tablespoons sugar
1 tablespoon unsalted butter

1. Place the ham in a large pot, add the vinegar and enough cold water to cover, cover, and bring to a boil over high heat. Reduce the heat to low and simmer for 30 minutes.

2. Preheat the oven to 350°F.

3. Drain the ham, reserving 2½ cups of the liquid. Score the ham in 1-inch crisscrosses. Mix the mustard and honey together. Place the ham on a rack in a roasting pan and brush with some of the honey mustard. Roast for 30 minutes, brushing once more with the mustard.

4. Meanwhile, peel the vegetables. Cut the carrots and parsnips into 1-inch lengths, and cut the rutabagas and turnips into 8 wedges each. Peel the pearl onions, being careful not to cut off the root ends. Cut an X in each end.

5. Combine all the vegetables in a 14-inch skillet or in two 8-inch skillets. Add the reserved braising liquid, the sugar, and butter, cover, bring to a boil over high heat, and cook for 5 minutes. Uncover and cook, stirring frequently, until all the liquid has evaporated and the vegetables are glazed and shiny. Remove from the heat and keep warm.

6. To serve dinner, place the vegetables in a serving dish. Present the ham on a large platter, and offer any remaining honey mustard on the side.

FRESH HAM WITH CARAWAY APPLES

SERVES 12 TO 16

A fresh ham is just a pork leg that has not been cured or smoked. Buy half a leg—it's probably all you'll be able to get in your oven but it will still feed a crowd. This is, after all, holiday food. Insist that your butcher leave the crackling on—it acts as a kind of natural roasting bag and it's a real treat to eat. Once the ham is cooked, cut up the squares of crackling for all your guests.

½ boneless fresh ham (about 8 pounds), skin intact
½ teaspoon ground allspice
1 teaspoon ground cumin
2 tablespoons chopped fresh or dried sage
¼ cup finely minced garlic
1 tablespoon salt
2 tablespoons freshly ground black pepper
2 pounds small new potatoes
6 apples, peeled and diced
1 teaspoon caraway seeds
1 cup dry white wine
2 cups chicken stock or canned low-sodium chicken broth
Dijon mustard, for serving
Prepared horseradish, for serving

1. Lay the pork skin side up on a work surface and score the skin in a 1-inch crisscross pattern. Combine the allspice, cumin, sage, garlic, salt, and pepper. Turn the leg meat side up and rub the inside cavity with the seasoning mixture. Roll the leg up into a compact shape and secure with string. Refrigerate at least overnight or up to 3 days.

2. Preheat the oven to 450°F.

3. Place the ham in a large roasting pan, cover, and roast for 20 minutes. Reduce the heat to 300°F and roast, covered, for 1½ hours. Then add the potatoes to the pan and roast, uncovered, for 1 to 1½ hours longer, or until a meat thermometer thrust into the center of the ham reads 165°F. (Total roasting time is approximately 25 minutes per pound.) Stir the potatoes from time to time, and remove them from the pan as soon as they are tender. Place in a bowl and keep warm.

4. When the pork is done, transfer it to a serving platter and let rest for 20 minutes. Meanwhile, pour off the drippings from the roasting pan, reserving 2 tablespoons. Set the pan aside. Place the reserved drippings in a skillet over medium heat, add the apples and caraway seeds, and cook for 5 minutes. Remove from the heat and keep warm.

5. Place the roasting pan over medium heat. Add the wine and stock and stir to scrape up the brown bits on the bottom of the pan. Transfer to a saucepan, bring to a boil over high heat, and cook until reduced by half. Pour into a sauceboat and keep warm.

6. To serve, untie the roast, slice off the crackling, and cut into squares. Slice the pork thin. Arrange a bed of the apples on a serving platter, arrange the pork on top, and place squares of crackling on the pork. Surround the pork with the potatoes. Pass the sauceboat of pan juices and offer mustard and horseradish on the side.

ROAST LOIN OF PORK WITH
FIG AND ONION COMPOTE

SERVES 6 TO 8

*A*s the pork roasts, the onions soften and the figs plump. Scrape up this savory, jammy stew with slices of pork and drizzle them with honey mustard.

Some small roasted new potatoes and other simply prepared vegetables should accompany the pork. Begin dinner with clam chowder.

3 tablespoons vegetable oil
2 teaspoons kosher salt
1 teaspoon ground white pepper
½ teaspoon ground allspice
1 3-pound boneless pork loin roast
24 dried black Mission figs
⅔ cup Marsala wine
1 pint pearl onions (about 1 pound)
½ cup chicken stock or canned low-sodium chicken broth
3 tablespoons honey
6 tablespoons Dijon or other spicy mustard
1 tablespoon chopped fresh parsley
3 tablespoons unsalted butter

1. Combine 1 tablespoon of the oil, the salt, pepper, and allspice in a small bowl. Rub the pork all over with the mixture, cover, and let stand at room temperature for 1 hour. Combine the figs and Marsala in a small bowl and let steep for 1 hour.

2. Meanwhile, place the onions in a bowl of warm water and let sit for 20 minutes to soften the skins. Drain.

3. Using a small knife, peel the onions. Cut an X in the root tip of each one, and set aside.

4. Preheat the oven to 350°F.

5. Heat the remaining 2 tablespoons oil in a frying pan over high heat. Add the pork and brown on all sides. Transfer the pork to a roasting pan, add the onions, figs, Marsala, and stock, cover, and roast for 30 minutes. Then remove the lid and roast 30 minutes more, or until a meat thermometer inserted into the pork reads 145°F.

6. Meanwhile, combine honey and mustard and pour into a small dish.

7. Transfer the pork to a platter and let rest for 5 minutes before slicing.
Add the parsley to the onion/fig mixture and beat in the butter.

8. To serve, mound the fig compote on a serving platter. Slice the pork into ¼-inch slices and lay the slices over the compote. Accompany with the honey mustard.

PORK CHOPS WITH
SAVORY SAGE BREAD PUDDING

SERVES 8 TO 10

*7*he bread pudding that accompanies this pork tenderloin is like a refined bread stuffing, almost a soufflé.

A heavy pot with a tightly fitting lid allows you to sweat and then caramelize the onion, celery, and garlic mixture without using any oil. Listen to the sound the pot makes—the pot sound will get louder and more frenetic as the vegetables approach doneness and lose moisture. They're then ready to be mixed into the pudding.

2 medium onions, diced
1 large bunch celery, trimmed and sliced
¼ cup finely minced garlic
6 ounces egg bread, such as challah, cut into 1-inch cubes
  (about 4 cups)
6 eggs
4 egg whites
5 cups milk
¼ teaspoon ground mace
Salt and freshly ground black pepper
4 tablespoons unsalted butter
6 double-cut pork chops
1 cup chicken stock or canned low-sodium chicken broth
2 teaspoons fresh rosemary or 1 teaspoon dried

1. Combine onions, celery, and garlic in a heavy 2-quart pot, cover, and cook over medium heat for about 10 minutes. Remove the lid, increase the heat to medium high, and cook, stirring, for 20 minutes, or until the vegetables seem dry and the onion is golden. Scrape into a bowl, add the bread, and mix.

(continued)

2. Beat the eggs and egg whites together. Beat in 3 cups of the milk, salt, mace, 2 teaspoons salt and 1 teaspoon pepper and pour over the onion/bread mixture. Let rest for 30 minutes.

3. Preheat the oven to 350°F. Generously butter a 2-quart Bundt pan, using 1 tablespoon of the butter.

4. Carefully pour the pudding mixture into the Bundt pan and bake for 1¼ hours.

5. Meanwhile, heat 1 tablespoon of the butter in an ovenproof skillet over medium heat. Sprinkle the pork chops with salt and pepper and add to the skillet along with the remaining 2 cups milk, the stock, and rosemary. Bring to a boil, transfer the skillet to the oven, and cook the chops, turning once, for 25 minutes. Remove from the oven and keep warm.

6. Remove the bread pudding from the oven and let cool for 5 minutes.

7. Run a knife around the edge of the pan and turn the pudding out onto a platter. Arrange the pork around the pudding. Whisk the remaining 2 tablespoons butter into the cooking juices remaining in the skillet and pour over the chops. Serve immediately.

VEAL ROAST WITH SHALLOTS AND LEMON

SERVES 5 TO 6

*T*his dish needs shallots—lots of shallots—for their garlicky edge and because they play better than onions with the tart lemon pan gravy.

A veal roast is a glorious piece of meat and deserves only the best accompaniment. Feel free to serve a creamy, cheesy potato gratin with dinner, and feature lots of vegetables. Begin with a seafood bisque or some smoked salmon. Follow the veal with a green salad and serve bitter chocolate truffles with coffee.

¼ cup olive oil

1 tablespoon fresh thyme or 1 teaspoon dried

1 teaspoon salt

½ teaspoon freshly ground black pepper

1 3- to 3½-pound boneless veal round roast

¼ cup fresh lemon juice

½ cup chicken stock or canned low-sodium chicken broth

¾ cup finely minced shallots

2 tablespoons unsalted butter

1. Combine 3 tablespoons of the oil, half the thyme, the salt, and pepper and rub all over the veal. Cover and refrigerate for at least 4 hours, or overnight.

2. Heat the remaining 1 tablespoon oil in a Dutch oven or deep heavy skillet over medium-high heat. Add the veal and sear on all sides until browned, about 15 minutes. Reduce the heat to low and add the lemon juice, stock, shallots, and remaining thyme. Cover tightly and cook for 45 minutes, or until a meat thermometer reads 135°F.

3. Transfer the roast to a carving board and let rest for 15 minutes. Swirl the butter into the cooking juices in the pan, and keep warm.

4. When it's time to put dinner on the table, cut the roast into ¼-inch slices and arrange on a serving platter. Spoon some of the sauce over the meat and serve the remainder in a sauceboat.

Roast Rack of Veal with Vegetable Mirepoix

SERVES 7 TO 10

*W*hen I serve a whole roasted rack of veal, people gasp with anticipation, for this is one of the most sublime cuts of meat you can cook. Although one is accustomed to eating veal chops in restaurants, when the rack is roasted whole, the texture of the meat is more relaxed, unctuous, and flavorful. There's more than enough meat here for seven people, but I prefer to give each person a bone.

1 tablespoon vegetable oil
1 teaspoon ground marjoram
1 teaspoon kosher salt
1 teaspoon freshly ground black pepper
1 7-bone rack of veal (about 6 to 7 pounds)
3 medium carrots, peeled and diced (about 2 cups)
2 medium onions, diced (about 1½ cups)
6 celery stalks, thinly sliced
3 medium potatoes (unpeeled), diced (about 5 cups)
2 tablespoons melted unsalted butter
¼ cup chicken stock or canned low-sodium chicken broth
1 cup fresh or frozen peas
2 tablespoons unsalted butter

1. Combine the oil, marjoram, salt, and pepper and rub all over the veal. Cover and let sit for 1 hour at room temperature, or refrigerate overnight.

2. Preheat the oven to 450°F.

3. Place the veal in a large roasting pan. Toss the carrots, onions, celery, and potatoes in the melted butter and scatter around the veal. Roast for 10 minutes, then reduce the temperature to 350°F. and roast for 1 to 1¼ hours, or until a meat thermometer reads 140°F.

4. Transfer the roast to a carving board and let rest for 15 minutes. Meanwhile, add the broth and peas to the pan and return to oven for 10 minutes.

5. Remove the pan from the oven and swirl in the 2 tablespoons butter.

6. To serve, spoon the vegetables onto a serving platter. Cut the roast into chops and arrange on the vegetables. Pour the pan juices over and serve immediately.

Rack of Lamb with Asparagus
and Bacon Vinaigrette

SERVES 4

I t's so nice that spring brings us the best baby lamb and the first asparagus of the year—a well-paired combination. I adore asparagus, even the tinned spears. The thick spears have more flavor than the pencil-thin variety, and although a prettier green color when undercooked, asparagus tastes better when it is tender.

The nut of meat that comprises the rack is solid and only about 2 inches in diameter. Perfectly cooked racks of medium-rare to medium lamb should have nearly the same pink color from the surface to the center.

> 2 trimmed lamb racks, 8 ribs each (about 3¾ pounds total)
> ¼ cup olive oil
> ⅔ cup red wine vinegar
> 1 teaspoon minced garlic
> 1 teaspoon ground coriander
> 1 teaspoon kosher salt
> 1 teaspoon freshly ground black pepper
> 2 pounds small new potatoes
> ½ pound sliced bacon, cut into ¾-inch-wide strips
> 1½ cups chicken stock or canned low-sodium chicken broth
> 2 pounds medium to thick asparagus
> Salt to taste
> 1 tablespoon Dijon mustard

1. Trim off the outer layer of fat from the lamb, leaving only a thin layer of fat. Lay the racks in a glass or other nonreactive dish and sprinkle with 1 tablespoon of the oil, ⅓ cup of the vinegar, the garlic, coriander, salt, and pepper. Cover and let stand at room temperature for 1 hour.

2. Preheat the oven to 450°F.

3. Place the lamb racks fat side down in the roasting pan, add the marinade, and surround with the potatoes. Roast for 10 minutes, then reduce the heat to 350°F, turn the racks fat side up, and roast 15 minutes longer for medium-rare, about 18 to 20 minutes for medium.

4. Meanwhile, place the bacon in a 10-inch skillet, add the broth, cover, and bring to a boil over high heat. Add the asparagus, sprinkle with salt and

(continued)

cook until the asparagus is just tender, about 3 to 4 minutes, depending on thickness. Transfer the asparagus to a plate. Add the remaining ⅓ cup vinegar to the pan, whisk in the mustard, and cook until the liquid thickens slightly, about 5 minutes. Immediately remove from the heat. Whisk in the remaining 3 tablespoons olive oil and set aside.

5. Remove the lamb from the oven and let rest for 5 minutes before carving.

6. When it's time to put dinner on the table, place the potatoes in the center of a serving platter and mound the asparagus on either side of them. Cut the racks into chops and arrange them around the potatoes and asparagus. Pour the bacon vinaigrette over the lamb and serve immediately.

ROAST LAMB WITH GARLIC

SERVES 6 TO 8

*T*his lamb is overcooked, tender to the point of falling apart and amazingly delicious. Lots of peeled garlic cloves roast with the lamb, then the sauce is finished with chopped capers and parsley.

1 5- to 6-pound boneless lamb shoulder
2 teaspoons ground sage
1 teaspoon salt
½ teaspoon freshly ground black pepper
½ cup red wine
¼ cup balsamic vinegar
1½ pounds broccoli
½ cup peeled garlic cloves
2 pounds small new potatoes
2 tablespoons olive oil, plus additional, for roasting
2 tablespoons unsalted butter
¼ cup drained capers, chopped
3 tablespoons chopped parsley

1. Preheat the oven to 450°F.

2. Rub the lamb with the sage, salt, and pepper and place in a large roasting pan. Add the wine, 1 cup water, and the vinegar and roast for 10 minutes. Then reduce the heat to 350°F and roast 35 minutes longer, turning once.

3. Meanwhile, trim off and discard the woody ends of the broccoli stalks and cut the broccoli into serving pieces. Place in a bowl, add the garlic and potatoes, and toss with the olive oil.

4. Add the broccoli, potatoes, and garlic to the roasting pan, brush with olive oil, and cook for 45 minutes, turning the vegetables and lamb once.

5. Arrange the lamb, broccoli, potatoes, and garlic on a platter and keep warm. Place the roasting pan over medium heat and add ½ cup water. Boil while stirring to dissolve and scrape up any bits that adhere to the bottom of the pan. Swirl in the butter and stir in the capers and parsley. Pour the *jus* into a sauceboat, and serve dinner.

Guess Who's Coming to Dinner

ROAST BEEF WITH BLUE CHEESE

SERVES 8 TO 10

*7*he salty, pungent sauce of blue cheese, wine, and vinegar is divine on the roasted potatoes as well as on the rich red meat. The walnut oil in the sauce blends together the flavors, giving a finish to each mouthful. What's so wonderful about a boneless rib roast is that we can eat our fat and have it too—there's enough to bathe the meat with its flavor as it roasts, but the rich deposits can still be trimmed off by each guest when dinner is served.

You need serve only a first course of asparagus or other vinaigrette of vegetables, and then a rich dessert—but one without cream.

> *1 4- to 4½-pound rolled boneless beef rib roast or spencer roast*
> *Salt and freshly ground black pepper to taste*
> *16 to 20 very small new potatoes or Finnish potatoes*
> *½ cup chicken stock or canned low-sodium chicken broth*
> *¼ cup red wine vinegar*
> *½ cup red wine*
> *¼ cup crumbled blue cheese*
> *¼ cup walnut oil*

1. Preheat the oven to 450°F.

2. Sprinkle the roast with salt and pepper. Place in a roasting pan, and roast for 10 minutes. Lower the temperature to 350°F and roast about 1¼ hours longer (about 17 minutes per pound), or until a meat thermometer inserted into the center of the beef reads 130°F; add the potatoes to the pan after the roast has cooked for 45 minutes.

3. Remove the roast from the pan and set aside in a warm place to rest for 20 minutes. Remove the potatoes and keep warm in the turned-off oven.

4. Meanwhile, pour off the fat from the roasting pan. Add the stock, vinegar, and wine to the pan, place over medium heat, and cook, stirring to dissolve and scrape up any dark bits that have collected on the bottom of the pan. Then pour into a saucepan and cook over medium heat until reduced by half. Remove from the heat and stir in the blue cheese and any juices that have collected around the roast. Whisk in the oil, taste for salt and pepper, and adjust to taste. Pour the sauce into a sauceboat.

5. To serve, place the potatoes in a vegetable dish. Place the roast on a platter and carve into slices at the table. Pass the sauce separately.

Roast Sirloin with Artichokes and Caper Sauce

SERVES 8

New York steak, a sirloin steak, is a grill favorite, but the meat reacts differently when it is roasted as a large cut of beef. A hot 425°F oven will drop to a perfect roasting temperature when the roast is placed in it. Then after 5 minutes the temperature is turned down to 350°F. Roasting this well-marbled piece of meat works best if the meat heats through at a moderate pace until medium rare, still rosy pink both near the surface and all the way through.

Begin dinner with a vegetable soup, and finish off with a crisp green salad.

1 lemon
4 large artichokes
16 plum tomatoes
1 4½- to 5-pound New York steak, exterior fat trimmed
3 tablespoons olive oil
Salt and freshly ground black pepper to taste
1 small onion, finely chopped
¾ cup white wine
¼ cup white wine vinegar
6 anchovy fillets, finely chopped
¼ cup drained capers
5 tablespoons unsalted butter
¼ cup finely chopped fresh parsley

1. Preheat the oven to 450°F.

2. Cut the lemon in half and rub the cut surfaces of the artichokes with it as you work: Trim ½ inch from the tops of the artichokes. Using scissors or a small knife, cut off the spiked ends of all the remaining leaves. Cut off the stems. Cut the artichokes into quarters and cut out the hairy chokes and small inner leaves.

3. Place the artichokes in a large pot of salted water and add the lemon. Cover and bring to a boil over high heat. Reduce the heat slightly and simmer for 5 minutes. Remove from the pot and set aside.

4. Using a small knife, core the tomatoes. Add the tomatoes to the pot of boiling water and cook for 1 minute, or just until the skins split. Immediately

(continued)

remove from the water and plunge into a bowl of ice water; drain. Remove and discard the skins, and set aside.

5. Rub the steak with some of the olive oil and sprinkle on both sides with salt and pepper. Place in a roasting pan and roast for 5 minutes, then reduce the heat to 325°F. and roast for 15 minutes. Add the artichokes to the pan and brush with the remaining oil. Turn the steak over, without piercing its crust, and roast 40 minutes longer, or until a meat thermometer inserted into the thickest part of the roast reads 130°F, for medium rare. Add the tomatoes to the pan for the last 10 to 12 minutes of roasting.

6. Transfer the steak, artichokes, and tomatoes to a platter and keep warm. Place the roasting pan over medium-high heat, add the onion, wine, and vinegar, and stir, scraping up any dark bits that have stuck to the bottom of the pan. Transfer to a saucepan, add the anchovies and capers, and cook over medium heat until the liquid has reduced by about one third. Remove from the heat, whisk in the butter, and add the parsley. Taste for salt and add as desired.

7. Slice the steak across the grain into ¼-inch slices. Arrange the meat on a large serving platter, surround with the tomatoes and artichokes, and spoon the sauce over.

Index